THE STORY

OF

SEVENHAMPTON

BY
ROS STEWART

The Story of Sevenhampton

ISBN: 1 903607 77 9 / 978 1 903607 77 0

Published by:

Able Publishing
13 Station Road
Knebworth
Hertfordshire SG3 6AP

Tel: 01438 812320
Fax: 01438 815232

www.ablepublishing.co.uk
email: books@ablepublishing.co.uk

The content of this book was the subject of my Exhibition for the Millennium held at the Rhodes Memorial Hall, Brockhampton.

The centre piece was this model of St Andrew's Church, Sevenhampton by John Candler.

This is a superb and intricate piece of carving, representing hours of patient hard work. The detail is meticulously correct in every way.

ACKNOWLEDGMENTS

The Research for this Book was done 'The Hard Way'

With the help of my late husband Ian McDonald Stewart the detective work got under way. We did a lot of travelling in the early days – to the Brecon Beacons tracing the history of Llanthony Abbey and its monks. To Hereford Cathedral to check its connection with our local history. Also to Hereford Record Office to do more researching. Many hours were spent in the search rooms at the Gloucestershire Record Office, also Gloucester Library. Transactions and books from the Bristol and Gloucester Archaelogical Society provided much information. The staff at all these places were most helpful.

Hours spent at The Vicarage of St Andrew's Church, Sevenhampton looking through registers and other papers, was a fruitful exercise. I was helped a great deal with information and advice from Canon Philip Hobbs.

Many hours were also spent at Whittington Court, courtesy of Mr & Mrs J. Stringer, searching through the Lawrence collection of papers, which proved to be a mine of information In this I was much helped by their visiting Archivist from the Record Office.

Many people have helped me with their memories, photographs, newspaper cuttings, also important papers acquired by visitors, some from overseas, collected for their own research, which adds to the full story.

I am grateful to them all for their interest and help and wish to thank them most sincerely. In so doing they have added to their own Local History of Sevenhampton.

Ros Stewart

DEDICATION

To

IAN

CONTENTS

THE STORY OF SEVENHAMPTON

THE NEOLITHIC PERIOD

To live in Sevenhampton is to love it, as did our ancestors who created, tended and cherished it over the many centuries.

High in the North Cotswolds Sevenhampton is a village and parish which includes Brockhampton, Brockhampton Quarry and some outlying parts of Hampen north of the road to Stow-on-the-Wold. Sevenhampton lies seven miles east of Cheltenham, three and a half miles south of Winchcombe and two miles north-east of Andoversford.

Sevenhampton and Brockhampton sit prettily along the upper valley of the River Coln which rises a few hundred yards to the north of the parish boundary near Charlton Abbots. Their altitude above sea level is 600-650 feet (184-200 metres) while that of the parish is 585-932 feet (180-287 metres). The soil and subsoil are clay and light oolite.

This is a thriving, happy Parish, pleasant to live in and attractive to look at because of its well farmed areas surrounding pockets of houses large and small. It appears to have evolved in a somewhat disjointed fashion, but it must have grown this way for a reason and that reason has to be that it was shaped by history.

These villages as we know them now came into being in the 12th century A.D. but the feet of our ancestors trod the hill paths for over four thousand years. The earliest trackways were created by wild animals and Stone Age man while Britain was still part of the continental land mass. These men were the nomadic hunter gatherers, living off the flesh of their kill and clothing themselves with animal skins. They struggled through thick scrubland and much woodland, for the hills, once bleak and bare following the last Ice Age, were covered with lush vegetation once the temperature rose.

The first people to leave real evidence of their presence here were the Iberians, dark haired and short in stature. They came from the Pyrenees area during the Neolithic Period – New Stone Age of 2000 B.C. They were a tribal race who made their way to the Cotswolds and settled here, possibly because it was their kind of country. We know little of their lifestyle, but in disposing of their dead they left behind the burial mounds or barrows which have survived to this day. The most famous in this area is Belas Knap at Hamley Hough, now in the parish of Charlton Abbots; BAAL being the God of Fire whom they must have worshipped. Man had by now discovered the use of fire.

Belas Knap was a Long Barrow discovered by archaeologists in 1863, found to contain several chambers with some 30 skeletons. In one cell were 5 children aged

Bellas Knap Long Barrow
At Hamley Hough near Charlton Abbots

between 1 and 7 years. In another 12 skeletons were found sitting in a circle. Their fingers were in their noses as they had been placed, presumably to hold up their heads.

Pieces of sundried pottery, a bone scoop and flint arrow heads were found, also evidence of large funeral pyres were near to the grave mound. During the New Stone Age chiefs and their families were placed ceremoniously in Long Barrows, but for lesser mortals cremation was the norm.

Evidence of the earliest human population here in Sevenhampton parish comes from the Tumuli, ancient burial mounds or barrows, discovered within our boundaries in the land between Oxlease and Soundborough (Ordnance Survey Map 42/02) known as the WHIST Tumuli. In an area some 20 yards across 4 tumuli were found in the same field. Near the centre was a grave formed of flat stone dry walling 18 inches deep, 2 feet wide and 8 feet long. It contained 7 human skeletons and was covered over with rough unhewn stones like the roof of a house. Many coins and a whorl spindle were found. Whist could have been a graveyard for many generations. So by now the people had learned simple spinning and were able to clothe themselves from the wool of their flocks. Earlier men clothed themselves in the animal skins of their hunting prey.

The graveyard could have been started by the Celts who were the next invaders of Britain c.500 B.C. Celtish tumuli were Round which distinguishes them from the Iberian Long Barrows. The stone lined graves could have been of a later period when the area had become more inhabited. WHIST proves that there were tribes here in the Bronze and Iron Ages. These people were Pagans who were buried with their belongings – men with swords, spears, shields – women with spindles, weaving batons and sewing items. Later Christianity taught them that these grave goods were not necessary in the next world.

The Celts came from the Upper Rhineland and were said to be fair haired and of larger stature than the Iberians whom they drove further West into Cornwall and Wales. They had domesticated certain animals, sheep, cattle, pigs and goats and followed them across land ever seeking new grazing grounds. With them came the beginnings of agriculture as they settled and began to till and plant the soil. Many of them preferred the higher, drier land of the Cotswolds and having improved their tools they were able to clear small areas to set up their homesteads and graze their animals. The tiny homesteads – villages – were connected by tracks, and being tribal people they were required to meet together with their chiefs at certain times; here they would have belonged to the DOBUNNI Tribe. An advanced, intelligent race they had mastered the use of minerals such as bronze and iron. Skills included spinning and weaving the wool from their flocks, from which they were able to make garments. Hides of oxen provided leather for their sandals.

The DOBUNNI were a powerful tribe of Celtic origin occupying most of Gloucestershire, with parts of Somerset, Hereford, Worcester, Oxford and Warwickshire. They were a warlike people centred on Bagendon which was a large Iron Age Oppidum – defended town. Banks and ditches enclosed the circular homes of the people and served to keep the animals in and the enemy out. They had to fight off constant attacks from the Welsh tribes and this may have accounted for their surrender to the Romans. They fought the Romans bravely but after a few skirmishes and probably on the promise of help in dealing with the western tribes they joined the Romans peaceably. The Dobunni, who were by now skilled in working bronze and iron, minted coins at Bagendon; they also made brooches and other ornaments, tools and domestic items.

The Romans first attacked this country in 55 B.C., but at the onset of winter they withdrew to Gaul taking some hostages with them. The people of the Cotswolds would not have been aware of this, yet within 100 years the Romans would return to change their way of life forever.

The Birth of Jesus

Within 50 years, or c.4 B.C., in another part of the Roman Empire came an event that was gradually to change the life of much of the world – a baby boy was born. Not a prince to one of the great Royal families, but a child, born out of wedlock, to a simple peasant girl. The State of Israel, under the orders of Rome, called each of its people to return to the place of his birth to be registered. Joseph, with his pregnant fiancée Mary, returned to the overcrowded small town of Bethlehem. By the time they arrived all accommodation was taken – "no room at the Inn". Mary was weary and possibly already in labour when a kindly landlord took pity on her and allowed them to shelter in his stables with the animals. She gave birth that night to the baby Jesus, wrapped him in the covers she had brought with her and laid him in a trough full of hay which was meant for the animals.

The Israelites had been waiting down the centuries for this to happen, as it had been foretold by sages and prophets of old. Strange lights filled the skies that night which brought firstly the simple people to the stable to see this child and later kings from other countries and all acknowledged him to be the long awaited Christ. When word of this child reached Herod, King of Israel, he was both angry and afraid it would undermine his powerful position. He decided to remove all chances of this child growing up to be king and there followed the "Massacre of the Innocents" – all boy children under the age of 2 years were killed by order. But the Holy Family had already left for Egypt, Mary with the baby rode on a donkey. After Herod's death they returned to set up home in Nazareth.

Jesus grew up as a hardworking, obedient son, also intelligent and learned. In his early thirties he became a Rabbi and took to the road as a wandering teacher. He gathered a group of earnest young men around him and together they preached a new, simple religion, worshipping only one God, living frugally and collecting no worldly goods. Jesus spoke to the people in a way they could understand, illustrating his teaching with stories. He went to the aid of the poor and sick and became much loved by all who met him. But he was hated by the rich and powerful who saw Jesus as a threat to their control of the lesser people. They plotted against him and when he was 37 years old they lured him back to Jerusalem to destroy him. They needed to put him on open trial to discredit him in the eyes of his many followers. They persuaded Judas Iscariot , one of his twelve disciples, but also the son of a very rich man who was one of the governing group of Jerusalem, to betray him. They gave Judas the handsome sum of 30 pieces of silver to lead the soldiers to Jesus.

The disciples with Jesus were all together taking supper in the upper room of a private house when Jesus gave them bread and wine, saying this is my body and my blood, "take and eat these in remembrance of me".

The Communion Service of the Christian Church dates from this supper. Afterwards they walked in the garden in the darkness when Judas came up and kissed Jesus; this was a signal to the soldiers hidden in the garden who stepped out and arrested him.

Now Judas was probably the greatest believer of them all. He agreed to do his father's bidding because he thought Jesus was God and therefore could not be hurt by mere men. He was so shattered and upset by what followed that he returned to the Temple, threw the pieces of silver at the feet of the Priests and later committed suicide. If he had waited a little longer he would have known that his belief in Christ was well founded because Jesus came back to life again on the third day – ever after to be known as Easter Sunday. Jesus Christ "died" at the age of 37 years in A.D.33.

The Crucifixion took place on Friday, ever after to be known as Good Friday, the day before the Jewish Feast of the Passover commemorating the liberation of the Jews from Egypt. The Resurrection took place on Easter Sunday, to be celebrated by Christians on the first Sunday following the full moon on, or just after, March 21st each year.

The Augustan Legion had been on garrison duty in Jerusalem in A.D.33 and some may well have witnessed the Crucifixion. Later in A.D.47 this same legion was brought to Britain and garrisoned at Glevum – Gloucester – for a time.

The Roman Conquest

A.D.43. Only 10 years after the death of Christ the Romans invaded Britain, gradually conquering the whole country. Many of the tribal people fled to Wales and Cornwall, as others had done before them.

After their withdrawal from the invasion of 55 B.C. the Romans left Britain undisturbed for many years but they were well aware of its mineral wealth and corn growing land, also they had experienced the way in which the natives protected themselves. The Celts built forts in many places, usually on high ground surrounded by deep earthworks. These defences were but little protection against the might of the Roman legions. In some areas the tribes fought fiercely led by such chiefs as Caractacus and Queen Boudicca. They rode into battle on horseback or in chariots and fought fiercely, but eventually all were defeated. Here the fighting was short-lived.

The Romans constructed military establishments and forts along their new roads. By A.D.50 they had built a frontier fort at Corinium on the Fosseway. They encouraged the Dobunni to move their capital from Bagendon (which is 3 miles to the North of Cirencester) to Corinium which was now a "modern" town with regular streets, markets and theatres. The Dobunni lived by their own laws but under the overall rule of the Romans. The town became known as Corinium Dobunnorum.

There were no towns or forts in this area nearer than the Iron Age fort at Crickley Hill, only homesteads of a few thatched, timber huts often surrounded by a wall.

Romans had advanced skills unheard of by the local tribes. They could read and write, design buildings and plan cities, construct and maintain good straight roads, often using the old British trackways, also construct and control waterways. They used the capabilities of their captives, from other countries, who were often noblemen forced to join the Roman armies.

They started setting up a network of garrisons across the country to control their captured territories, connected by good straight roads for the movement of troops and later for trade routes. These forts contained barracks, hospitals, granaries, storerooms, bath houses, stables and workshops. Outside the fort were houses, temples and amphitheatres. All needs were catered for including their own religion of worshipping Gods such as Mars and Jupiter.

Just such a settlement was discovered in 1864 on the land from present day Syreford taking in the whole of Andoversford. It was excavated by Walter Lawrence Lawrence Esq., who when Lord of the Manors of Sevenhampton, Whittington and Sandiwell, and living in Sevenhampton Manor House, noticed that tracks or roads seemed to criss-cross his cornfields in the Syreford area. This phenomenon had been noted some years previously by Rev. T D Fosbroke, Antiquarian, in 1826. The excavation was started after the harvest and a large Roman township was unearthed. Its boundary at the Syreford end was the River Coln and the whole area was given the name of Wycomb.

Wycomb
Site of Roman Settlement near Andoversford

Wicham – deriving from the Latin *Vicus* meaning quarter, village or estate.

Wicham – was the Old English name for a Roman settlement.

The Roman township was found to be built on the burnt out remains of an early English village. This village may have been sacked by the Romans and the original villagers made to rebuild their homes nearby where they could continue to till the soil to produce food for the Romans. This was done in other parts of the country. The land in all directions would have been scrub or woodland, apart from the area already cultivated by

River Coln at Syreford
Boundary of Roman Settlement

the native British, with ample water supplies from the River Coln and the very many freshwater springs in the area. Some of the early tribes could have moved towards Whittington and Andoversford areas, while others may have cultivated the land from Syreford towards Winchcombe, mostly on hilly terrain.

Evidence of the Celtic occupation comes from barrows and stone lined graves found by archaeologists on the side of Wycomb Hill. In Black Close, meadows near Andoversford, calcined stone, ash and charcoal were found near to the surface and it is said Black Close was so named because it was the site of a burnt town. Under the Roman site rich, black earth contained pottery and ashes of a pre-Roman date. A cinerary urn was found in an old Syreford gravel quarry. Two Dobunni coins, one inscribed EISU and pre-historic flint work all suggest that the area was settled from at least 7 B.C.

Walter Lawrence Lawrence drew up a plan of the "Roman Remains at Wycomb near Andoversford" which was as far as his excavations went. Later the Roman Settlement was found to include all Andoversford to its modern boundaries. He later published a report of his findings in the Gentlemen's Magazine and also got some help from the Antiquary Society. Foundations and buildings were all of oolite stone, which he suggested came from Brockhampton Quarry. Finds were – much pottery including some good specimens of Samian ware; about 1000 coins in all, covering the whole Roman period and later some Romano-British coins; knives, styli, and articles of toilet – the Romans appear to have been clean-shaven. Stone troughs and drains, foundations, pavements, forges and fireplaces, tesserae, hypercaust and other tiles were also found.

One building Mr Lawrence took to be a Temple, with broken columns and statues, also stone idols and bronze figures, was built over the remains of a two-cell structure which may have been the earlier site of a shrine.

Wycomb was taken to be a Roman Military Settlement and in Walter Lawrence Lawrence's own words:

"No position could have been better calculated for the concentration of troops. It was near to a point where the ancient road from Cirencester to Cleeve Hill intersected those from Campden, Stow and the higher Cotswolds to Gloucester. It was distant little more than a mile from a large camp at Dowdeswell and was only three miles from the watch towers on Cleeve Hill from whence an extensive view is obtained over the vale of the Severn and the approach of an enemy easily detected".

Excavations came to a halt because of the new railway being laid from Cheltenham to Bourton-on-the-Water and the embankment being built to take it across the lower ground at Andoversford cut across the middle of the settlement site. He hurried the work along because of this but was forced to stop before the whole

Roman Settlement could be uncovered. (Ironically W.L. Lawrence had shares in this new Railway Building enterprise.)

Roman villas were built in the area, in true Roman style, for the wealthy and powerful Romans. Mostly the only evidence left of these is from their beautiful mosaic pavements, many of which have been excavated and well preserved. Some pavement evidence has been found in the Whittington Court area, but sadly there is little of this left. The best preserved site is at Chedworth, near to Cirencester, where the quality of these buildings give a good idea of how well the Romans lived. Everything they did was organised on the style of life in Rome itself; buildings and streets would be of the same layout in whichever country they happened to be building. Bath (Aquae Sullis), and Gloucester (Glevum) have also preserved much of their Roman building and culture.

Tacitus – Roman Historian A.D.55-120 – wrote: "Little by little, the Britons were seduced into alluring vices: arcades, baths and sumptuous banquets. In their simplicity they called such novelties 'civilisation' when in reality they were part of their enslavement."

In A.D.400 the Romans left Britain. They were called back to defend their territories when Rome itself was under attack. This was the beginning of the decline of the great Roman Empire.

The Wycomb Romans were among the last to leave Britain. Their final departure was in A.D.414.

The Dark Ages

As the Romans slowly drifted away the native British must have been in a state of utter bewilderment. First the legions were called away, so the familiar sight of marching troops was no more. Then the officials responsible for law and organisation were called to Rome and were not replaced as they had been over the years. Society broke down because the natives had for over 350 years and several generations known nothing but slavery to the Roman way of life. Urban organisation, which had been orderly, was there no longer, so neither was the usual employment available. Gradually the people went back to their tribal way of living cultivating the land for food. A few people in other parts of Britain tried living in the now empty Roman villas, somewhat unsuccessfully it seems, for in some excavations archaeologists found crude D.I.Y. repairs, but they lacked the expertise and wealth to support such living. Some Roman villa residents may have stayed in Britain having established themselves as landowners, but even they would have found it too difficult once trade had broken down and their luxury living could not be sustained.

The villa owners around the Syreford settlement probably left for Rome once Wycomb was closed and deserted. The British here were living in their thatched huts in country conditions so they reverted to their old tribal systems of homesteads and kingships again. Some moved to, or were already in, Whittington centre, some to the Andoversford side, and some moved up the hill towards Winchcombe to the area we now know as Sennington. An old trackway from Sennington to Whittington across the hill shows that they kept in touch and probably traded with each other. From these early homesteads larger villages grew.

The Roman army had kept this country peaceful once conquest was completed. They guarded our shores and borders and patrolled our seas against marauding enemies who were constantly trying to invade Britain, originally for plunder and later seeking to occupy this rich territory. Left to defend themselves the British were ineffective for the Romans had not given them military training, so their warfare skills were long forgotten. The Vikings from Scandinavia continued to attack the North East, while the Jutes then the Angles and Saxons from Northern Europe attacked, invaded and overran Britain.

THE ANGLO-SAXONS

By A.D.450 the Angles and Saxons had infiltrated much of the country abandoned by the Romans, with whom they had had many skirmishes over the years but the powerful Roman army had held them back. Now however there was no Roman army so their efforts as invaders were more successful.

The area now known as West Midlands was occupied by the HWICCE tribe who descended from the DOBUNNI – this could have been their new name when they joined tribally again after the Romans left. Our local natives would be of the HWICCE now living on the hill above Syreford.

The Saxons were gaining ground and in A.D.577 they won a famous victory at the battle of Dyrham killing three Celtic Kings – Condidan, Conmail and Farinmail. The defeated Celts retreated into Cornwall and Wales. Thus the three great Roman towns of Aquae Sullis, Glevum and Corinium fell into Saxon hands. They moved into these towns but, since the Saxons were not urban people, they ignored the Roman built towns and instead set up their own centres.

By A.D.600 the Cotswolds were colonised by the Saxons and a large area which included the whole of Middle England became known as MERCIA. In A.D.625 a Saxon army marched into Stow-on-the-Wold and defeated the HWICCE; Stow was then ceded to Mercia.

The kingdom of Mercia was ruled over by the cruel King Penda from A.D.632. He incorporated Hereford and Shropshire in to Mercia. In A.D.655 Penda, the

The HWICCE / DUBONNI

10

last of the Pagan Kings, was killed in battle. He was succeeded by his now Christian sons.

Christianity had been brought to these shores in A.D.596 by Augustine, sent to these shores by the Pope of Rome, and became well-established. Abbeys were built by the Christian Saxons, including Gloucester and Hereford, later to become Cathedrals.

From A.D.757-790 Offa was King of Mercia. The infighting had never ceased and his kingdom was attacked continually by the Celts of Wales. Offa's Dyke, a massive earthwork, was constructed to cut off the whole of Wales. It stretched from sea to sea c.160 miles from the River Severn to the River Dee.

Although coins had been produced by Kings of the past, but not used generally, Offa introduced Saxon coinage based on the Frankish system of 12 pennies to the shilling and 20 shillings to the pound. Thus giving us the difficult to calculate system of £.s.d. which stayed in force until A.D.1971 when Britain turned metric in keeping with Europe.

The Shire System

The Saxon period in Britain was no less impressive than the Roman. The Saxons left behind not buildings, roads and towns as was the Roman legacy, but great administrative order which still has its effect on today's Britain.

Slowly from the 9th century the Anglo-Saxons started to divide their kingdoms into Scires or Shires.

Shire meant sawn off – Glowecestrescire was sawn off Mercia.

Mercia was divided into Glowecestrescire, Wincelcumscire, Herefordscire, Oxenfordscire, Wirocestrescire, and Sciropscire. Sennington was originally in Wincelcumscire.

When the Normans conquered the country in later years the Shire became a County, or Compte, controlled by a Norman Count.

With the Shires came law and order. The Saxons introduced from their Eldormen the SHIRE REEVE or SHERIFF (still in existence today) who was responsible for the whole Shire with a REEVE to each village or township. The Reeve became Steward of the Manor, or Constable, who was answerable to the Sheriff.

The Constable was responsible for local law and order and could bring offenders before the COURT LEET or Local Court. More serious offences referred to the Sheriff would be brought before the Shire Court (County Court) or COURT BARON.

In the 17th Century a VESTRY was held by the Church in Sevenhampton. In Brockhampton a separate COURT HOUSE was built on Brockhampton Park land, by Paul Pearte. The centre of the present building was the original 'Court Room' with a raised dais for the Judge. Above this was a small room known as the Wig Room where the lawyers changed into their gowns before a Court Session. For many years it was known as The Court House, now a private house renamed Brockhampton Court.

The Shires were later divided into HUNDREDS or 100 Hides. 1 Hide equalled 60-120 acres, or sufficient land to support one extended family. Sennington was first in Wacrescymbe then in Bradelege or BRADLEY HUNDRED after amalgamation. NORTHLEACH was the centre for the Bradley Hundred. Each Hundred had its appointed Meeting Place at which the people of the Hundred attended compulsory assemblies for the issuing of laws, military orders or dispensing justice in Saxon days. The people were mostly illiterate therefore it was necessary to gather them together to have these read out to them.

The Meeting Point for Northleach was at Hangman's Stone at the junction where the Salt Way crosses the Fosseway near Stowell Park.

The Hundreds were divided again into tithings or groups of 10 households administered by a tithingman. This system was called FRANK PLEDGE in which each member of the group was held accountable for the good conduct of his fellows. It was a good system because it transformed the matter of personal obedience to the rules into one of personal loyalty to each other. If anyone offended in spite of this the tithingman brought him before the Court Leet.

Wincelcumscire

Wincelcumscire was one of the Shires founded by the Anglo-Saxons. Each Shire, with a few exceptions, was named after the town at its centre and Winchcombe had become an important Saxon centre.

It probably had been a settlement in Roman times, there being a number of villas in the surrounding area, but its importance as a township came when it was chosen by the Mercian Kings to be the seat of Royalty. A palace, later castle, was built for the royal family, but now no longer exists.

The Saxon administration centre had been moved from Cirencester to Winchcombe, because Cirencester was too near to the Wessex border and suffered too many raids. Also Winchcombe was nearer to Tamworth the then capital of Mercia. Winchcombe gradually became the most important township in all Mercia.

In A.D.787 King Offa, now a Christian, built a Nunnery in Winchcombe. Then in A.D.800 foundations were laid for a Benedictine Abbey on behalf of King Cenulf. The Abbey was dedicated to St Mary amid great pomp and ceremony in A.D.811 attended by Royalty and important Bishops and clerics from great distances. (Kings had much ecclesiastical power long before the days of King Henry VIII.)

The Venerable Bede records that workers in stone and glass were brought from Italy by Benedict Biscop to create this building. The original Abbey would have been very beautiful. Sadly this Abbey was burned down some years later and all its records with it. Another Abbey was then built on the same site.

Winchcombe suffered much damage many times – at the hands of the Danes in the 11th century, in the Civil War of King Stephen's time, the 12th century, and again in the Civil Wars of Charles I, early 17th century.

In A.D.1016 the Danes were slaying, burning and pillaging Winchcombe. Although it was in Wincelcumscire, Sennington was not affected at this time.

One EADRIC STROENA Eldorman under Saxon Ethelred and Danish Canute became very powerful. He held dominion as under-king, using his great power to his own ends, joining township to township and shire to shire. He amalgamated WINCELCUMSCIRE to GLOWECESTRESCIRE (Gloucestershire) and so it has remained to this day.

Sennington

In the early Anglo-Saxon years our villagers arrived and settled at a high point of the hill bringing their sheep and cattle with them to a convenient spot where water was plentiful and the land fertile. Now they were able to create a permanent homestead, clearing land for the village homes, for pasture and for cultivation

The village of Sennington existed on the high ground of what is now Manor Farm and became a settled community for several hundred years.

The people, who would have been members of the HWICCE tribe, had learned to renew the health of their soil by using a new system, grazing the ground for one year then cultivating the ground fertilized by the animals and moving the flocks to fresh pasture. In this way they could stay in one place whereas earlier generations had to move the whole village every few years when the land became exhausted. The people of Sennington may have moved up the hill in this way.

Before the days of written evidence, which could have been used to discover the past history of an inhabited area, the old placenames can tell much of its story, SENNINGTON in Old English ING = a common meadow. TON = enclosure surrounding a homestead or village. Archaeological research now reveals material evidence of man's life in times past.

Sennington is shown as 'Site of Medieval Village' on Ordnance Map SF.02.SW.

The remains of Sennington village were unearthed, in 1936, by Archaeologist Mrs O'Neil of Bourton-on-the-Water.

The Gloucester Sites and Monuments Record gives a description in SMR No.56.

"The site of a former village exists at a spot known as 'Old Sennington'. A path known as 'Church Walk' indicated that the original chapel of Sevenhampton may have been built there and foundations can be traced. During construction of a drain rather lower down ashes and coins were found. Sevenhampton was recorded as 'Sen(N)yington' in C.16. Excavations in 1936 by Mrs H.E. O'Neil and Rev. J. Miller (report not published) revealed walling similar to that of a probable farm at Temple Guiting (site 2656) and numerous finds of C.12-13 pottery. The remains are those of a DMV covering an area of about 6 ha. on a N facing slope near the head of a dry valley. Banks and scarps between 0.2 & 0.5m high indicate the sites of between 20-30 house platforms and associated paddocks and fields. It is not possible to identify any particular boundary or associated field systems."

DMV = Deserted Medieval Village.
ha = hectare
The Rev John Miller was Vicar of St Andrew's, Sevenhampton from 1934 to 1944.

The house platforms are well preserved under the turf of Sennington meadow. One larger base is thought to be that of the Chapel and some platforms appear to be of two rooms. One circular walled pit was probably used for storage of grain. The dwellings were dotted about, not in a row or circle, and the doorways always faced in the same

Sennington – Site of Deserted Village showing where early buildings were

direction, perhaps to escape the cold of a prevailing wind. The walling found is probably that of the surrounding wall of an enclosure.

Homes were of wooden walls, on stone foundations with thatched roofs. By now the villagers were all Christians.

The ditch lower down could have been their burial ground. For simple villagers, ashes placed in pottery jars following cremation would have been the normal way of burying their dead. Possibly the people continued to use this area for the funerals of their dead after they had resettled in Sevenhampton.

By late Saxon times they had started to use the ridge and furrow method of ploughing – this is still evident in the fields near Nash above Sennington. Old ridge and furrow can be detected when there is a layer of snow on the ground. The plough was pulled by oxen, any number from two to eight

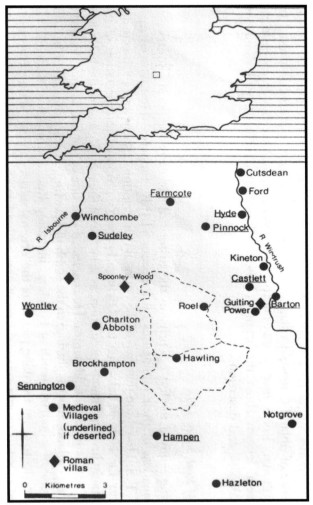

Map showing Sennington and Brockhampton (Sevenhampton did not exist at that time)

beasts harnessed together, and was driven in one direction as far as the oxen could go without stopping. After a short rest they were turned around and driven back in the opposite direction, each strip was a 'furlong' or one furrow's length, equal to 220 yards.

The Open Field System, introduced during the eighth and ninth centuries, was the means of controlling the balance between grazed and cultivated land. There were no walls, hedges or fences in open fields which usually by now belonged to an Overlord who sublet to the tenant villagers. These fields were again divided by strip farming where the land was ploughed in strips and each tenant would be given a number of strips in different parts of the open field. In this way the good and the poorer land was equally divided. Also similar crops would be planted side by side to

15

make for easier harvesting. This was different from the original ways of cultivating and since the land was owned by one lord, usually the Church, it was controlled by customary rights (based on custom or tradition). Some of the land was set aside as Common or Waste land where the 'commoners' or villagers were allowed free grazing for their animals. The people also had rights of Panage which allowed their pigs to forage freely in the woods for beech mast etc. The whole system was the forerunner of the Manorial System and was the basis of mutual economic life.

Christianity was first brought to this country by the Romans in the early days of their occupation of Britain. Only a few Romans had been converted, mostly they held to their old beliefs and worshipped their pagan gods. Therefore Christianity was unknown to the local British tribes. By A.D.596 Augustine, sent by the Pope of Rome, had been accepted in Canterbury, the Christian religion he taught spread over the whole country and chapels and monasteries were erected in many places. The monks were able to receive a good education, they could read and write in Latin and through them some idea of life in early Britain was recorded.

One of the greatest was the Venerable Bede, a scholar, priest and monk of Jarrow and Lindisfarne, a prolific writer. His finest work was The Ecclesiastical History of the English Nation, written in A.D.731, which gives a good idea of the country at this time. "Britain, formerly called Albion, excels for grain and trees and land adapted for feeding cattle and beasts of burden. Produces vines in some places. Remarkable for rivers abounding in fish and plentiful in springs, water fowls of several sort and greatest plenty of salmon and eels. There is an abundance of cockles of which the scarlet dye is made; a most beautiful colour which never fades with the heat of the sun or with the washing of rain. It has both salt and hot springs and from them flow the rivers.

Britain has also many veins of metals such as copper, iron, lead and silver. It has much excellent jet which is black and sparkling.

This island at present, following the number of books in which the Divine Law was written, contains five nations, the English, Britons, Scots, Picts and Latins, each in its own particular dialect cultivating the sublime study of Divine truth. The Latin tongue is, by this study, become common to all the rest. At first the island had no other inhabitants but the Britains, coming over into Britain, as is reported, from Armoria, possessed themselves of the southern parts thereof."

After Christianity was brought to this country in A.D.596 and later became the country's main religion, the Anglo-Saxons divided England between the Abbeys. Winchcombe Abbey owned Charlton Abbots and surrounding areas. Most of lower Mercia was given over to the Worcester Abbey (later Cathedral).

By A.D.800 Sennington is documented as belonging to the Bishops of Hereford. At this time the many Bishops owned much land outside their own diocese. Hereford owned 24 manors which they used for revenue and for the Bishop's lodgings whenever he moved about the country. Each village was forced to pay Tithe to support the Abbey or Cathedral and the priests.

The Bishop of Hereford held the manor of Prestbury (Presteberie – the fortified place of a priest) together with Sennington as one unit, plus much land around and between including Puckham (Goblin Valley).

They became known as UNAM SUB MONTIBUS and UNAM SUPER MONTIBUS – together under the hill and together on the hill.

End of the First Millennium

The new Millennium saw the end of Anglo-Saxon England.

In A.D.1000 Saxon King Ethelred A.D.968-1016 was on the throne of England. He was known as 'Ethelred the Unready'. Ethelred meant 'Noble Counsel' whereas 'Unraed' meant 'No Counsel' or 'Evil Counsel'. He was a weak King, married to Queen Emma of Normandy. From A.D.900 the Saxon Kings became King of all England, rather than many kings of small kingdoms into which the country had been divided hitherto.

England was not at peace for it was being attacked from all sides by Vikings. In A.D.995 a comet was seen in the sky which became known as the Hairy Tailed Comet. This brought out much superstitious fear and there were those who expected the world to come to an end in A.D.1000.

The people of Sennington may have been unaware of the passing of the 1st millennium, so would not have celebrated it. They were living simply and peacefully on their hilltop surrounded by scrubland. There were no roads, nearer than the Roman Fosseway, only tracks. There was one deep track, still visible today, which connected them with Whittington, so no doubt they visited and possibly traded with their old friends and relatives.

The Danish Vikings had for some years attacked and finally invaded Britain, conquering and occupying many parts, Hereford now being under Danish rule. On the death of Saxon King Ethelred in A.D.1016 the Danes seized power under Cnut (Canute) until A.D.1042. The Saxons were now in power again and Edward the Confessor son of Ethelred was crowned King. He it was who founded Westminster Abbey; on his death a shrine was built for him in his own Abbey. Britain's land was fairly equally divided between the Saxons and the Danes and for a few years they managed to live side by side peacefully. Edward had no children and to keep peace during his reign he promised his throne to both Harold of the Danes and William of Normandy.

On Edward's death in January A.D.1066 both potential successors were alerted. Harold, who was at his seat in Hereford, declared himself to be King of all England and galloped across country to Westminster to be anointed and crowned in Westminster Abbey, while masses for Edward were still being said. On his arrival in London he was brought news that the Vikings were attacking northern England.

He turned his troops around and galloped north meeting the Viking army near York at Stamford Bridge. He won a famous victory.

William of Normandy was also making his way to London to claim the promised crown. When Harold was brought word that William had landed he turned his battle-weary troops around yet again and marched them hastily south. When the two armies met at Hastings on 14th October 1066 William's army was rested and ready. Harold's men were depleted and tired, even so they were winning at the beginning of the battle. After Harold was slain, however, the Normans won the day.

William declared himself King and was crowned in Westminster Abbey on 25th December 1066.

This was the beginning of much change in England.

THE NORMAN CONQUEST

William's first act on becoming King of England was to claim the whole country as his own "as bequeathed to him by King Edward". All previous landowners kept their land only by doing homage to William in a colourful ceremony, even so most of the land of the English Nobility was confiscated and granted to William's followers. William favoured the Manorial System.

Many Bishops were removed in favour of French Bishops. Hereford was not affected because the resident Bishop was a Frenchman, Walter of Lorraine. Edward the Confessor had already brought in many Frenchmen because of his own relationship with France. His Mother was Queen Emma of Normandy and Edward had spent most of his early years in France.

To keep the peace in England William had many castles built. One of these was Gloucester Castle, which was a favourite place of William who travelled a great deal about his kingdom. He spent Christmas of A.D.1085 at Gloucester and here it was that he conceived the idea of the Great Survey. William needed to find out just how the country was divided and what its wealth was before and after the death of Edward.

He sent his men out to survey and bring back the required details. This was carried out in an incredibly short time, aided no doubt by the previous Saxon efficient administration. This led to the compilation of the DOMESDAY BOOK.

It shows the land of the Church of Hereford as 30 Hides in Presteberie and Sevenhatone. 20 hides were in what we know as Sennington. Durand, Sheriff of Gloucester holds 3 of these 20 hides from the Bishop of Hereford. Although it was called Sevenhatone in 1085, after it was deserted later and the new village of Sevenhampton built, it was probably referred to as Old Sevenhatone or Old Sennington to distinguish it from the new Sevenhampton.

William the Conqueror died two years after the compilation of Domesday Book and was succeeded by his second son William Rufus, so called because of his red hair and ruddy complexion. He, William II, was killed in a hunting accident in the New Forest. He died childless and was succeeded by his brother Henry I who married firstly Anglo-Saxon Princess Edith, a descendant of Ethelred; she later changed her name to Matilda. His second wife Aldela of Louvain was the mother of Empress Matilda who later claimed the throne as left to her by her father Henry I who had named her as his successor.

Hereford And Llanthony Abbey

During the reign of William Rufus a Norman Knight, William de Lacy, built a little chapel in the Vale of Ewias in the Black Mountains of Wales. By A.D.1108 the

Hereford Cathedral and Bishop's Palace

Knight and a Priest Ernisius who was chaplain to Queen Matilda, gathered together a band of followers and formed a monastic settlement. They built the first priory church and dedicated it to St John the Baptist. It was consecrated by the Bishop of Hereford.

During the 12th century Anselm, Archbishop of Canterbury persuaded them to regularise to the monastic practise of the time. It was agreed that

The Cistercians were given to averice
The Benedictines were inclined to laxity

They finally decided on The ORDER OF AUGUSTINIAN CANNONS.

Their second prior in A.D.1121 was Robert de Bethune of Flanders. He dearly loved the isolation of the valley. In A.D.1131 Robert (who now lies buried in Hereford Cathedral) reluctantly moved to become Bishop of Hereford at the Pope's insistence.

LLANTHONY ABBEY
Ruins in the Black Mountains

Five years later he was to give shelter to the Prior and monks of Llanthony Abbey who were fleeing from Black Mountains brigands who destroyed their Abbey.

After another two years Bishop Robert prevailed upon Milo, or Miles, Sheriff of Gloucester and Earl of Hereford to grant them land on which to build a new Abbey. This he did and the new Abbey became known as Llanthony Secunda. The revenues of Prestbury and Sennington were used to endow the new monastery. The ruins of Llanthony Secunda can still be seen in Llanthony Road, Gloucester City.

Miles was the great-nephew of Durand the former Sheriff. He may have given Durand's land for the building for the new Priory.

LLANTHONY SECUNDA
Ruins of Llanthony Priory in Gloucester

The Destruction Of Sennington

On the death in A.D.1135 of Henry I (said to be caused by a surfeit of lampreys) there was no direct heir. Henry's son William, with his illegitimate brother, were drowned in the White Ship disaster of A.D.1120. They had been visiting Normandy on state business but when ready to return the Channel was too rough for them to set sail. The story goes that they killed time on shore, waiting for better weather, by drinking with the Captain and crew of the ship. When the weather improved they set sail, all, including the Captain, were under the influence, so the ship was lost with all hands.

The throne was claimed by both Stephen, grandson of William I, and Matilda daughter of Henry I. She claimed the throne on behalf of her son Henry of Anjou. Stephen snatched the throne and was crowned on 26th December 1135 in Westminster Abbey. Robert of Hereford backed Stephen, out of loyalty to Stephen's brother the Bishop of Winchester. Miles of Gloucester also backed Stephen, but later changed his allegiance to Matilda. A bitter war broke out.

Sennington was in danger because of its connection to Miles of Gloucester.

Much of the fighting in this Civil War was in the Cotswolds. Miles took up arms on behalf of Matilda doing much damage and laying waste much of the countryside. After the burning and sacking of Worcester by Miles he was deprived of his office on 7th November 1139. Robert, Earl of Gloucester and John de Suddeley, illegitimate brothers of Matilda, joined her.

"Stephen collected a great army, invaded Winchcomb on Thursday 13th January 1140 and burned the greater part of the town including the Abbey.

(Quote from LANDBOC – the cartulary of Winchcomb Abbey.)

"If Winchcomb escaped in the preceding reigns, it was involved in the troubles of King Stephen's time. Sudley, within ½ mile had for its Lord, John, son of Harold de Sudley. He had married Grace, daughter of William de Tracey, who with Robert, Earl of Gloucester, was a natural son of Henry I and so far a brother of the Empress Matilda, next in succession to the throne as the King's lawful daughter. Milo, made Constable of Gloucester by Henry I, violated his oath to Stephen the late King's nephew. On Stephen's seizing the crown, Milo rose up in rebellion against him. Espousing the cause of Matilda, he laid waste to all the country around. After the sacking and burning of Worcester by Milo, now deprived of his office (7 Nov. 1139) reprisals were made by the King's party on Sudley, for John de Sudley had gone over to Matilda and the Earl of Gloucester. Milo, collecting a great army, invaded Winchcomb (Thursday, January 13 1140) burnt the greater part of the town, plundered it, drove out the inhabitants or took them prisoner; and committing the King's castle of Winchcomb to the keeping of his partisans, marched to Sudley, but was compelled to retreat. Overmatched by the enemy, Stephen removed from the siege of Tetbury to Winchcomb. His object was to lay siege to a stronghold there erected by Milo's son, now Earl of Hereford "on a shelving precipice with a very high wall, surrounded on all sides with defences of exceeding strength". By his orders to the most able soldiers selected "some were to keep up a continued shower of arrows, others were to scale the mound on their hands and knees, while the rest were to keep up a constant and untiring circuit round the walls. Every missile that came to hand was to be discharged into the interior." The besieged (but a scanty garrison, for many at the news of Stephen's sudden approach had taken flight) unable to endure the impetuous attack, surrendered the Castle, under mutual pledges. Winchcomb is again, for the nonce, the headquarters of a King. Stephen sallied forth for further conflict.

What it cost the town and the adjoining country is witnessed by the almost impassioned plea of William de Solars and the self-sacrifice of the men of Postlip, as well as by the tax-returns of the next reign. In this reign the great fire burned the houses about the Abbey, and with its records, the Abbey, which the houses were built to fortify."

Stephen's son Eustace was known to be fighting at Postlip. From there, because Sennington belonged to Llanthony Abbey connected with Milo, they could have galloped the short distance over the hill to Sennington and destroyed it in a single night in the mid-1140s. The survivors took flight down the hill to the scrub land on the banks of the River Coln.

Sennington Now Became A Deserted Village

1152. King Stephen tried to obtain permission from the Pope to have Eustace crowned King of England. The Pope refused because of Eustace's bad character interested only in fighting, pillaging and destruction. Eustace went on the rampage mainly in East Anglia and Cambridgeshire. He died suddenly in August 1153. The death of Eustace persuaded Stephen to give up the struggle. By the Treaty of Westminster, Christmas 1153, Stephen was allowed to keep the kingdom on condition that he adopt Henry of Anjou – Matilda's son – as his heir. Stephen died in 1154 and Henry II took over without difficulty.

SEVENHAMPTON

The people now started to rebuild their houses of wood and thatch as before and a new village sprang up above the flood plain of the River Coln. The land was still owned by Hereford and leased to Llanthony Priory (Secunda). They may have been helped in this rebuilding by the monks who continued to give them spiritual guidance. Having no chapel now, their appointed priest would have used a preaching cross in the open air around which the people, who by now were all Christian, worshipped. The Bishop then ordered the monks to build a new church. The Norman law of the land said that a church built on Manor land could be taxed if it had a graveyard. Inhumation had now become the common practice and cremation was no longer acceptable. So the new church was set in a graveyard and the taxes went to the King and the Bishop; hitherto the taxes of Sennington went to the Hereford Bishop and one round building among the remains was thought to be that of the store house for grain etc used as tithe as well as winter storage. Houses were still built of wood, which was plentiful, but for the church they used local stone. The Priors of Llanthony and Winchcombe had legal access to some local quarries including the one in Upper Brockhampton which was known to be a working quarry in those times.

Sevenhampton Church c.A.D.1150

The late David Verey, well-known and much respected local archaeologist, in his 'Buildings of England', describes St Andrew's as "A church of Norman and Early English origin, greatly enriched and altered under the Will of John Camber, a merchant of Worcester, who probably had a wool business in the Cotswolds, and died here in 1497".

The architecture of St Andrew's Church is proved to be of many styles. Norman 11-12th century; Early English 12-13th century; Decorated or Early Gothic 13-14th century; Perpendicular 14-16th century; and Tudor 15-16th century.

We know from Domesday Book of 1086 that, together with Prestbury, Sevenhampton was the property of the Bishops of Hereford. Also, from the Hereford Records, that this ownership dates back to A.D.803. The Norman record also shows that there was a church or chapel at Sennington which was destroyed and, in the mid-12th century the present church of St Andrew was built, or the earliest part of it was, this part is of Norman construction. The church was held by Llanthony Priory under the jurisdiction of the Hereford Bishops. Some of the revenue from Sevenhampton/Sennington was used to endow and support the new monastery of Llanthony Priory in Gloucester, after the flight from the Black Mountains of Wales. We also know that Winchcombe and Postlip were almost destroyed in the Civil War in the 1140s and the destruction of Sennington probably followed in c.1145, the survivors rebuilding their village and church at Sevenhampton.

The Norman building must have been started c.1150 A.D. King Stephen, who was the last of the Norman Kings, died in 1154. The first part of the church is known to be Norman. It was a long, hall-type of building stretching from the window at the West end, taking in what is now the inner door of the present church – the Norman doorway still stands on the South side, with a Norman chevron lintel above it. There was a doorway on the South side opposite the North door, also there were windows on each side. Of its early features three flat pilaster buttresses 12-13th century remain at the West end. This, the oldest part of the building, is now the Nave of the completed church.

The people of Sennington then brought down their original, precious stone altar from the remains of their former chapel on the hill. This was placed at the East end of the new church beside a blank wall – there were no East windows in churches at this stage. The inner South wall has a Stoup which may have been part of a Piscina used by the Priest for washing the communion vessels. These were always placed to the South of the altar. There is a matching stoup on the outer wall (now inside the Porch) beside the Norman doorway. These outer stoups were used by the congregation to dip their fingers and cross themselves before entering the church. The church in those days was Roman Catholic.

As the population grew the need for a larger church was recognised and the building was now extended to the present chancel steps. The floor was level throughout

Norman Nave of St Andrew's Church

Norman Doorway with Chevron Lintel   *Stone Bench in porch with Stoup*

and the original roofline adhered to. The new East end wall would still have had no window and the stone altar would have been moved near to this wall. The whole building was still rectangular, whether there were more windows is not known because of further changes to the building at a later date.

The building was extended yet again to its final length by the early 1400s. This extension now had an east window behind the altar and this was Early English. Later this was to be replaced by the present Perpendicular window behind the altar on the east wall.

This new area became the Chancel to which the ordinary churchgoers could not enter. A priest's door (now unused) was added in the south wall, giving the priest his own private access to the chancel.

The Black Death

In 1348 the Bubonic Plague, which had swept across Europe, was brought to England by rats escaping from ships, and spread with extreme rapidity across the whole country; the total population was decimated. The cities suffered most because of the density of the inhabitants, but the country areas suffered too mainly because people escaping from London and other large towns brought the plague with them when they fled to the countryside. It used to be believed that Sennington was depopulated because of the plague, but that was not so as Sennington had been destroyed at least two centuries earlier. Sevenhampton was affected to some extent; they buried their dead from the plague on the north side of the church. But such was the terrible fear of the disease that the windows and door on the north wall of the church were blocked up for protection. It was believed at that time that the disease was airborne. The evidence of this can still be seen in the Nave. For long years after the plague had ended people still disliked burying their dead on the north side until the clergy took it upon themselves to bury their own dead in the north graveyards of churches everywhere, then the old superstition was forgotten.

North Doorway in Nave
Blocked up at time of Black Death Plague

The Tithe Barn

A Tithe Barn was built during the early days of Sevenhampton Church's development. Tithe was a tenth part of each inhabitant's actual produce which had to be paid by law and, since it was paid in kind, e.g. grain, wool, fruit, animals etc., a large barn was required to accommodate it. Built beside the church Sevenhampton tithe barn was said to reach from the site of the Vicarage lower lawn to the now outer wall of the churchyard – the remains of the supporting posts could be seen in the lawn in recent years in very dry weather. The tax was repealed by the Tithe Commutation Act of 1836.

The Plantagenets

The civil war ended when Stephen and Matilda agreed that her son Henry would become heir to the throne. Stephen died in 1154 and Henry of Anjou was crowned King of England in Westminster Abbey on 11th December 1154. He was known as a Plantagenet after his father Geoffrey of Anjou who wore a sprig of planta genesta in his hat. This was the King who appointed Thomas a' Becket as Archbishop of Canterbury and later quarrelled with him. To insure the continuity of his own line Henry committed the unprecedented act in 1170 of crowning his own son and heir Henry as King while his father was yet living. The boy was only nine years old and the ceremony was performed by the Archbishop of York while Thomas Becket was out of the country. Feelings between King and Archbishop grew steadily worse and the King is reputed to have said something like "Will no one rid me of this troublous priest?" Four of Henry's knights on hearing this left for Canterbury and murdered Beckett in his own cathedral. Henry was distraught and Beckett's tomb became a shrine to be visited by many including Henry II.

Sevenhampton's early life was during this period. We tend to think that Crown affairs did not touch the peace of the countryside, but Kings and their war making had some effect on everyone, down to the lowest in the land. The people of Sevenhampton were living through troublous times of their own and would be looking to settle down peacefully. However the manor was always subject to outside influences.

Henry II died in 1189, but his son Henry, whom he had crowned as a child, died before his father. The next son Richard 'Coeur de Lion' inherited the throne. He was a Crusader who spent more time fighting in the holy wars of the Middle East than on ruling his kingdoms in France and England. His younger brother John became king on the death of Richard in 1199.

Charter Roll of John 1204

"One half hide of land in Sevenhampton belonged to Ralph, then to Philip, and John the Clerk and his sons, and then by their grant to Philip Sentelf. The population must have exceeded 100."

Hereford Castle and Cathedral were very close together; both were often greatly damaged in the border wars. Finally the castle was demolished and rebuilt at a greater distance.

"In 1216 By the King's Precept, Ralph Musard, Sheriff of Gloucester, was directed to give to Walter Lacy seizin (possession) of Prestbury and Sevenhampton, belonging to the Bishop of Hereford, the profits to Re-edify Hereford Castle."

(Quotes from Bigland's Genealogical Collections)

This may have resulted from King John's quarrels with the Barons, ending with Magna Carta in 1215. But the precept was not carried out, probably because of John's death in 1216.

The churches at that time were Roman Catholic and answerable to the Pope of Rome.

1291 Pope Nicholas Taxation

Manor 3 carucates held in demesne
(carucate = hide = 60-120 acres)
(demesne = land belonging to the feudal lord)
A Water Mill   paid yearly   13s 4d.
                 (believed to be beside the river in Lower Sevenhampton)
There is a Saxon Crook Bridge – a bridge made of one large Stone here.

Services & Rents of Assize of free and customary tenants	£7 5s 1d.
Ecclesia de Sevenhampton Valor	£9 6s 8d.
Item porcio Decani de Herford	£1 15s 4d.
Item porcio Precentoris de Herford	£1 13s 4d.

Pope Nicholas' Taxation lists all churches in existence by the end of the 12th century. Sevenhampton church was on this list.

From the Conquest onwards England's affairs were closely linked with France and much feuding and fighting continued, with appropriate taxes raised to fund the wars. King John managed to lose Normandy and Anjou, his father's homeland. In the next 100 years 4 Kings, all in direct French descent were all married to French highborn ladies, thus keeping the French connection and much French territory. Edward III started the 100 Years War with France, hoping to reclaim some of the former territories which had been lost. Consequently more local taxes were levied.

In 1327 the Subsidy Roll of Edward III gives a list of taxpayers – "whence is found the Value of Estates, or Holdings in Brockhampton cum Sevenhampton" (this is the first mention of Brockhampton separately.) This list gives some interesting local names of the time:

De Roberto de Solers (12)	iiis vid.
- Johne le Eyre (13)	ixd. 9
- Johne atte Well	iiiis 1d.
- Henr. Le Palmere	xiiiid. ob 9
- Robbo. Copland	iis viid 9
- Galfrido Colynes	xiiid. ob.
- Thoma Bird	iis iiiid.
- Rico Lyplofe	xviiid. ob
- Robt de Hales	xiid. 9
- Galfrido de Wytwelle (10)	xxd. 9
- Johne Henryes	xxiid.
- Nicho Fraunceys	xxid. ob. 9

In 1337 the Manor Estate was enlarged by the addition of lands in Clopley (between Sierford and Sevenhampton) and Whitebourne. Land changed hands many times. In 1362 Edmund de Crupes, of Whittington Court, held in capite (in chief) lands in Brockhampton. Also in 1362 Walter Frenche of Brockhampton in the Wold (as it was now called) granted all his lands in Brockhampton to William House and John le Heyre in fee (freehold). The document was witnessed, interestingly, by John Solers of Shipton Solers, John of Upcote (in Withington), Richard Shakelok, Robert Hillmond and William Genyns of Halling.

Robert Coles of Northleach granted, in 1388, to Thomas le Frenche a Parcel of Wood called Anneys Wood, lying between Puckham and Nash Quarry, abutting on the Bishop of Hereford's land and extending to the King's Highway leading to Stowe. Among the witnesses were T de Walleye (of Walley Farm) and R Olive (of Shipton Oliffe).

1430 Thos. French, Clerk, granted all his lands in Brockhampton, Sevenhampton, Clopley and Whitewell and the grove called Agneys Wood to Walter Baker of Wynchcombe. (Could this be Baker's Wood as we now know it?)

These deeds produce some interesting names from the past which still have relevance to nearby areas, farms, villages etc.

The Wool Trade

Cotswold farming flourished down the ages mainly through its sheep population. The flocks grazed the cleared ground, which provided them with good pasture, they in turn fertilized the soil which was then ploughed and planted with barley. Farming families used sheep's wool for making clothing and, after lambing was over, they used the sheep's milk for butter and cheese making. Cheese could be stored for long periods, so supplementing their diet later in the year. But it was the wool of the sheep which brought the greatest benefits.

The wool trade became a very thriving business in the 14th century. Llanthony Priory became one of the richest Augustinian Abbeys in the country, much of their wealth coming from sheep farming in this area. They held a number of pasturelands both in Sevenhampton and other areas, the largest being at Barrington. Flocks were mostly walked to Sherbourne for dipping, though our local flocks were probably walked to Syreford Mill which had its permanent sheep dip used until the 20th century when chemical dipping became compulsory by law and farmers had to create their own individual sheep dipping facilities. Blockley was the usual place for shearing. If the sheep were sheared nearer to home the fleeces would be taken to Blockley to be graded and stored before being sold to dealers. Sale to dealers would have taken place at Northleach which was the nearest large wool centre.

The Lord of the Manor or the Prior of the Abbey would be paid for the fleeces. The tenants who also kept sheep would send their fleeces with the Lords or Priors wool and would be paid a smaller fee by the Lord or Prior later. The animals were kept for their wool rather than meat but the oldest of the flock would be eaten as mutton eventually. Dr W G Hoskins suggests that these small farmers accounted from 4 to 7 times as much wool as that owned by the landowners.

The King, Edward II, benefited from the wool boom by taxing wool exports, this would be in cash or kind. 30,000 sacks of Cotswold wool was sent annually to the King, and various monarchs exploited this source of wealth.

Much of the country's wealth was made through wool, Cotswold wool being especially prized on the Continent, and many of the now high family names became important through the wool trade e.g. the Spenser family. Many of them turned out whole village populations to create pastureland for sheep. These villagers became vagrant looking for homes and work. This did not happen on the Cotswolds because the villages were small and widely scattered, so there was plenty of land available for large flocks. The fleeces were shipped to Europe, mainly to Flanders, whence it was spun and woven into cloth and exported back to England.

In 1337 King Edward III prohibited the export of wool to Flanders, which was the incident which sparked off the 100 Years War, when Edward was claiming the French throne. This was devasting to both England and France. The Flemish craftsmen were encouraged to emigrate here and England became a manufacturer of cloth as well the producer of raw wool. By the 15th century she was beginning to export wool and cloth abroad.

The owners and dealers became very important and very wealthy at this time. Many of them in the larger wool centres such as Fairford and Northleach put much money into enlarging the local churches, partly for the good of their souls but also to show their wealth and power. One such was JOHN CAMBER, a wool merchant of Worcester, who traded in fleeces from the Cotswolds and other areas. According to the famous Red Book of the Exchequer, which contains an account in Latin of all the Bishop's tenants, John Camber is said to have held land in Sevenhampton. Probably he kept his own flocks of sheep on this land.

John Camber

John Camber died in Sevenhampton on 26th February 1497. He must have travelled widely in his profession for he left money in his Will, dated September 15th 1496, to benefit the church in whichever parish he should die.

"I bequeathe my soule to Almyghte God, oure lady Saint Mary and to all the Hallowes of Heven, and my bodye to be buried within that Holy Churche in whatsoever Parishe it shall so tyme me to decease: And I bequeathe to the same churche werk that my bodye shalbe buried in, Cs."

He also left to the curate of the same to pray for his soule, 6s.8d. To every priest that shall be at the Dirige and Mass at his burying, 8d.

"Two honest priests that be quere (choir) men to help the quere", were to be appointed by his executors, to sing and pray for his soul "within the parish churche in Worcester, by the space of two yeres, to either of them £6 by the yere".

To the Friars Preachers at Worcester to pray for his soul 20s. and a like sum to the Convent of Grey Friars in that city.

His "Month's Mind" was to be kept within St Andrew's church – every priest present at Dirige and Mass to have 6d., every parish clerk 2d., and every other childe that be at Dirige and Mass, 1d.

JOHN CAMBER Wool Merchant

The same day no less than 100s was to be distributed amongst "poore people … to every poore woman and childe, one penny". For the marriage portion of maidens in the same city within a year of his decease, 6s.8d. each.

Various bequests to cousins and others; 40s. to his servant. To his executors Master Thomas Morton, Sir Richard Gardiner and Sir John Sindithurst: the whole residue of his goods to be disposed of "after their discretion and minds for the welthe of his soule". (Thomas Morton was the incumbent of Sevenhampton church.)

This Will was proved in the Court of the Archbishop at Lambeth within two years of its date, viz. May 5th 1498. It was discovered in the Probate Registry at Somerset House by the Revd. J Melland-Hall (one time incumbent of Sevenhampton Church) in 1894.

John Camber was buried in front of the altar in the chancel of Sevenhampton

Church. His likeness, portrayed in effigy in the contemporary merchants dress of the day, was originally placed over his grave, but in later years when the chancel floor was raised this likeness was removed and hung on the south wall of the chancel where it hangs to this day. Others later buried in the Chancel included the Carter family of Charlton Abbots, and some of the Lawrence and Chandler families.

The TRANSEPTS to the church were added in the late 15th century, thus making the church cruciform. Local wool profits were probably used for this. It has been suggested by some researchers that the transepts were originally used as Chantry Chapels with an altar in each. The windows in each are Perpendicular style, which dates from 14th century, with the exception of the south window in the south transept which is Early English, being the original East Chancel window which was removed and put into the south transept.

John Camber's legacy was used to build the tower of the church.

Chantry Chapels were built for private masses for the soul to be said daily. No doubt masses for John Camber were said here. The erection of chantry chapels coincided with the flowering of the Perpendicular style of architecture in England and here wool money would have funded the building The termination of Chantries followed the Dissolution of the Monasteries and the buildings were then used for other purposes.

The Porch

The Tudors were now on the throne, Henry VII was crowned in 1485. Possibly to commemorate this a Tudor Arch was added to the church. The porch has a Tudor arched entrance with pierced quartrefoils in the spandrels, a straight head and stops carved with roses.

In earlier times weddings were conducted before the door of the church. The family and witnesses were seated on the stone benches, while the bride, groom and priest stood at the closed door. The priest married the couple, using holy water from the stoup, in front of the family. Then the priest and wedded couple only went into the church for the blessing at the altar.

This was the custom in the days of Chaucer, author of The Canterbury Tales. To quote from his 'Wife of Bath' –

The Porch with TUDOR ARCH

"For let me say, if I may make so bold
My Lords, since when I was but 12 years old,
Thanks be to God Eternal, Evermore,
Five Husbands have I had at the church door".

Turret and Bell

A bell turret, similar to the one still at St Martin's, Charlton Abbots, would have been over the centre roof of the church between the transepts. This housed the 32" early 15th century bell inscribed with the legend SANCTE GABRIEL ORA PRO NOBIS (St Gabriel pray for us) in Early Gothic characters. This was the Gabriel bell rung every morning and evening and was thus called the 'daybelle' and the 'kerfowbelle'. The midday bell was never rung in England.

The Tower

John Camber's legacy of 100 shillings was used to build the Tower of the church after his death in 1497. Towers on churches were becoming popular at this time to make the church stand out as the most important building in the parish, higher than all other buildings.

What gives the church its charming and unusual character is the way in which the tower has been inserted. Its east arch more or less coincides with the width of

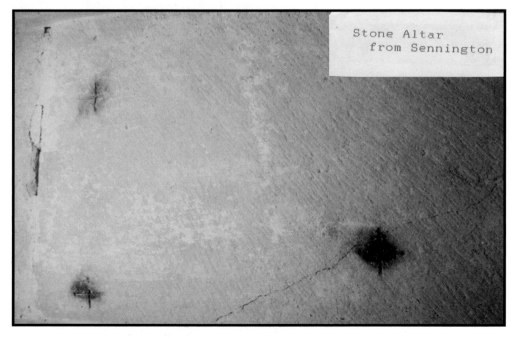

Stone Altar
from Sennington

Stone Altar from Sennington now used as roof in Hagioscope

34

the narrow chancel, so that the other arches of the square are much smaller than the widths of the nave and transepts, and the south-west and north-west corners are supported inside the church by flying buttresses from the west walls of the transepts. The crossing has a tiercon vault high under the belfry, lit by the Perpendicular windows of the tower and supported by angel corbels bearing shields.

In the early days of the church there was no seating, people walked around as they pleased, except for the chancel immediately in front of the altar. Two stout pillars helped to support the tower and a walkway or AMBULATORY was left open between the north transept and the chancel entrance through which people were able to walk. The Chancel floor was raised to the height of the now chancel steps, elevating the altar. Later the floor at the altar end was raised yet again, creating the second steps. The original height of the altar is shown by a low shelf on the wall behind, under the East window. The raising of the floor turned the ambulatory into a Hagioscope or Squint through which people could watch the Host being raised at the Communion Service.

Hagioscope in North Transept

Completion And Dedication

By the early 1500s the building of the church was completed. In 1504, at a ceremony held by the Bishop of Hereford, Bishop Adrian Costello, and other dignitaries, the Church in Sevenhampton was dedicated to ST ANDREW.

The Parsonage House
Among parcels of land granted off by Bishop Costello is a site for a church house in 1504.

"On the 20th September in the nineteenth yeare of the Reigne of King Henry the Seventh, was given one parcel of wast ground lying between the High way and the Church yard, 36 foot in length, and 21 foot in breadth, to build a house called a Church House there, for the use of the Church of St Andrew's in the foresaid p'sh of Sevenhampton by Hadrian Castell then Lord Bishop of Hereford as appeareth by an indenture in our possession … Paying to the Lord of the Manor one halfpenny at the Feast of St Michael yearly."

(The Highway was the main road from Whittington to Church Lane. It crossed the Syreford to Winchcombe 'road' which was merely a sheep track. The Highway continued past the church and over the river and fields, joining the old road to the Quarry – now non-existent, except as a right-of-way.)

Witnessed by principal inhabitants at that period, viz: Thos. Morton (Clerk), Rich. Wenman; John Hawkins; John Watts; Rich. Mason; Will Yonge; Will Townsend; Will Rymall; and Thos. Grove.

In 1683 the deed was held at the Church:

There is no other lands or anything else as we know of given to Pious or Charitable use in our P'sh.

William Longford) Church
William Nind   ) Wardens

Approved by me   Charlton Barksdale Priest
Examined 29 Oct. 1683

(The deed is now held by the County Archivist at Gloucester Record Office)

The Church House was in fact built on land which is now part of the graveyard – to the right of the present gateway facing the church. It is shown on a sketchmap in Rebecca Lightbourne's book of tenants and estate accounts, now held at Whittington Court.

Sennington was never lived in again. The villagers probably looked upon it in fear and superstition. The grass gradually covered the old village.

In 1504 Bishop Costello ordered that SENNINGTON be "PUT IN HAND FOR SHEEP" and so it has remained to this day. (Document in Record Office)

It is now controlled as An Ancient Site by English Heritage and used only for grazing animals.

1509 – Rents of the Lords lands
Church house lately built   New Rent   10 1/2d
(This new rent included some land)

SITE OF CHURCH HOUSE

Site of First Parsonage House

The Highway
Runs from the Quarry to
Whittington now Church Lane

THE TUDOR DYNASTY lasted for 118 years and 5 monarchs

This was a crucial period in the life of the Church generally and St Andrew's in particular. The final building and dedicating of St Andrew's took place during the reign of Henry VII – Henry Tudor.

In 1509 he was succeeded by his second son Henry VIII who had been made by his father to marry his brother Arthur's widow Catherine of Aragon. Henry needed a son to succeed him and this became an obsession with him. Catherine had given him a daughter Mary and at the age of forty was too old to provide a male heir. So Henry appealed to the Head of the church Pope Clement VII to grant him a divorce on the grounds that it was unlawful in the eyes of the church to marry your brother's widow. After a long deliberation the Pope refused.

The Reformation 1533 A.D.

Angered by this refusal Henry took the law into his own hands; cutting the country off from Roman Catholicism. He reformed the Church of England as Protestant and declared himself as its supreme head. Followed by The ACT of SUPREMACY passed by Parliament on 26th March 1534. Henry divorced Catherine and married Anne Boleyn.

The effect on the country generally must have been traumatic, forced to give up the form of worship to which they were accustomed and first brought to these shores by Augustine in 596 A.D. One can only imagine how confused the local Christian congregation must have been, but they were law abiding and would have accepted the changes under the wary guidance of the Llanthony monks.

Henry then turned his attention upon the Abbeys, which at that time were all Roman Catholic, very wealthy and very powerful. In 1535 came The DISSOLUTION OF THE MONASTERIES. The monks were turned out, the Priors pensioned and if they refused to hand over their Abbeys they were executed. The Crown took all the wealth of the Abbeys and sold some of their lands as farmland. The people were relieved for a time from paying heavy tithes to the Abbeys.

LLANTHONY PRIORY at Gloucester had a Prior and 22 Canons, with 80 other people as servants or benefactors when it was handed over to the Crown in 1538. The Prior was pensioned and some of the canons became parish priests. Hereford Cathedral, now presumably Protestant, still held Sevenhampton manor and church.

The people of Sevenhampton would have felt the loss of the monks because of the help they had received from them over very many years. They had been a Medieval Health Service tending the sick in the villages, also providing some sort of schooling for the peasant population. They helped with farming and the wool trade, dipping and shearing the sheep and dealing with the fleeces. The Sevenhampton people were a farming community, however, so they would have carried on with their various associated trades such as miller, baker, thatcher etc as before.

In 1540 following Henry's orders, Thomas Cromwell had thousands of bibles in English printed and distributed to all parish churches. This became known as The GREAT BIBLE translated by William Tyndale and revised by Miles Coverdale.

The land began to change hands. In 1545 was a Grant in the Patent Roll of Henry to William Berners Esq, King's Auditor, and his heirs – of "all the manor, messuage and farm of Sevenhampton, all rectory and church, with all its rights and members, now in the tenure or occupation of Roger Fowler, Yeoman, and lately belonging to the Prior of Llanthony near our city of Gloucester. The advowson of the Parochial Church of Sevenhampton; also all buildings, lands, tenements, pastures, grazings, tithes, oblations, obventions and all other profits and emoluments and the wood, Priors Wood, containing 7 ½ acres --- all to be held in free socage." (socage – lands without service).

This grantee sold the lease of Rectory and the Advowson (the right of appointing a priest to an ecclesiastical benefit) to Joanna Davys, widow. She later married again to Richard Harbert and the Harberts sold to William Wenman of Fringdon, Oxon and Thomas Chandler of Soundborough.

Henry VIII died in 1547 and was succeeded by his only son Edward. His mother was the late Jane Seymour. Edward VI proved to be even more Protestant than his father and in his few short years as King he brought a number of changes to the church.

In 1547 he ordered the dissolution of Chantry Chapels. So no longer would St Andrew's transepts have their altars.

In 1548 all images of the Virgin and other relics were to be removed. The church walls were to be whitewashed, so removing the murals painted thereon telling the bible stories to those who could not read. The pictures were replaced by texts of scriptures in black lettering with borders, as approved by the Protestants.

In 1549 Edward ordered that the Book of Common Prayer in English was to be used in all churches.

In 1550 Edward decreed that all stone altars were to be replaced by wooden tables. This was a particular blow to the congregation of St Andrew's who would not want to see their precious stone altar destroyed. This was the altar brought down from Sennington and revered by the people for 400 years – so they compromised. A wooden altar was brought in and the stone one, complete with its consecration crosses, was placed as a roof to the Ambulatory, or Hagioscope, where it can be seen to this day.

On the death of Edward in 1553, Northumberland had Protestant Lady Jane Grey proclaimed Queen, with unfortunate consequences. She was the granddaughter of Mary, Henry VIII's younger sister, so she had some legal claim to the throne.

Edward's elder sister Mary now became Queen and the country was to experience another violent change to its religion. Mary, like her mother Catherine of Aragon, was a staunch Roman Catholic and she swiftly set about changing the country back to its old religion with the Pope at its Head. Parliament began to dismantle the Edward Reformation Settlement and the Roman Mass was again to be celebrated in all churches. Edward's texts were to be removed – in St Andrew's all that is left are parts of the Creed on the West wall of the South Transept. All dissenters were regarded as heretics and burned at the stake, including Bishop Hooper of Gloucester who was burned outside his own cathedral in 1555. Their heroism is remembered in Foxe's Book of Martyrs. Many were disillusioned by Mary's harsh behaviour, but this lasted for only five years. She died on 17th November 1558.

Elizabeth, Henry's third child, was now Queen of England. At 26 years of age this daughter of Anne Boleyn was a Protestant. So much like her father in temperament it was expected that she would revert to his Church. Gone were the extremes of Mary and her Roman Catholic rule, but also the severe Protestant rule practised by her brother Edward VI.

Elizabeth believed everyone had a right to his own soul and should worship in any way he pleased. She became Governor of the Church of England, no longer supreme head. She disliked Puritan severity and preferred to keep some colour in the church with its vestments and hangings. Worshippers were allowed to kneel to receive the Eucharist. The 1549 Prayer Book and the Bible in English were reintroduced. She did not accept the 1552 Protestant Bible. No doubt there were many religious disputes in some areas, but on the whole life generally had become calmer and safer.

The whole manor continued to be in the possession of the Hereford Bishops, although by now some land was leased which previously had been Priory sheep land. Enclosures of land in Sevenhampton included Ford Hey, Gold Hey and Well Hey. (Hey = meadow)

In 1538 Henry VIII had ordered that an account should be kept of all the baptisms, marriages and funerals undertaken in every church. These records were kept very casually on odd scraps of paper. The law ordered that these should be entered in proper record books in every parish. Past records were to be copied into the books, so many entries were written in the same hand by the current incumbent. This law was not quickly adhered to in many places and Sevenhampton's Register dates from 1558.

1549 Lease of demesne by the Bishop of Hereford, John Skip, to Richard Willison and his heirs for 90 years

In 1559 John Scory became Bishop of Hereford and Elizabeth persuaded him to give up many of the manors held by the Cathedral, particularly the wealthier ones.

In 1562 Bishop Scory granted to Queen Elizabeth the manors of Prestbury, Sevenhampton and Brockhampton in exchange for other estates.

Elizabeth was now LADY OF THE MANOR. Her Steward was Richard Pate of Minsterworth. Member of Parliament for Gloucester and Recorder of that city. He was the founder of Pates Grammar School in Cheltenham. Through him the Queen granted certain tenants the right to enclose land on payment of £5.

Robt Lawrence Gent (Lessee of the manor)	18 acres
W Lord	2 acres
Richd Timbrell	2 ½ acres
W Grove	2 acres
Jno Rymell	1 acre
W Tuffley	1 acre
Arthur Meysey	1 acre
Margt Parkes	1 acre
R Chandler &)	
R Lawrence)	8 acres
Parsonage)	
--- Moor	1½ acres
Myles Burstede	1 acre

1568 William Wenman assigned his moiety (half) to Stephen Hales who passed it to Robert Lawrence, Gent, of Shipton by assignment in 1569. This is the first mention of the Lawrence family in Sevenhampton.

The Queen had her favourites at Court, Lord Robert Dudley was one and Christopher Hatton another, he became one of her Corps of Gentlemen Pensioners (her personal bodyguard). She made him Lord Chancellor and as Sir Christopher Hatton she rewarded him with a number of manors in various parts of the country, including land in his native Lincolnshire where he built Holdenby House as a 'shrine' to his beloved Queen.

Sevenhampton Manor House

In 1576 the Queen granted him lands in Sevenhampton, Brockhampton and Clopley and in Sevenhampton he built the first part of the Manor House by 1590. He became ill and returned to London where he died in 1591, unmarried because, so say, of his love for the Queen.

Another of the favourites at Court was Sir Walter Raleigh, courtier and navigator, who found favour because of his

St Andrew's Church with Manor House before the fire

seafaring exploits. He it was who brought tobacco to this country and cultivated it firstly around Winchcombe, becoming a thriving industry and keeping many local people employed. It went well until the Colonies, particularly America started tobacco plantations, British owned, there. Then it was heavily taxed in this country and eventually declared illegal in England. It is said that the Queen's men uprooted all the crops, but when the soldiers left the locals replanted them. Raleigh was replaced as favourite by the Earl of Essex and then when Elizabeth discovered that Sir Walter was having an affair with one of her ladies in waiting, Bess Throckmorton, she banished them from the Court. Walter and Bess married and lived at Sherbourne.

In 1590 the Queen granted all the manors to favourite Robert Devereux, Earl of Essex. His trustees were Thomas Crompton, Robert Wright and Giles Meyrick.

Essex fell out of favour when his campaigns, particularly in Ireland, were disastrous. He was heavily in debt and when Elizabeth refused to help him he turned to conspiracy against the throne. He was executed for treason and Meyrick with him for complicity. Hereford then held only the Church and the Glebe land.

Compton and Wright then assigned their interest to Sir Thomas Throckmorton of Corse and Richard Nicholas of Prestbury in 1591. In 1593 Sir Thomas' moiety passed to his son William Throckmorton by gift. William then purchased the Nicholas moiety and so became Lord of the Manor of Sevenhampton.

By 1602 Elizabeth was getting very frail, she fell ill at Richmond, yet she still would not appoint her successor, to the chagrin of her Court and advisors. On her deathbed she nominated the son of the late Mary Queen of Scots. She died on 24 March 1603.

Sevenhampton Manor House after the fire

Her Minister, Lord Robert Cecil, sent immediately to Scotland and James travelled south to become James I of England, he was already James VI of Scotland.

Sevenhampton manor lands

1549   Lease of manor granted by Bishop Beauchamp of Hereford to Richard Willyson
1550   granted to William Berners Esq
1553   He sold to Joanna Davys, widow. She sold to William Wenman and
1554   Thomas Chandler
1568   Wenman's moiety (half) sold to Stephen Hales
1569   Sold to Robert Lawrence of Shipton
1562   Bishop John Scory of Hereford granted many of his best manors to Queen Elizabeth in return for other estates.
1576   Lands in Sevenhampton, Brockhampton and Clopley granted to Christopher Hatton. Manor House built.
1590   Queen granted all manors of Sevenhampton and Brockhampton to Robert Devereux, Earl of Essex. His trustees were Thomas Crompton, Robert Wright and Gilly Meyrick of London. Devereux got into financial difficulties and looked to the Queen to save him from ruin. When she refused him he turned conspirator and was executed for treason and Meyrick with him for collusion.
1591   Compton and Wright assigned their interest to Sir Thomas Throckmorton and Reginald Nicholas. Throckmorton passed his moiety to his son William Throckhampton.
1608   William Throckmorton purchased Nicholas half from Reginald Nicholas and Thomas Nicholas his son.
1608   William Throckmorton conveyed the manor to Anthony Lawrence of Shipton.
1605   Sevenhampton Manor House sold to Robert Lawrence by John Carter of Charlton Abbots

The Lawrence Family

Robert Lawrence, Gent, of Shipton acquired his first lease of part of the manor of Sevenhampton from Stephen Hales in 1569. He was a descendant of Sir Robert Laurence of Rixton, Lancs, who in turn descended from a long line of 'de Lancaster' dating from Norman times. Several members of the Laurence family came down to Gloucestershire, acquiring land in Withington, Shurdington, Painswick, Shipton and Sevenhampton.

By 1608 Robert Lawrence Gent and his son Anthony Lawrence Gent were resident in Sevenhampton, having purchased the Manor House in 1605 from John Carter of Charlton Abbots. In 1608 the estate was conveyed to the Lawrences by William Throckmorton.

The Little Shurdington Estate was owned by one branch of the Lawrence family.

William Lawrence inherited it in 1584 and built the house known as The Greenway (now an Hotel). His son William inherited the estate in 1638, his only son died in childhood and the estate passed to his second wife Dulcibella on William's death in 1682. In 1736 Dulcibella died and the estate passed to William's godson Littleton Lawrence. It was later sold in 1854 thus severing the Lawrence connection with Shurdington.

The Sevenhampton line thrived and prospered, adding to the estate. Three plaques in St Andrew's church show Robert Lawrence died 1688; William Lawrence son of Anthony and Culpepper Lawrence died 1693; Robert Lawrence 'Lord of the Manor' of Sevenhampton died in 1700; (the Lawrence family owned enough of the land by now to be Lords of the Manor), also a monument to Walter Lawrence died 1810, late of the Manors of Sevenhampton and Brockhampton. There are Lawrence vaults in the churchyard where other members of the family are buried including the last Lord of the Manor, Christian William Lawrence Esq of Sandywell, died 1920.

In the earlier days the surname was spelled with a U – Laurence, later it was changed to Lawrence. Also in earlier days the heads of the Laurence households were knighted. This is thought to have been deliberately dropped in the days of Charles I. because the Lawrence family did not wish to take sides in the Civil Wars

The Walter Lawrence, who died in 1810, married Mary Hayward; their only surviving child Mary Lawrence married William Morris of Gloucester. They had only one son Walter Lawrence Morris born 1799 who changed his name by Royal Licence in 1815 to Walter Lawrence Lawrence, to keep the family name alive. This was the Walter Lawrence who discovered and had excavated the Roman settlement at Syreford. Mary and William inherited the Brockhampton estate from Rebecca Lightbourne of Sandywell. Thus after both parents died Walter inherited and united all the estates of Sevenhampton, Brockhampton, Whittington and Sandywell for a time.

In 1824 Walter married a very wealthy heiress Mary Splidt. She was the daughter of Christian Splidt of Stratford le Bow in Essex. When she died in 1881 her family had the very beautiful Chancel window put into St Andrew's church in her memory.

This window depicts in stained glass the Transfiguration of Christ in white, with Moses to his left, holding his tablet of stone, and Elijah to his right. Also three of his disciples Peter, James and John below showing great fear of the blinding light.

In 1832 when Walter was experiencing some financial difficulties, he sold

Brockhampton Park, house and estate to his good friend Fulwar Craven, whose family were in residence there and had rented it from Rebecca Lightbourne before her death.

Walter and Mary had three sons – Walter born in 1835, died in 1859, aged 24 – Christian William Lawrence, born in 1836, no doubt named after his grandfather Christian Splidt. Christian William inherited Sandywell, Whittington and Sevenhampton from his father. Walter's third son was Anthony Cocks Lawrence who became Rector of Whittington church for many years.

Christian William Lawrence lived in Sevenhampton Manor for many years. He was a good Lord of the manor, building a school, for the children of Sevenhampton and the surrounding areas, which survived into the 1980s. C W Lawrence was the first Chairman of the Parish Council of Sevenhampton when it was newly formed in 1894. He would have been out of the country in the early days while he was Her Majesty's Ambassador Resident at Quito, Equador. He moved into Sandywell Park in the late 19th century and the total estates became known as the Sandywell Estate and the house numbering in Sevenhampton dates from that time. Many now have individual names but some still retain their Sandywell identity, e.g. 56 Sevenhampton. He died in 1920 unmarried and therefore without issue, leaving his estates to his brother's two daughters.

The Revd. Anthony Cocks Lawrence was married to Mary Anne Ogilvie, daughter of Charles Almore Ogilvie, Canon of Christ Church, Oxford and Rector of Ross, in Hereford. As Rector of Whittington Anthony lived with his wife and two daughters at the Whittington Vicarage. He died suddenly whilst walking in Andoversford one February day in 1904; there is a stone marking the spot where he fell in Station Road near to the Post Office and opposite the new Andoversford Vicarage.

Because the Whittington Vicarage was needed for the new Incumbent the bereaved family moved into Whittington Court which had been used latterly as a farmhouse on the Sandywell Estate owned by C W Lawrence. On his death the elder daughter of Anthony, who was Katherine Mary Cecily Lawrence, inherited the Sandywell/Whittington estate. Her sister Wynnefrede Henrietta inherited the Sevenhampton estate. She caused great consternation among the Lawrence family when she sold most of her inheritance, but fortunately (in view of the later fire at the Manor House) she had removed much of the ancient panelling from that house to Whittington Court.

Katherine Lawrence married Commander Stephen Bowle Evans R.N. in 1911. Sadly he was killed during the Great War (1918). His wife changed her name to Mrs Katherine Evans-Lawrence. Their children were John Evans-Lawrence, who, tragically, was killed during the Second World War, and his sister Stephanie Evans-Lawrence. After the death of her mother, Stephanie lived alone at Whittington Court until her death in 1985.

The Lawrence Dynasty from Norman Times

Roger de Lancaster

Thomas de Lancaster

Laurence de Lancaster   John de Lancaster

1191	Sir Robert Laurence of Ashton Hall, Lancs. Sir Robert Laurence = daughter of James Trafford
1252	James Laurence = Matilda daughter of John Washington (of the U.S.A. Washington family)
1286	John Laurence = Margaret
1360	John Laurence = Elizabeth Holt of Stably Sir Robert Laurence = Margare Holden of Lancs
1454	Sir Robert Laurence of Rixton, Lancs = Amphilis daughter of Edward Longford of Longford, Lancs 2nd son Robert Laurence = Margaret daughter of John Laurence of Rixton
1507-1559	2nd son William Laurence = 1. Isabella 2. Alice of Withington
1521-1584	Robert Laurence of Shipton = Eleanor daughter of John Stratford of Farmcote Eleanor (died 1606) conveyed estate in 1606 to Anthony Lawrence
1588-1645	Anthony Lawrence = Mary daughter of Giles Broadway of Postlip
1638-1700	Robert Lawrence = Mary daughter of John Rogers of Hastleton
1651-1717	Anthony Lawrence = Culpepper daughter of John Colles (physician of Tewkesbury) sons died in infancy 1717 estate passed to sisters Mary and Anne who surrendered it to nephew Walter.
1689-1764	Walter Lawrence = Mary daughter of John Cocks of Woodmancote

1729-1810   Walter Lawrence = Mary daughter of Thomas Hayward

1768-1839   Mary Lawrence = William Morris of Gloucester

1799-1877   Walter Lawrence (Morris) Lawrence = Mary daughter of Christian Splidt of Stratford le Bow, Essex

1835-1859   1st son Walter died aged 24

1836-1920   2nd son Christian William Lawrence H.M. Minister Equador
Lord of the Manor, Sevenhampton

3rd son Anthony Cocks Lawrence = Mary Anne daughter of Charles Almore Ogilvie

1877   Katharine Mary Cecily   1879 Wynnefrede Henrietta
Katharine = Commander Stephen Bowles Evans
John Evans Lawrence d.1946 Stephanie Evans Lawrence d.1985

THE STUART AGE

King James, a Prestbyterian, soon ran into difficulties with Parliament over money and other problems and with the Church over the Roman Catholics who were still struggling for supremacy.

The Gunpowder Plot 1605

James' intolerance led some Catholic gentry to plot against him and on the 5th November when the full house was in session for the opening of Parliament by King James, they tried to carry out their plan to blow up the Houses of Parliament and all parties with it. They were foiled however because one of their number warned his Catholic friends, hoping to save them. John Catesby was their leader, with Guy Fawkes (caught in the act) and John Throckmorton of Lypiatt Park (where they met to make their plans) and several others. Catesby and Fawkes were executed. James ordered that church services be held annually on 5th November to commemorate his deliverance. This continued until Victorian times, when it became the 'Bonfire Night' still celebrated each year. Most churches settled down to Protestantism as we now know it and James became more friendly with both parliament and the church for a while.

James and his parliament needed to know what the strength of the country was in manpower and weaponry, to combat any war or invasion that might occur. For this he drew up a military census, parish by parish, of all his territory. The Returns made in August 1608 for this area were sent to the Lord Lieutenant of Gloucestershire.

Men and Armour for Gloucestershire in 1608

Shenhampton and Brockhampton:

Whereof Sr William Throckmorton knight is Lord

Shenhampton:

Anthony Lawrence gent.	1.p.
Edward Jeynes 1.ca.)	
Henry James 1.m.)	servants to the said Anthony Lawrence gent.
Robert Carpenter 1.ca.)	
Robert Lawrence gent.	hath one musket fur'.
Edward Tuffley his servant	1.ca.
William Chandler yeoman	2.m.
	Hath one musket fur'.
John Parks sen'	tr.
John Parks jun' his sonne.	tr.
Richard Stevens husbandman	1.ca.

John Joynes husbandman	1.ca.
Humphry Lord husbandman	1.ca.
William Bate laborer	1.py.

Brockhampton:

Richard Busteed yeoman	2.p. tr.
Richard Busteed jun. His sonne.	1.p.
Gyles Tymbrell yeoman	1.ca.
Will'm Brevell his servant	1.m.
Anthony Moore	1.ca. tr.
John Mason	1.m. tr.
Thomas Mason yeoman	2.m.
John March	2.py.
William Harvey mason	1.p.
Thomas Longe mason	2.ca.
Will'm Lord laborer	2.py.
Richard Pemberton laborer	1.ca.
John Lord laborer	1.ca.
Thomas Chandler	1.ca.
William Chandler	1.m.

Inhabytants chardged with the finding of Armour not before mentioned. The wholl Thythinge standeth chardged with the finding of one Corslett And one Calyver with the fur'.

Explanation of abbreviations:

Figure 1 indicates an age of about twenty.
   "   2   "   "   "   "   "   forty.
   "   3   "   "   "   "   "   between 50 and 60.

Letter	"p"	shows a man of the tallest stature, tall enough to be a pikeman.
	"m"	shows a man of medium height, tall enough to be a muskateer.
	"ca"	shows a man of shorter stature, not tall enough to be a muskateer, but tall enough to be armed with a caliver – a kind of light harquebus, or portable fire-arm, which could be fired without a rest or support.
	"py"	shows man of meanest stature and fit only to be a pioneer "or of little other use".
	"tr"	trained soldier at time of list.
	"sub"	shows man was a subsidy man, as opposed to a trained soldier.

At the time of 'Men and Armour' the Lawrence family were living in Sevenhampton Manor House. Later in November 1608 Sir William Throckmorton conveyed the manors and their appurtenances to Anthony Lawrence, son of Robert Lawrence of Shipton. Hitherto the Lawrences had leased land in Sevenhampton in Queen Elizabeth's reign.

Deeds of 1605, now in the Record Office, show that John Carter of Charlton Abbots conveyed the Manor House of Sevenhampton to Robert Lawrence of Shipton. Carter also sold land in Brockhampton at this time to Thomas Chandler of Soundborough. In 1610 Robert Lawrence and Thomas Chandler were joint impropriators of the Church lands, Tythes and the Rectory.

Formerly this had been held by Chandler and Wenman, but Wenman sold his moiety to Stephen Hales in 1568 who within a year transferred his interest to Robert Lawrence of Shipton. So from 1569 the Lawrence family held land in Sevenhampton.

The Chandlers were influencial in the area for many years and in the church, holding the Advowson (the right to appoint a Priest to the Benefice) jointly with the Lawrences. W Chandler presented a bell to St Andrew's Church in 1650. This is inscribed:

"BE YEE FOLLOWAIRES OF GOD AS DEARE CHILDREN"

W Chandler 1650

(from the Chandler Foundry at Drayton, Parslow, Bucks)"

He died in 1651, was buried in the chancel and his memorial in Latin hangs on the Chancel South wall – to GUILIEMI CANDELARII de Senhampton.

In 1606 the National Flags of England and Scotland were united. The Red Cross of St George and the White Cross of St Andrew on a blue background joined forces for the new Union Jack.

In 1611 James ordered a new version of the Bible to be prepared, because he considered the Geneva Bible, in common use, to be seditious. Scholars prepared a new translation which became known as the Authorised Version used in churches to this day. A King James Bible rests on the Lectern in St Andrew's and is used for most services.

Sir Walter Raleigh, who had been a favourite of Queen Elizabeth, fell out of favour with King James and was imprisoned in the Tower. However,

Lectern with King James Bible

when James needed to improve his wealth situation, Raleigh was released to lead an expedition to the Orinoco to search for the gold mines reputed to be there. He failed to bring back the desired gold and was returned to prison and executed in 1616.

King James died in March 1625 leaving the country little better for his years on the throne, but considerably poorer financially.

Charles Stuart 1625 – 1649

James was succeeded by his second son Charles. The heir to the throne had been Henry, Prince of Wales, who had been thoroughly schooled for kingship, was athtletic and popular with the people, but unfortunately died suddenly of a fever at the age of nineteen years. Charles was not well fitted for kingship, being small of stature and with an impediment in his speech. The early days of the new monarchy started peacefully enough, but Charles demands for money became excessive. The parliament granted him the country's Tonnage and Poundage for one year – tonnage = tax per tun of all imported wines, poundage = a money levy on the pound sterling value of all imports and exports – but Charles continued to take it long after the year was up. He also pawned some of the Crown Jewels and sold off some of the Crown Land to raise money for himself. Parliament continued to defy him, although they knew he had the power to dissolve it at any time. This he duly did and raised taxes directly himself, such as reviving The Ship Money tax in 1634 to improve his Navy and pay for his war with Spain. This tax had originally been levied on ports only, but Charles brought the whole country into it, making the Sheriff of each county responsible for the whole sum. In this way he ensured the money would be collected, but it made the King very unpopular with his subjects. John Dutton M.P. for Gloucestershire and of the local Dutton family, went to prison rather than pay Ship Money. It was declared illegal and repealed in 1641. His quarrels with Parliament lasted throughout his reign, when the members opposed him he dissolved it, but prorogued it when he needed very large sums of money.

Civil War 1642-1648

The continual problems between Charles and his Parliament eventually resulted in war between them. Civil War broke out with the first major clash between the Royalists (Cavaliers) and Parliamentarians (Roundheads) being at Edgehill in Warwickshire on 23 October 1642. The war raged for many years.

The Civil War affected the whole country, although there was no known fighting in Sevenhampton, battles were fought at Andoversford and Suddeley, where part of the castle was left in ruins, and Winchcombe where the castle was totally destroyed. Both armies were known to have demanded food and accommodation for their troops and as the battles grew worse crops were destroyed and much looting took place. Sevenhampton may have been spared somewhat because Anthony and Robert Lawrence, by then Lords of the Manor, did not declare themselves for King or Parliament. After the war the landowners who did not take sides were forced to pay large fines to the Commonwealth or forfeit their estates.

Sevenhampton was used to help the injured soldiers of both sides at different times who were housed in the Tythe Barn to recover or die. Remains of the Civil War were found near the South door of the church, in the footpath, many years later c.1850 when repair work was being carried out. Four skulls were placed closely together with a portion of a spear or javelin head and a stirrup as if of silver and quite bright even then. There were no other bones found there.

In 1634 the Tewkesbury Feoffes Book records a phenomenal fall of snow which remained until August in the Brockhampton quarry in spite of a very hot summer.

Charles I surrendered to Col Fairfax and Oliver Cromwell who had him tried and executed in Whitehall in 1649. His son, also Charles, had escaped to the Channel Islands. Queen Henrietta Maria and her other children had already moved to France.

The Commonwealth 1649-1660

The war had bankrupted the country and poverty prevailed. Under Cromwell the kill-joy parliament banned all pleasure. Ale houses were closed, sports, cock-fighting and horse racing were banned. The Royalists were heavily taxed.

A narrow religion was enforced which brought a great upheaval for the clergy. All Bishops were removed, the Bishop of Gloucester, Geoffrey Goodman escaped to Wales and his houses were plundered. Many clergy lost their livings and in Sevenhampton there was no Priest during the interregnum. Maybe there were no services but burials of course continued. Table-top tombs on the South side of the church are of the Stuart period dating from the Lord family tomb of 1615 onwards. A rough stone slab covers the grave of a child – Henry Lord died 1650 the first of the Commonwealth period. By now the Lord family were living at Soundborough.

The years of the Republic were hard to bear. Celebrations of May Day and the Twelve Days of Christmas were forbidden. Life did not get back to normal in the countryside although tobacco growing was still thriving stealthily near Cheltenham and Winchcombe in the areas still named Tobacco Close etc. In 1652 the Long Parliament banned it again, but after the Growers petitioned it was allowed for another year.

In 1655 Cromwell banned it yet again and troops were sent to destroy the crops. They were outnumbered by the local people earning a living from the trade and as some of the troops were dealers and planters themselves, therefore unwilling to uproot the crops, the troops withdrew without further action.

Cromwell died on 3rd September 1658. He was succeeded by his son Richard

Cromwell who was a lesser man than his father. Parliament was unpopular, the New Model Army was disbanded and the Commonwealth fell apart.

The Restoration

Charles II 1660 – 1685

After 20 years of turmoil and deprivation the country welcomed back the Monarchy. Most people wished for peace and social order after suffering anarchy, chaos and

Font in Churchyard

military rule. Charles II returned to England and entered London in triumph on his thirtieth birthday 29 May 1660. He was crowned in Westminster Abbey on 21st April 1661. He handled kingship with skill and proved to be the only Stuart with the common touch, whereas the previous Kings had been aloof and haughty. He was a shrewd politician and tried to achieve agreement between the Church of England and the Prestbyterians. He promised 'liberty of conscience'. A new prayer book was drawn up and an Act of Uniformity was passed.

In Sevenhampton, probably to celebrate the Restoration, a simple but elegant, 17th century, chalice shaped font was installed. This Stuart font was removed to the churchyard in 1891, when Waller was altering and updating the church, including much scraping of the walls. A new and elaborate Victorian font was given to the church by Miss Agatha Lawrence in memory of her parents. The Stuart font remained in the churchyard until 1953 when it was decided to bring it back into the church again. It was mounted, by Mr E W Barnfield, on a stone adjoined to a pillar at the chancel steps. It is now used to great effect by the flower arrangers with beautiful displays throughout most of the year. However, in Lent it stands empty, when its simple beauty can be appreciated.

Charles II lived through major distractions

Restoration Font

during his monarchy such as the Great Plague of 1665 which caused many deaths in London and other major cities, followed in 1666 by the Great Fire, which destroyed two thirds of London including St Paul's Cathedral.

Charles II died in 1685 and was buried in Westminster Abbey.

D444 M3 18th October 1676

Names of TENANTS and RESIDENTS within the Manors of Sevenhampton and Brockhampton – taken from the COURT ROLLS covering land disputes, water rights, stopping of bridal ways etc.

George Slytor Bayliffe
Giles Mason Constable
Richard Rogers Gent
Paul Dodwell Gent
John Carter Gent
John Jordon Gent

Thomas Harrison
Joseph Hinksman
Thomas Longford
William Longford
Thomas Timbrell
Robert Mason
William Nind
John Joynes
William Bursteed
John Mason senr of Brockhampton
Robert Mason senr of Sevenhampton
William Joynes senr
William Young
Edward Manley senr.
John Mason of S'ton
John Ebsworth senr
Josias Mason
Thomas Bloxam
John Williams
Edward Thorndell
James Wicksey
Samuel Hall
John Arkell
Richard Johnson senr
Robert Mason junr

John Thorndell
Thomas Woodward
Robert Protherow
John Hill senr
John Hill junr
William Marsh
Thomas Hill
Zachary Hooper
Henry Ashward
ffrancis Willis
Samuel Timbrell
John Mason junr of Brock.
Robert Timbrell of Brock.
Isaac Arkell
Daniel Hinksman
Thomas Horseman
Richard Keare
Nathaniel Mason
Robert Timbrell junr S'ton
Richard Johnson senr
Giles Mason junr
Richard Hall
ffrancis Hill
William Mason
Joseph Curtis

Richard Johnson senr	Giles Harman
William Woodward	William Joynes junr
William Arkell	Henry Davis
William Manley	Thomas Mansell
Bartholemew Whittorn	John Ebsworth junr
fferdinande Mustoe	George Roover
Thomas Andrews	George Kitson
ffrancis Joynes	John Child
Edward Manley junr	John Carpenter

James II

The remaining Stuart years brought more problems to the Church. The reign of James II, a Roman Catholic, lasted only three turbulent years. Finally seven Bishops – 'The Immortal Seven' – together with Parliament, invited James' Protestant nephew William of Orange to come to England to protect liberty and his wife Mary's right to succeed to the throne. Mary was James' elder daughter. William was offered the honour of becoming Regent to his wife QUEEN MARY. This he refused and decided to return to Holland. However it was accepted finally that they should be given equal status, so together they ruled as KING WILLIAM and QUEEN MARY.

James meanwhile had fled to France, still claiming the throne as his, to collect an army and returned through Ireland. William and his army met him in the Battle of the Boyne in July 1690 where James was thoroughly defeated. The Irishmen, who joined forces with William and fought with him, thereafter became known as the Orangemen. James fled to the Continent yet again and died of a stroke in 1699.

Queen Mary died of smallpox in 1694 followed by William in 1702. James' second daughter came to the throne as QUEEN ANNE. She was married to Prince George of Denmark and had many children all of whom died in infancy. Anne died in 1714 without an heir, thus ending the one hundred and eleven years of Stuart domination.

Brockhampton Park

It was during the reign of Charles I that Paul Pearte Esq, Comptroller of the King's Counting House and undoubtedly a very wealthy man, purchased land known as Ford Hey from Thomas Chandler of Soundborough in 1639. The Chandlers had acquired the land from the Carter family of Charlton Abbots. It had earlier belonged to the de Croupe family of Whittington. Paul Pearte also purchased more land in Brockhampton from Anthony Lawrence of Sevenhampton.

On Ford Hey he built 'Brockhampton House', in the new Cotswold Style stone buildings, a double fronted, 5-bay building with two gables at each side, which is now the centre and oldest part of the much extended house. He surrounded his house with

BROCKHAMPTON PARK
Centre section original Brockhampton House

ornamental parkland, a very beautiful setting for a gentleman's country seat. (This is featured in Sir Robert Atkyns book 'The Ancient and Present State of Gloucestershire of 1712.') On land purchased from the Lawrences he built about six stone cottages for his key people. These were long, low, two storey buildings of one room width and an innovation for his time as staff had not been so well housed hitherto. Most villagers were still living in houses of wood, wattle and daub with thatched roofs.

Paul Pearte would have known little of the Civil War and enjoyed his house for a very short period only for he died in 1642 without issue, but he willed his property to his niece Anne Skipwith. She married Ralph Dodwell of the Dowdeswell family and their daughter Anne married Thomas Timbrell of the powerful family of Winchcombe and other areas, landowners dating back to the mid 1500s. The Timbrell name is of the oldest, continuous family in the area, surviving from the 16th to 21st century.

Ralph Dodwell's son Paul inherited Brockhampton Estate in 1663. He married Dame Elizabeth Rogers of another well-known family of Dowdeswell and Southam, widow of Sir Walter Raleigh of Sandywell Park. He was the grandson of the famous Elizabethan Sir Walter Raleigh. Their son William (later Sir William Dodwell) inherited in 1690. He greatly enlarged the estate by land purchase from the Nind family of Oxlease and the Lord family of Soundborough and was something of a personality in his time.

Sir William married twice, first Anne, widow of John Deleau of Whaddon, Gloucester and secondly Mary, widow of Thomas Miller Esq, a memorial on the Chancel North wall of St Andrew,s Church tells something of their story. By Anne he had a daughter Mary Dodwell to whom the estate passed on William's death in 1727. Mary married Thomas Tracy of Toddington.

Park Lodge, Main Gate

East Lodge

Sandywell Park

Referred to in early documents as Sandiwell but later changed to Sandywell.

The land belonged to the Rogers family of Dowdeswell from the late 16th century, when in 1588 Robert Rogers bought a farm called Ligons – now Sandywell.

In 1650 William Rogers' daughter married Paul Dodwell of Brockhampton Park, Sandywell then became the property of Paul through marriage. Their son, William Dodwell, sold the land in 1704 to Henry Brett of Brett Hall in Warwickshire. He it was who built the first part of the house.

In 1712 Henry Brett sold Sandywell to Lord Conway, of Ragley Hall in Warwickshire, who greatly enlarged the house. He also enlarged the estate in 1720 by purchasing the manor of Whittington. So Sandywell and Whittington were one estate.

Lord Conway died in 1732 and his son the Earl of Hertford sold the Estate for £17,250 to Thomas Tracy, Member of Parliament, son of John Tracy of Toddington, and married to Mary Dodwell. Mary and Thomas had but one surviving child, a son Dodwell Tracy, but he died in 1768, aged 21 years, unmarried, in Paris on his return from the young man's Grand Tour. Thomas, his father, died 2 years later in 1770, leaving his widow Mary, who was by now Lady of the Manors of Sandywell, Whittington and Brockhampton, living alone in Sandywell Park. She leased Brockhampton Park and the Revd John Craven was for many years her tenant.

There is a story told of George III who visited Cheltenham in 1788, with his Queen Charlotte, to take the waters. They stayed in Bayshill Lodge and travelled around the countryside nearby during their stay, including Stanway House where a plaque was put up to commemorate the visit. The King had heard of a famous black stallion at Brockhampton Park, so he paid them a visit. It seems he wanted to buy the horse but the price was too high for him. However he was entertained to a meal at the house and recorded that he was given an excellent meal of boiled mutton and carrots. Emma Dent tells of this visit in her 'Portrait of Suddeley'.

Mary died intestate in 1799. This caused an upheaval in her large estate affairs. The inheritance problem was taken to High Court and 1806 the Court of Common Pleas awarded the estates to three 'sisters' Judith and Patience Timbrell and Rebecca Lightbourne née Timbrell. Patience née Gladdon was the widow of William Timbrell who died in 1774. He was brother to Judith and Rebecca. The Timbrell family were living in the Cotswolds from the 1500s.

Anne Skipwith, who inherited the Brockhampton estate from her uncle Paul Pearte in 1641, had married Ralph Dodwell of Whittington. Their daughter Mary Dodwell married Thomas Timbrell in 1651 from whom the three Timbrell claimants descended. Ralph and Anne's son Paul inherited Brockhampton Park and his son Sir William Dodwell greatly enlarged Brockhampton estate, but sold the Sandywell estate, later purchased by Thomas Tracy.

The Timbrell sisters moved into Sandywell Park – Judith was a spinster, Patience a widow and Rebecca a divorcée. They were illiterate and ran their large estate with much guiding help from William Morris of Sevenhampton Manor, husband of Mary Lawrence. Rebecca and her sisters objected to the Railway Bill of 1811, in case they should lose any of their land to this new invention.

Rebecca outlived her sisters, Judith died in 1812 and Patience in 1816. Their branch of the Timbrell family had become Goldsmiths, Silversmiths and Fishmongers in London. Rebecca herself was known to have worked in the fish market, acquiring a drink problem and a rough temper. One of her tenants said of her "she was quite easy to get on with – when she was sober". In her better moments she did much good for the village.

Whittington School

Rebecca Lightbourne started a school in Whittington for all the local children. The school and the school house were on the land now occupied by the Village Hall. It opened in 1818 and the first Master was Jeremiah Greenway. Accounts show "in 1818 Revd. Hicks for Jeremiah Greenway – salary Whittington School £10." No doubt this was one year's salary.

Parents were not too anxious to send their children to school when they could be more usefully employed helping them on the land. They made up excuses for non-attendance, such as not knowing what day the school was to be held, or at what time. So Rebecca had a large bell installed, which could be heard from a considerable distance, to be rung before school commenced.

It was described as a Charity School, but there were a few fee-paying parents. Children came from long distances, walking of course. The registers show children from Brockhampton Quarry, Sevenhampton, Syreford, Andoversford, Kilkenny and Charlton Kings as well as Whittington children.

The school closed in 1829 but re-opened in 1830 with William Cox as Master. After him came Richard Hendrick and later William Winstone, each of these had children of their own attending the school. In the registers is a column headed 'reason for leaving' – went to work; went into service; wanted at home; one family left to attend Dowdeswell school, so there must have been a school at Dowdeswell; one poor little girl's reason for leaving said simply 'Dead'.

Tenants of Rebecca Lightbourne from the Rent Books

1814	Thomas Bee	–	Upper Farm, Brockhampton
	John Rowland	–	Oxlease Farm
	John Trotman	–	Lower Farm, Sevenhampton
	William Cox	–	Whitehall Farm
	Joseph Timbrell	–	Coulsgate Farm

1818	James Agg (Hewletts)	–	Puckham Farm	
	James Morris	–	Little Calcum	Oathill Field
			Lower Calcum	Plovers Piece
			Court Field	Pocketts Piece
			Elsdown Field	
	Thomas Bee	–	Upper Farm	Fields two sides of
	Yeoman		Quarr Ground	Brock Village
1818	William Arkell	–	Paddock, Perch Pool	
	John Lovering	–	Gassons Fields	
	John Hincksman	–	Blackthorn Field	Hawthorn Field
	Sunborough		Hampen Common	Oathill Field
			Land around Oxleys & Sunboro	
	John Trotman	–	Lower Farm, Sevenhampton	
	John Brown Esq	–	lands Shipton end of Brockhampton	
	Thomas Denley	–	Lands in Quarr Ground	
1824	John Humphris	–	Whitehall Farm	

Living in Sandywell Park, Rebecca, who having outlived her sisters, leaned heavily on William Morris to help with her business affairs. Rebecca's husband left early in the marriage and there were no children. This accounts for Rebecca leaving her estates to William Morris, who in turn handed them on to his son Walter Lawrence. Sevenhampton thus became united with Brockhampton, Sandywell and Whittington for a time as one very large estate. When Walter Lawrence got into financial difficulties, in 1832, he sold Brockhampton Park to his friend and companion Fulwar John Colquit Craven Esq. Thereafter Sevenhampton and Brockhampton became two separate manors again, but were still one Parish.

After Rebecca's death in 1823 part of her Brockhampton estate was possessed by Theodore Gwinnett, solicitor of Cheltenham, to discharge her debts. On Gwinnett's death in 1827 his trustees resold this to Walter Lawrence.

The Cravens acquired Charlton Abbots also. The stained glass, East Chancel window of St Martin's Church was given as a memorial to Georgina Craven, who died in 1878. Two plaques, also in the Chancel, commemorate Charles Goodwin Colquit Craven, who died in 1889, on the South wall and Fulwar John Colquit Craven, died 1890, on the North wall. They were Georgina Craven's husband and son. All three were buried in St Andrew's churchyard in Sevenhampton, in a group of red marble edged graves each with a red marble cross. Beside these is the grave of Kate Kennedy Locke who was for many years their loved and trusted housekeeper, she died in 1883.

The Revd. John Craven was Minister of Sevenhampton Church for a very short time after the Revd. John Lawrence died in 1803. His family were resident at the Park as tenants of the Timbrell/Lightbourne sisters.

He was the only one of three brothers who survived to adulthood. He had five sisters, three of whom were later Mrs Hincksman, Mrs Bishop and Mrs Lloyd. They were the children of the Hon. Charles Craven, one-time Governor of South Carolina. Charles had married Elizabeth daughter of Col. John Staples, and in their early married life lived at Lenchwick in Worcestershire, where all their children were born. Later they moved to Brockhampton Park, where they were involved in a local scandal.

The mother was of a stern tyrannical temper and the children were brought up in fear not love. They were sometimes not allowed proper food, but were required to eat what was loathsome to them, and were often relieved from hunger by the maids privately bringing them up bread and cheese after they were in bed.

Mrs Craven was frequently away on visits and usually took one daughter with her when they were young women. It was while they were away on one such visit that young Mr Hincksman of Soundborough aspired to the hand of one daughter. His friend, a horse dealer named Bishop wanted another daughter and they all ran away together to get married during their Mother's absence. The Hincksman marriage turned out quite well, but the Bishop one was deplorable.

The third daughter, fearing the brunt of her Mother's anger, left home before her Mother returned. She later married a Mr Lloyd. Their daughter, Caroline, eventually married the elder brother of Jane Austen the famous novelist. Her sister, Martha, married another Austen brother who became an Admiral and was later Knighted.

Fulwar Craven, son of the Revd John Craven, was a Magistrate for the city of Gloucester and had been Deputy Lieutenant in Wiltshire. He was described by Gwen Hart in her History of Cheltenham as "the 'eccentric' Fulwar Craven of Brockhampton and cousin to the colourful Berkeley Craven patron of the Cheltenham Races". Brockhampton House had been considerably enlarged by 1835.

Fulwar's daughter, Georgina, was the next owner of the estate. She married Charles Goodwin of Cheltenham, one time High Sheriff of Gloucestershire. He changed his name to Charles Goodwin Colquit Craven to keep the family name alive. As many highborn ladies did at this time, Georgina had a schoolroom built to educate the children of her estate workers. It closed in 1877 and the pupils were moved to the new school in Sevenhampton. Georgina died in 1878.

The schoolroom stood idle for 7 years until Charles Craven opened it as a Library, with books, newspapers and magazines, open daily for men only. Mr Craven was able to keep a regular supply of books from his contacts in London. It then became known as the READING ROOM. He died in 1889 and his son Fulwar John Colquit Craven died in 1890 without an heir.

The estate now passed to relatives who rented to Major de Freville. He took an interest in the village and became President of the Reading Room, but he left the area a few years later. The estate was then sold to Colonel Fairfax Rhodes in 1900.

Col. Rhodes was the son of John Rhodes a wealthy Leeds Stockbroker and himself a Barrister of the Inner Temple in London. He was remembered as a Good Squire by many of the older villagers. There were then two good Squires in the Parish, Col Rhodes of Brockhampton and Christian William Lawrence Esq of Sevenhampton, Sandywell and Whittington. Col Rhodes also bought Charlton Abbots Manor House and estate.

Fairfax Rhodes married Mary Cooper of Gledlow Hall, Leeds and there were four children, two of whom died in infancy. Their daughter Alice, born 1871, married Arthur Hayes Sadler (later Admiral) and they lived in Charlton Abbots Manor House. Fairfax Rhodes' son John was born on 24 December 1877.

John Fairfax Rhodes was educated at Eton College and entered the 2nd Dragoons of the Royal Scots Greys in 1899. He was soon promoted to Lieutenant in September and his Regiment was sent to South Africa in October 1899. He served throughout the war in operations of Cape Colony, the Relief of Kimberley and the Advance of Bloemfontein. They were sent into action against the Boers at Klippan near Springs, outnumbered and outmanoeuvred. Lt Rhodes was shot in the stomach and fell from his horse. He died in the ambulance taking him to hospital, accompanied by the Padre Father Hill, and was buried in South Africa. His uncle Cecil Rhodes (of Rhodesia) had his body exhumed and returned to England accompanied by a Sergeant and five men of the Royal Scots Greys.

It was a great local tragedy when John Fairfax Rhodes was killed in action in the Transvaal in 1902 during the South African (Boer) War. His body was brought back for burial in the family tomb at St Martin's Church, Charlton Abbots. Returning by train to Notgrove Station, thence it was carried by wagon to the church. Ferns and hay were strewn on its route past Brockhampton Park, to deaden the sound of the wheels and the horses' hooves, for the sake of his invalid mother who did not attend the funeral. In 1903 Col Rhodes extended the Village Hall in memory of his beloved son.

Col. Rhodes was the owner of three motor cars, when these were a rarity especially in the countryside. He had two Rolls Royces, one of which was especially adapted for the convenience of his invalid wife, the other was an Arrell Johnson which the villagers thought was quite wonderful, some never having seen a motor car before. Mrs Mary Rhodes died in 1915 and was buried in the family tomb at Charlton Abbots.

Col. Rhodes married again in 1916 to Mary Louise Snowdon widow of the Revd. R.K. Snowdon. He died in 1928 and was also buried in the family tomb at Charlton Abbots. Mary left the village in 1934 to live in Cheltenham and the Park and Estate were sold. Mary died in 1941.

ARRELL JOHNSON Car

Brockhampton House/Park

1639   Paul Pearte Esq. builds Brockhampton House. Died 1642

1642   Anne Skipwith (niece) inherits. Married Ralph Dodwell died 1663
        Daughter Anne married Thomas Timbrell

1663   Paul Dodwell (son) married Dame Elizabeth Rogers. Paul died 1690.

1690   Sir William Dodwell (son) married 1. Anne Deleau 2. Mary Miller
           William died 1727

1727   Mary Dodwell (daughter) married Thomas Tracy M.P. died 1770
           Dodwell Tracy (son) died 1768
        Mary died intestate 1799

1806   Court of Common Pleas awarded estate to three sisters.
        Judith Timbrell   Patience Timbrell   Rebecca Lightbourne
        died 1812   died 1816   died 1823

1823   William Morris married 1796 Mary Lawrence of Sevenhampton Manor

Walter Lawrence Lawrence (son) inherited Sandiwell/Whittington estate
Also Sevenhampton /Brockhampton estate. Sold Brockhampton Park to

1832   Fulwar Colquit Craven died 1860 son of Revd John Craven

1860   Georgina Maria (daughter) married Charles Goodwin (Craven)
died 1878 died 1889

1889   Fulwar John Colquit Craven (son) died 1890

Brockhampton Park rented to
1891   Major Edward de Freville

Sold to
1900   Col Fairfax Rhodes married Mary Cooper (died 1915)

1902   John Fairfax Rhodes (son) killed in action South African War

1928   Death of Col Fairfax Rhodes

1934   Brockhampton Park Estate
split up and sold

The Court House

Built for dealing with law and order on the estate, was also used as an Estate Office controlling the affairs of the whole of Brockhampton Village.

The Court House
Centre section built by Paul Pearte

The Reading Room – Rhodes Memorial Hall

The first part of the building was a single storey room, possibly with a small entrance hall, erected in 1864 for Mrs Georgina Craven as a School for the children of Brockhampton Park estate workers. It was used thus until 1877 when the school was closed and the children were sent to the new Sevenhampton School. Mrs Craven died in April 1878.

In 1881 Mr Whitbread of Salem Chapel in Cheltenham obtained permission to hold a Baptist Sunday School for the chapel children in the now unused room. Then in 1885 Mr Charles Goodwin Colquit Craven, husband of the late Georgina Craven, reopened the Room as a library, well stocked with books, changed every six months by a London Book Club, also newspapers and magazines such as Tattler, London Illustrated News and Punch. The room then became known as The READING ROOM and was open in the evening to men and boys only, at a membership fee of one shilling per year.

Until 1887 the room was known as the Brockhampton Reading and Coffee Room and apparently the coffee on sale was less than the normal Coffee Tavern prices and served in greater comfort than in the coffee taverns of the time. 'In October 1887 a member of the Brockhampton Reading and Coffee Room (familiarly known as the Institute) claimed in a letter to the Cheltenham Free Press that "we can, without exaggerating at all, boast of having a Reading Room second to none in any of the villages on the Cotswold Hills." Fifteen years later a Cheltenham visitor

Georgina Craven's School Room / Reading Room

65

to Brockhampton described the Reading Room as "the envy and admiration of the whole Countryside". Reports of its activities, which appeared regularly in the Cheltenham press over a quarter of a century, show that it was an exceptionally enterprising and successful institution.

A founder member and guiding spirit of the new institute was Edward Whitbread – his picture is on the Reading Room wall besides that of Col Fairfax Rhodes. Mr Whitbread was a Cheltenham Draper and a member of Salem Baptist Chapel when from 1887 he and a team of teachers had made the journey on foot from Cheltenham to run a Sunday School in the village. Once involved as Manager of the Institute he made his arduous journey twice a week. He was the driving force bringing energy, enthusiasm, imagination and organising ability to the task as well as his time and money. He acknowledged that running the Institute had become his life's work, although he was also an active Governor of Cheltenham British Schools and first Treasurer, then Chairman, of the Cheltenham Sunday School Union.

Mr Craven and others were generous with their donations, thus enabling the room to be well furnished and well lit with a number of oil lamps hanging from the ceiling, also some wall brackets. Mottoes were used to decorate the walls such as 'Economy is the easy-chair of old age'. Later some etchings were given by the Cheltenham artist and Guide Book writer Edward J Burrow. Mr Burrow and Mr Whitbread were colleagues and together they started the Salem Institute in Cheltenham in 1905.

Mr Whitbread of The Institute and Baptist Chapel

Charles Craven died in 1889 and his son Fulwar John Colquit Craven died in 1890 so the supply of books to the library ceased. The organisers inherited only a static library and this required building up to make it a viable library again. A fund raising programme included a Sale of Work on Easter Monday arranged by the Misses Coombe. This must have been most successful because shortly afterwards the library was reported to have 400 volumes and £13 in hand to purchase further copies. Mr Christian Lawrence gave a Panorama of the World's History, probably in several volumes and Capt St

Clair Ford added some useful technical books including a series on farming. A Miss Pembry of Cheltenham was thanked for her contributions to the library stock which had been built up to 700 volumes. By 1912 the library reached its maximum of 1,000 volumes.

The Institute was open to villages covering a large area, enjoying the patronage of the owners/occupiers of Brockhampton Park, Sevenhampton Manor and Sandywell Park. Because some members had to travel some miles to and from the Hall, the closing time was fixed at 9 p.m. to accommodate them. On club nights a variety of wholesome edibles and non-alcoholic beverages were available. They were provided as a service rather than as a source of income and members could enjoy an ample supper for threepence. The refreshments may have been provided by the then non-resident caretaker, for Mrs Norris was presented with a Queen Anne teapot and tea set in 1907, probably for her long service.

The management provided by way of entertainment chess, draughts, bagatelle and playing cards for the over-18s. It said much for the intelligence of the farm workers that they were able to master and excell at chess. The first match in the handicap tournament of 1889 against an outside team was played and won against the Cheltenham Working Men's Club who visited Brockhampton. This further added to the fame of the Institute by reports in the Press. By 1906 chess gave way to a draughts tournament for cash prizes. Then whist became the popular game for in 1909 a Whist Secretary was appointed and Mr Whitbread was authorised to grant an extension on the opening time to hold Whist Drives.

The Institute then began to hold a programme of social evenings, carefully balanced between enlightenment and entertainment. Mr Whitbread originally provided a lecture or concert once a month, but this proved so popular one evening a week had to be set aside for them. Mr Whitbread had a large number of friends prepared to make the journey to instruct or entertain the members. According to the local press "Mr John Sawyer, the Cheltenham Printer, spoke on 'Bits of Brockhampton History' illustrated with lantern slides'. Other lecturers spoke on 'Earthquakes' and 'The Transvaal Question' at the time of the Boer War. Mr Sawyer also spoke on the geology of the area 'The Sevenhampton Valley – what is it made of and how was it made'.

From 1896 the Institute, apparently recognised by the County Council as constituting a Local Technical Education Committee, was able to take advantage of the courses available under the technical education programme. Over the year courses were provided in butter making, cookery, wood carving, cottage gardening, poultry rearing and marketing. Under the County Council's 1903 scheme for adult education the Institute became a sub-centre for Cheltenham Grammar School's evening classes. In the 1908/9 season it pioneered a course in agricultural woodwork – making farm gates, hurdles etc. This was later taken up by other rural centres. Classes were also started to study agricultural pests and Mr Whitbread provided the students with a microscope.

The membership of the Institute was initially one shilling per season, increased to 2/6d in 1889, the fee for juveniles remained at 1/-. Until 1889 the membership had been for males only, but the Vicar of Sevenhampton, the Revd Joseph Storr put in a plea for the ladies when they were then allowed access to the newspapers and magazines during the daytime.

Ambulance instruction for men and women was offered over the years with occasional demonstrations in first-aid by two of Mr Whitbread's friends. However, in 1896 Dr W Cox, Medical officer of Health for Winchcombe and Superintendent of the Cottage Hospital, volunteered to give first-aid classes to as many villagers as Mr Whitbread could assemble. The response was excellent with up to 70 persons enrolling for a season. The courses consisted of 10 lectures and continued until 1912. All sections of the community were involved.

Major E H G de Freville M.F.H. followed the Cravens as resident of Brockhampton Park. He was described as a popular President of the Institute. If, as in February 1898, he was prevented from attending an Institute function 'by an extra long day's hunting', he was careful to send a contribution. His wife and daughter set a good example by enrolling in the ambulance classes in the early days, also the Unwin ladies from Dowdeswell Court. The annual distribution of medals and certificates became an important social event.

The earliest entertainment at the Room, as far as records show, was in March 1884 when Mr Whitbread brought a company of ladies and gentlemen from Cheltenham, transporting them in brakes. They gave two shows, one for children then one for adults. This, of course, was well received and was followed by concerts of local talent. In February 1896 the room was crowded to excess when "very pleasing and capitally rendered dialogues" were given by children and young people. Mr Whitbread organised all the activities and, when a concert coincided with a house party, the local gentry brought their guests along.

Col Fairfax Rhodes purchased Brockhampton Park in 1900. For nearly 20 years the Institute had functioned in the single room until Col Rhodes built the extension, with two identical porchways added. This was built in memory of his only son Lieut. John Fairfax Rhodes.

The Institute enlarged its activities when in 1908 Col Rhodes provided a miniature rifle range, described as "full sized, 55 ft, well housed and well equipped". It ran along the back of the Hall (the entrance being where the modern garage doors were). It was officially opened by Mr J D Birchall, President of the North Gloucestershire Association of Miniature Rifle Clubs.

The Institute Rifle Club proved to be immensely popular with the young men and a membership of 96 was achieved in the first year. A membership fee of 1/- per year was made, excluding the ammunition which had to be purchased from the club.

Col Rhodes gave a silver cup to be won by internal competition and the winner in the first year was Mr Hyatt on Boxing Day 1908. Also during the first year the

Institute won all three matches against local rifle clubs. In 1909 they joined the North Gloucestershire Association when they came up against stronger opposition, for in December of that year they defeated a combined team of E and F Companies of the 5th Gloucestershire Territorials.

Col Rhodes built on to the Hall, at the Reading room end, a cottage for a Caretaker as it was decided that a resident caretaker was now required to provide services such as cleaning and setting up for meetings etc. also to undertake minor repairs. A date on the wall of the cottage gives 1908. In later years when a kitchen was added to the Hall – previously all washing up had to be done on tin trays and water heated either on the open fire (a tiled fireplace was in the wall opposite to the entrance door) or on a tortoise stove when drinks or food were provided – and a bathroom added to the cottage, part of the disused rifle range had to be demolished.

Caretakers: Mrs Norris (non-resident) in 1907 she was presented with a Queen Anne teapot for long service.

      Mrs James in 1909 moved in to the cottage

      Mr Harry Vernon & Ethel Vernon, daughter, she later became Mrs Chris Locke

      Miss Birkenhead

      Mr & Mrs John Smith

      Mr & Mrs Mick Denley the last caretakers left the village in January 2000.

The Colonel had the Hall wired up for electricity to come from the Park's own supply. This was long before electricity was brought to the whole village in the 1940s. He was a great benefactor and when the hall got into debt he cleared it himself, but required that the fees for its use should be increased, to 5/- per person, but the original cost of 1/- would apply to industrial and agricultural workers for the time being.

When Col Rhodes died in 1928 his second wife Mary took on his responsibilities as Squire. The Parish Council obtained her permission to use the Reading Room for their meetings, they had previously met in the Sevenhampton schoolroom. In 1934 she left the village and the estate was divided up and sold. The Col had in his Will left the Hall to the village, with £1,000 in trust for its maintenance and support.

At a Parish Council meeting of Monday, 7th May 1934, a letter was read from the late Col Rhodes Trustees asking "if the Council were willing to take over the Brockhampton Room as from 2nd June 1934 as directed in accordance to his Will". This was agreed to and a form from Lloyds Bank was filled in for a Reading Room Account. Mr Nairne to take over as Honorary Secretary and Treasurer.

The Rhodes Memorial Hall

On the proposition of Mr Nairne it was unanimously agreed to, that the Reading Room be named –

"THE RHODES MEMORIAL HALL".

Parish Council adoption of the Reading Room

(a) The Parish Council consider themselves responsible for the management of the Rhodes Memorial Hall, following a decision taken at a Parish Meeting on the 17th September 1934, when it was resolved that a committee should be formed to manage the Hall and a committee was selected at that meeting.

(b) The Parish Council are now willing for a Scheme to be made, if this is required by the Department of Education and Science, to enable a management representative committee to be formed. Such Scheme to be based on the Model Trust Deed issued by the National Council of Social Service.

(c) Such a Scheme would create a charity, and it is the wish of the Parish Council to become custodian trustee of such a charity.

At the 17th September meeting 1934, Mr Nairne was unable to undertake the duties, so Mr R G B Combe was voted Hon. Secretary and Treasurer to the Hall.

A management committee was formed:

D Locke, L Newman, Mrs Barnett for Brockhampton
E E Bloodworth, E Harvey, Miss Hathaway for Sevenhampton
R Hanks, L Gladwell, Mrs Overton for Charlton Abbots.

THE HOUSE OF HANOVER 1714-1901

Queen Anne had hoped that her half-brother, Catholic, James Stuart would succeed her, but after she died the Government, still mainly Protestant, was anxious to keep the Catholic Stuarts out. So they looked to Hanover where Charles I's sister Elizabeth had married Frederick, Elector Palatine of the Rhine. They were Protestants and her grandson George was next in line to the throne of England. He was invited in 1714 by Parliament to accept the throne, which he did and so the Elector of Hanover became GEORGE I of England. He never learned to speak English and much preferred Hanover to Britain, so he was never a popular king but at least the country enjoyed a few years of peace.

He was succeeded in 1727 by his son, a fighting man who became GEORGE II. He was the last English king to lead his troops in battle. It was during his reign that Charles Edward Stuart – Bonnie Prince Charlie – returned to Scotland in a bid to reclaim his Scottish throne. He was soon defeated, after some initial successes, by George's son the Duke of Cumberland's army.

When George died in 1760 he was succeeded by his grandson who became GEORGE III, his father Frederick Prince of Wales having died in 1751. George was brought up in England and spoke English as his first language, therefore he was more acceptable to his English subjects. George III travelled about his kingdom and while visiting Cheltenham to take the waters for his health he stayed at Bayshill Lodge. He came to Brockhampton in 1788 when he visited Brockhampton Park.

He was the longest serving monarch before Queen Victoria, although during the last years of his life he suffered from an illness, now known as porphyria, when he was considered to be mad. His eldest son served as Prince Regent from 1812 until George III died in 1820. As George IV he was King for only 10 years. As Prince of Wales George, who had waited for a very long time to succeed to the throne, had lived a dissolute life, extravagant in all things, gargantuan meals, heavy drinking and affairs with many women. But he was also a man of style and culture which his influence on architecture shows. From his restoration work on Windsor Castle, the Royal Lodge and Brighton Pavilion which give a variety of styles, resulted in much Regency building in other towns and cities. Fashionable Cheltenham Spa produced Royal Crescent and other Georgian terraces, many Promenade buildings and Pittville Pump Rooms, all elegant structures.

After George IV's death in 1830, his brother William, third son of George III came to the throne. He was a Naval man and Admiral of the Fleet. His reign lasted only 7 years.

During the Hanoverian years Britain had been involved in many wars. The War of the American Independence was long and bitter. George III's forces were defeated by George Washington's army – the Washington family were related to the Lawrence family of Sevenhampton. America became Independent, a triumph for them which is still celebrated on 4th July every year. The French Revolution was a conflict across the Channel, too close for comfort, when many of the French aristocracy escaped to England and settled here, bringing many French surnames to add to our heritage. There followed the Napoleonic War with the Battle of Trafalgar at sea and ending with the Battle of Waterloo in June 1815 when Napoleon was finally defeated.

All this conflict must have involved much manpower and loss of life. It was also very costly, so this area must have been affected by higher taxes and the sacrifice of many of its young men.

It was during the reign of George III that the Longford Trust – or Donnywell Dole – was founded.

The Longford Trust

There is a plaque on the north wall of St Andrew's Church to the memory of Thomas Longford who died in 1770. He bequeathed £1 annually, to be spent on bread for the poor of the parish, being the rent earned from the land known as Dunnywell.

On the monument:

MR THOMAS LONGFORD
who departed this life
March the 9th, 1770
Aged 76 Years

He gave in his lifetime Twenty Shillings
Per Ann for ever to the Poor of this
Parish in Bread five of which Quarterly
To be given out of the Ground called, or
known by the name of Dunnywell.

At the time £1 was a lot of money and it was administered by the Vestry. After Parish Councils came into being in 1894 much of the original Vestry responsibility was taken over including in Sevenhampton's case the Donnywell Charity. The bread had been baked for the Vestry by Mr Pitman, a local baker of The Quarry, at 4½d per loaf. It was distributed by Mrs Pitman from her cottage on Christmas morning, after the Charity became annual rather than quarterly. The £1 was paid down the years by the Lawrence heirs as Lords of the Manor and later Mr T Hyatt.

After the Parish Council administered the Charity the supplying of the bread was put out to tender. Mr Pitman continued the supply for a time but later a succession of bakers provided the bread, which was distributed by a Councillor at the Reading Room on Christmas Day. A churchwarden had previously given out the bread for the Vestry. Mr Pitman, Baker, was a churchwarden.

The Charity Commission required an account to prove that the Trust was still being honoured.

3 February 1908   Donnywell Charity

Sevenhampton in the County of Gloucestershire.
Balance Sheet of the Donnywell Charity

For the year ending December 1907

	Income		Expenditure
1907	October	1907	December 25th
	Income of the Charity		By bread distributed
	Per C W Lawrence Esq		amongst 26 families £1.
	of Sandywell Park £1.		

Examined and passed by the Council of the above Parish on February 3rd 1908.

Chairman: Fairfax Rhodes
Clerk: C Clapps

The Parish Council continued to administer the Charity annually until by 1989 the £1 had devalued until it became worthless as a charity, so the Charity Commissioner agreed to close the Trust altogether and the very small sum of money that remained was donated to the local Pensioners Society viz 'The Century Club'.

The Longford Trust was honoured for about 200 years but the times had changed and the Charity was no longer needed.

The Longford Family

The records of the 'Visitation of Gloucester 1682-3' show that in 1454 Sir Robert Laurence married Amphilis daughter of Edward Longford of Longford, Lancs. They lived at Ashton Hall, Rixton, Lancs.

From them descended the Lawrence brothers who came to live in various parts of Gloucestershire. One was Richard Laurence who lived in Foxcote in 1599. (In early documents Lawrence was spelled with a 'u' later it was changed to 'w'.) A Thomas Longford also came to live in Foxcote – the Lawrences and Longfords would have been first cousins.

Robert Lawrence of Shipton and Thomas Longford of Foxcote both purchased much land in the Sevenhampton area.

In 1631 land including Dunnywell was owned by Henry Blackburn, Clerk. He left it to his son and heir Richard Blackburn from whom it was purchased by Thomas

Longford, Yeoman, of Foxcote in 1664.

In 1678 it became the property of William Longford, son of Thomas, as settlement on his marriage to Hester Kemmett, Spinster.

William and Hester's son Thomas inherited the family property and it was he who founded the LONGFORD TRUST (otherwise known as the Dunnywell Dole) which was the twenty shillings worth of bread annually given to the poor of this parish. This £1 was to be earned by leasing the land known as Dunnywell which included the farm land known now as the Cow Ground, as well as the area around the Dunnywell spring.

Thomas Longford died in 1770 and is commemorated by the plaque in St Andrew's Church.

His son the Revd. William Longford then inherited the Longford land and he sold it to Walter Lawrence in 1776.

Thomas Longford was buried in the church as were early members of the Lawrence family, the Chandlers, the Hincksmans and the Carters of Charlton Abbots. One Lawrence widow, Eleanor, who was a member of the powerful Stratford family of Farmington, of tobacco planting fame, was also buried in the Chancel of St Andrew's.

Monuments in the Church

On Chancel south wall:

John Hincksman died 1828 aged 63 late of Shipton Solers
1836 Ruth his wife aged 73

Brass to John Camber died 1497

Wooden memorial to Anna wife of Ioannis Avrigaris of Charlton Abbots died 1562.

Stone memorial to Guilielm Candelary of Senhampton died 1652 and Eleanor his wife, Latin inscription translated into English:

His light is quenched, his earth to earth consigned –
Yet shines his name, yet shines his godly mind,
And e'en his body shall one day be bright,
And in Christ's light for ever shall see light.

Wooden tablet to Carter family 1652

Painted stone to Joseph Hinksman died 1740 aged 85 years
1739 Mary his wife aged 82 1737 Nancy granddaughter aged 15 years

White marble to John Hinksman died 1774 aged 53, Margaret his wife died 1819 aged 83. 1795 Capt William Hinksman, son, fell in battle East Indies aged 35 years 1780 Elizabeth daughter 11 years. 1796 James son aged 39 years.

1923 Joseph Storr, Rector of Sevenhampton.

Shield shaped brass plaque, inscription in Latin, high on north wall
To John son of Robert Lawrence Gent., Aged five years MDCLVIII 1658

> Here lies interred, a most precious gem
> Than any prince doth weare his diadem
> Foiled by the hand of death in tender age
> E'er he had acted five years on the stage
> But he's not lost, when time shall cease to be
> And earth and heaven we shall new moulded see
> This laurel branch shall bud and blossom then
> And flower in the Paradise of Heaven
> And when the heavenly jeweller shall take
> Into his hand and up his jewels make
> He shall re-polish this and cause to be
> Sett in the ring of his eternity.

To Roger son of Robert Lawrence, died 7th May 1688

> Harke passenger, to celebrate a day
> Nature did hand her finest lump of clay
> And made this flower pot, heaven did like the piece
> And drest it with the bloomes of Paradise
> T'adorn her place, but fearing to procure
> Wherewith to match such costly furniture
> Dasht it against t'Rock of Destinie
> To save her credit, here t'pieces lie
> T'tell thee vessels whether fayre or foul
> Are as soon broken if theyre made of mould.

> Particularly to Roger, son of Robert Lawrence of this parish, Gent.,
> Whose rare perfections were shewn for 8 years and 10 mts.

> In hope of glorious resurrection.

Three brass plaques to Robert Lawrence died 1688 (shield)
William Lawrence son of Anthony & Culpepper Lawrence
Died 1693 (rectangular)
Robert Lawrence, Lord of Sevenhampton Manor died 1700 (shield shaped)

Monument to William Morris of Sevenhampton Court died 1834
    1839   Mary wife of William Morris

Monument to Walter Lawrence died 1810, Lord of the Manors of
Sevenhampton and Brockhampton
    1804   Mary wife of Walter Lawrence
            Elizabeth, daughter, died in infancy

North Transept

1860   Fulwar Craven 1844 Laura wife of Fulwar Craven

Black marble to Rev John Craven died 1804
        Catherine wife of John Craven
        Catherine Laura daughter aged 5 years

Grey marble to Sir William Dodwell died 1727, and his wives
    1719   Anne Lethieulier – Deleau 1st wife buried at Croydon
    1724   Mary Fuller – Miller 2nd wife

South Transept

War Memorial to the fallen of the Great War 1914-1918

During the great upheaval at the time of the Reformation, Chantry Chapels
were suppressed, because they were part of the Catholic religion and not allowed by
the Protestants. Subsidised prayers for the souls of the dead were not to be used and

Church Bells of St Andrew's

the altars were removed from the Transepts.

The Tracy family of Toddington became powerful landowners, following the Reformation, acquiring much additional land in this area including Charlton Abbots and part of Sevenhampton. Within a few years the Tracys had sold this land to the Carter family who later sold to the Lawrence family.

In 1718 a third bell was added to the 15th century Gabriel bell and the Chandler bell of 1650. This was inscribed

JOHN TIMBRELL, CHURCHWARDEN A.R. 1718
(cast in Gloucester)

In recent days Pearce Boulton, a local character (who died in 1991 just short of his 100th birthday) was known to toll all three bells at once, with two hands and one foot.

In 1716 the church was given a Silver Paten and Plate by Thomas Mason of Sevenhampton.

St Andrew's Church was altered and restored in 1771. A notice on the church wall, now removed, stated:

Henry Pearce Bolton ringing three bells at once
(two hands, one foot)

"This Inscription gives an account of the Repairs of the Church, which were begun in the Year of our Lord 1771, and finished in the ensuing Year. A Subscription was opened, and Money subscribed, but not sufficient to compleat the Work according to the plan, and the Money was put into the hands of the REV. MR. JOHN LAWRENCE to lay it out in the best manner he could, which he did, untill all was expended. Then WALTER LAWRENCE, Gent, (which was an assistant to his brother's undertaking,) took it in hand, and finished the whole at his own expence, which was, the Doors, his own Seats, and all the new Timbered Seats in the lower part of the Church except Mr REDDAL'S. Likewise he gave the Hangings of the Pulpit, Reading Desk, and Communion Table, with many more things not here contained."

THE PRESENT LORD OF THE MANOR
MR LAWRENCE,
REV. JOHN LAWRENCE, RECTOR

Mr Reddal was a local landowner of the time living at Puckham Farm.

The Church at this time had many BOX PEWS, which in the 18th century were wainscoted and provided with doors to protect the congregation from draughts.

Sometimes the Gentry converted the Chantry Chapels into Parlour Pews for their families and in the days of Sir Roger de Coverley, country gentleman, it was said that the Squire had a fireplace in his box pew, for use in cold weather. Also if the sermons were too long he had a hot meal brought to his pew during the service.

PULPITS became the focal point over the altar in those days of public speakers and clergy who spoke at great length. The priest would sometimes take an hour-glass into the pulpit with him and when it ran out, during the sermon, the priest would turn it over and the congregation knew they could expect another hour. Pulpits were required to be placed against either the first or second left-hand pillar beyond the chancel. They were usually two or three decker in the early days. Three deckers housed the Priest at the top, the Reader in the middle and the Clerk at the bottom. For the two decker they cut out the middle man and the pulpit became known as "The Parson and the Clerk".

All these with the pews were replaced when the church was to undergo more drastic changes in the 19th century.

Following the Dissolution of the Monasteries a number of new dioceses were created. In 1541 Gloucester Diocese came into being, out of the southern half of the old Worcester diocese. This arrangement has lasted for over 460 years.

In 1712 Sir Robert Atkyns in his "Ancient and Present State of Gloucestershire" says "Sevenhampton Church is in the Deanery of Winchcomb" yet "a small Quit rent* is still paid by Mr Lawrence out of the Impropriation to the Bishop of Hereford" (so the Hereford Bishops still had some claims on St Andrew's). The Impropriation at that date was vested in Mr Lawrence and Mr Hincksman, worth £70 yearly out of which £10 is allowed to the Curate. Mr Petty is the present Incumbent.

> The Parish is 16 miles in compass. It consists much in Arable-lands and large Downs, with some Meadows, Pasture-grounds and Woods. The River Colne riseth in this Parish and runs down to Fairford.
>
> Brockhampton is a considerable Hamlet in this Parish, containing 18 Houses. It now belongs to Sir William Dodwell, who has a large House and a great Estate in this and other places. Mr Carter has likewise a good House and Estate in this Hamlet.
>
> A Farm call'd Puckham and Puckham Wood, and an Hamlet call'd the Quarr, containing 8 Houses, lie in this Parish.
>
> There are 47 Houses in this Parish, and about 180 Inhabitants whereof 8 are Freeholders.   Yearly   (Births 5
>   (Deaths 4

(1692	To the Royal Aid	75 00 00
(1694	To the Land-Tax	70 04 00
(1694	To the Poll-Tax	18 13 06

*(Quit-rent A fixed annual rent that released a tenant from manorial service. Abolished as recently as 1922.)

Samuel Rudder writing on Gloucestershire in 1779 says "Mr Robert Lawrence died seized of the manor of Sevenhampton in 1700. Mr Anthony Lawrence was proprietor of the manor of Sevenhampton when Sir Robert Atkyns compiled his History. It belonged afterwards to Walter Lawrence Esq. and is now vested in Mr Walter Lawrence, who has a good estate in this parish, and resides there. His arms are, Argent, a cross raguley gules.

Brockhampton is a considerable hamlet in this parish, formerly belonging to the antient family of de Croupes. Edward Croupes, son of Richard de Croupes, died seized of the manors of Upper Dowdeswell, Whittington and Brockhampton 35 E.. 1593. The manor was afterwards vested in the Lawrences.

Puckham is the name of a place in this parish, antiently written Pulcomb, which belonged to the Bishop of Hereford. Puckham is the property of Mr Reddall."

At the beginning of the 18th century the English churches were at a low ebb with diminishing congregations, not in the Sevenhampton area however, Nonconformist denominations came into being, but it was another 100 years before these arrived in Brockhampton. It was in the 1700s that the Wesley brothers, John and Charles, with George Whitfield founded the Methodist Church. They had been friends at Oxford University and ordained into the church. They spent some years in America and when they returned their form of preaching was still not acceptable to the Establishment and many churches banned them altogether. So they held their meetings in the open air all over the country, drawing huge crowds, especially and happily singing Charles Wesley's stirring hymns. Maybe they used some of the preaching crosses in the churchyards which are mostly medieval. There is not one remaining in St Andrew's churchyard, though there may well have been one in the early days before the church was built. What did remain was a set of wooden stocks used for punishing offenders (first introduced by an Act of 1405) now incorporated into the Church itself. In Elizabethan days Whipping Posts were compulsory, to be used beside all the country stocks.

It was in 1780 that Robert Raikes, Philanthropist and Proprietor of the Gloucester Journal, founded the Sunday School Movement out of pity for the poverty and ignorance of so many children. He was also interested in Prison Reform, which no doubt received some publicity in his newspaper, when Gloucester prison was in a disgraceful condition. Others took up the cause and in 1791 a new county gaol and four new houses of correction were opened. One of these was at Northleach which may well have reformed some miscreants from the Sevenhampton area, sent from our local Court.

In 1791 the first Ordnance Survey was undertaken. Population had increased greatly, farming was the industry of the Cotswolds and most of the working population was engaged on agriculture or its associated industries such as the blacksmith. New crops were grown and new ways of animal husbandry were being adopted. Some of the new farm machinery was being tried out by the more venturesome, but many of the old peasant farmers lost their holdings. Under the Manorial System freemen and commoners held strip farming and grazing rights on the common or waste land for their oxen, sheep, goats and geese all the year round, except for a short period in the Spring when the pastureland was cleared to allow the new grass to grow. Enclosures had taken place down the years, particularly for the very profitable sheep farming when whole villages were taken over and the inhabitants became vagrants. This did not occur in the Sevenhampton area. By the reign of George III much more land was enclosed legally by country gentlemen who realised a profit was to be made by the new farming techniques. This inspired some wag to circulate the appropriate verse:

> Law punishes the man or woman
> Who steals a goose from off the common,
> But lets the greater culprit loose
> Who steals the common from the goose!

The local landowners of the 1700s were the Lawrences of Sevenhampton and Whittington and the Dodwells of Brockhampton. There was by then no common grazing ground and the land was let to many farmers.

In the 18th century there was no minimum wage, rather a maximum wage was set for farm workers and other servants. A head man in agriculture or domestic employment received £5 per year, or less, the cook was rewarded with £2.10s per year; a harvest mower received 1s. 2d. per day and a labourer 4d. or 8d. per day at most. Those servants who 'lived in' were housed and fed for free, extra to their wages, but it was extremely hard work for the low wage and there was little choice because most were bound for a year at a time.

Most workers found work at the hiring fairs where they had to stand in line with a mark of some sort to show what kind of work they did. A shepherd would have some sheep's wool pinned to his hat, or else workers would carry a tool of their profession. One local lady remembered standing in the market square at Stow-on-the-Wold, with a mop in her hand to show that she was a housemaid looking for work.

Farmworkers who changed jobs, had to change their homes too. The cottages were all tied cottages which went with the job, therefore when they found a new employer they had to move into one of his cottages and sometimes it would be in a different area altogether. The day after the fair someone would come along with an open cart and all the family's belongings would be piled on to it. The smallest children would be given a ride on the cart, but the older ones, with their Mother, would have to walk. This system survived into the end of the 19th century. One old man remembered the day when they moved to Sevenhampton when he was just a tiny lad. It was all very exciting at first and when he arrived on the cart he was taken in by the new neighbours and given food. He ran around exploring the new playground but got very tired, when his Mother arrived he said to her 'I am tired Mum can we go home now?' He meant go back to the only home he knew, the one which they had left in the early hours of the morning. He was a pensioner when he recalled this story, but he still remembered the bitter feelings he had when told that he could not return to his original home again.

Children had to work at a very early age, so education was limited. When they reached teenage many would be sent away from home to work, mostly the girls of the family were sent into domestic employment because there was a great demand for labour in the big houses of the time and girls were cheaper than adults. They were given very little time off, but it was a recognised thing that girls were allowed to visit their mothers during Lent on Mothering Sunday or at Easter, when they would have been allowed to bake a cake – a Simnel Cake – as a gift for Mother.

Enclosures brought new stone walls and hedges to the countryside which had previously been open fields. This was helpful to the wildlife habitat which later was to suffer a reversal in the 20th century with the advent of prairie farming. Sheep ceased to be the mainstay of the hills, although wool was still needed for the cloth mills, but landowners found that arable farming produced a better income mainly because the growing towns needed more food brought in to their markets.

Brockhampton Quarry

The quarry itself was on part of the land owned by Hereford Bishops from around 800 A.D. and was known to be a working quarry. From the time the land was leased to the Prior of Llanthony Secunda he had access to the stone which was then used for building the first part of the Church.

There were 8 cottages in the quarry area. These would have been the homes of the quarry workers and were built with their backs to the present road. This road was non-existent and the road from the quarry passed, beside the site of the later Bethell Chapel, in front of the houses, running down the hill and ending where the farm yard of Manor Farm now stands. The stone was brought down via this road, to be used locally for building and walling or in towns nearby. Later there were 10 cottages. Robert Atkyns says "the whole parish of Sevenhampton, which includes Brockhampton and the Quarry, has 47 houses and about 180 inhabitants, whereof 8 are freeholders."

Turnpike Roads

As the practical local government the Vestry was responsible for church affairs, administration of the law including dealing with the local poor and maintenance of the local roads. For all these it was empowered to set a local rate to finance it.

The roads suffered because there was never enough money raised to improve them and the population resented the tax. Tolls were then raised for road improvement by setting up Turnpikes, also much resented by the local people as they were charged for all animals e.g. horses and cattle passing through as well as all vehicles. Pedestrians were not charged. The first Turnpikes in Gloucestershire were set up in 1698 on the roads to London. On the country roads around the Sevenhampton area Turnpikes arrived in the 1750s; probably just gated turnpikes with a keeper on duty. Many roads had Tollhouses, small six-sided buildings, sometimes still to be seen at the roadsides in key places, though mostly converted into private dwellings, but none has survived in the immediate area.

By 1700 horsedrawn carriages were the popular form of transport, but the roads were appalling. The stage and mail coaches from London could go no further than the Frogmill Inn at Shipton for passengers hoping to get to Cheltenham, or visiting the many country houses, so they had to be collected by private carriages to reach their destination.

The road from Cheltenham at this time turned off towards Dowdeswell up Dowdeswell Hill. There was no A40 until the coming of the passenger railway c.1880 when the Viaduct was built. Tunnel Hill as we now know it, was called the Deep Cutting because of the way it was carved out of the hill to make a high embankment for the railway line. The road then ran in to and out of Andoversford under two further railway bridges.

Another road came up from Charlton Kings via Ham Hill through Whittington. This could previously have been a track made by the Romans marching their troops in a straight line as always. By Whalley Farm the road twists and turns into Whittington. In Saxon times Whalley Farm was owned by a man named Wall Eye. Turnpikes were set up on this road when the local people could not pay for the upkeep of the roads The turnpike keepers often set milestones for the use of travellers – and no doubt to guide them through the next turnpike to extract further payment.

Even so travelling was horrendous and the horses and passengers alike became very weary. They needed Inns at frequent intervals to rest and eat and the horses would be changed. The Syreford Inn, now known as Syreford Farm, was one such. The outside steps led to a long room inside, which has now been converted into smaller rooms. Maybe the passengers collected in this long room to await the oncoming coach. It is a possibility that the steps were also used to help the passengers to get on to and into the coach. The mail coaches were still routed through Whittington in the 1830s. In 1829 Joseph Denley was the Innkeeper at Syreford leasing it from the Shipton Estate. He was also a stonemason and worked the underground quarry opposite to the Inn – re-opened by Arthur Price, archaeologist, in 1994, but not as a working quarry. In the census of 1841 Joseph's widow Elizabeth is given as the Innkeeper. She was 65 years of age and had her son Thomas 30 and daughter Hannah 40 living and working with her. By the 1861 census the Inn was no more for it had become Syreford Farm owned and lived in by Edward Handy of Hampen.

Syreford Farm had a succession of owners. When a George Fletcher was the farmer he stored wool in the Granary, the long room at the top of the steps. He paid his workers once a week, when he would sit at a table just inside the door and the men would come up the steps to collect their wages. Underneath were stalls and feeding racks and the far end was divided off by slats of wood for the poultry to be housed there. The stables would have been used in the days of the mail coaches.

In Brockhampton in 1769 a building now known as the Malthouse was the property of John and Jane Wood. The farmhouse became a Bakery when the Combe family moved in. Later the buildings were converted into a Brewery, so industry had arrived in the village.

The end of the 18th century saw George III still on throne, his reign was to last for 60 years, he was however a very sick man. He was the best loved of the Hanoverian kings, but was a broken man after the loss of his American colonies.

As the 19th century came in Revd William Longford was the incumbent of St Andrew's Church, followed in 1803 by Revd John Craven, but he died in 1804. Mary Lawrence was the Lady of the manor of Sevenhampton but the Brockhampton Park Estate was without a Lord as Mary Tracy had died in 1799. It was not until 1806 that the Court of Common Pleas awarded the estate to the Timbrell sisters. In 1823 when Rebecca Lightbourne died her estate was left to William Morris, who had married Mary Lawrence of Sevenhampton Manor, and it was later inherited by their son Walter Lawrence Lawrence. For a short time Walter owned Sevenhampton Manor, Sandywell Park, Whittington Court and Brockhampton Park estates until he sold Brockhampton Park to Fulwar Craven in 1832. The Craven family had been tenants of Mary Tracy and then Rebecca Lightbourne before the sale.

The first National Population Count was taken in 1801, to provide population statistics, when Sevenhampton parish had an acreage of 3,377 and a population of 349. A census was taken in 1841, giving age, sex and, employment, and every 10 years thereafter. By 1851 more information was included such as address, marital status, and place of birth. Each census return becomes available for public inspection after 100 years.

THE VICTORIAN ERA

A great change came over the whole country when William IV died in 1837 and the throne passed to his late brother Edward Duke of Kent's daughter Victoria. She was only 18 years of age and it must have been a refreshing change for the people of Britain who had not seen a Queen on the throne for the 123 years since the death of Queen Anne. They became Victorians and were to be much influenced by her life for the next 64 years. The coronation was held in June 1838 and in 1839 she married her cousin Prince Albert of Saxe-Coburg Gotha. The marriage was a happy one producing nine children, many of them marrying into the Royal families of Europe including Germany and Russia. Together Victoria and Albert brought a new moral code to the country, which had been somewhat lacking during the Georgian years. One of Albert's many achievements was the Crystal Palace, an enormous glass conservatory built to house his Great Exhibition of 1851 showing the best of British Industrial achievements. This palace was destroyed by fire in 1936. Cheltenham built a replica in glass beside the Town Hall called The Winter Gardens, but this was taken down during the 2nd World War as it was thought to pose too easy a target for enemy bombers. The British Empire expanded during the Victorian period, as can be seen by the countries shown in red on the world maps of the time. Last to be taken was India, the Jewel in the Crown, which Prime Minister Disraeli marked by making Victoria Empress of India. The coins of the day bore the words FID DEF.IND IMP. for Defender of the Faith and Empress of India. For many years on Empire Day, 24th May, Victoria's birthday, the children of Sevenhampton School were walked in a 'crocodile' or column of pairs to Sevenhampton churchyard to stand around the Flag pole where the Union Jack was raised. There the children sang hymns and took part in the outdoor Empire Day service. The 'crocodile' reformed and proceeded to Brockhampton Park where a nice tea awaited them and afterwards fun and games and a scramble for sweets thrown by the Lady of the House.

The Bethell Chapel

The Church of England had been the centre of life for several hundred years when eventually other denominations crept in. From Brockhampton many dissenting people made their way to Naunton Chapel on Sundays either by walking, on horseback, or in pony traps. The Brockhampton people began to get dissatisfied with Naunton because as they said it was getting too Strict for them. So they decided to build their own chapel at the Quarry, raising the money to pay for it themselves. It was mainly built by the Denley brothers, local stonemasons, and was ready to be opened in 1834. James and David Denley were both Chapel lay preachers and conducted some of the services. The Bethell closed in 1966 probably through lack of support because another Baptist Chapel had been built in the village and being so near would have divided the non-conformist congregation.

The Bethel Chapel
The Quarry, Brockhampton

The Baptist Chapel

In the early 19th century some of the local people, who were non-conformists, met in each others houses for prayer meetings. They were of the same belief as the members of Salem Baptist Church in Cheltenham and were visited by them from time to time.

Quote from Salem Records:

On 13th February 1849 a Church Meeting resolved that 'The Brethren and Sisters at Brockhampton be advised to form themselves into a District church and that they be assured we feel desirous of rendering them all the assistance we can.' The resolution led to the formation of the Village Chapel at Brockhampton which flourished there for well over a century, linked to Salem as a branch cause. Today the membership has dwindled to four and the future of the Church is uncertain. (1986).

In 1881 Edward Whitbread, a Cheltenham Draper and a member of Salem Baptist Church, took part in their 'Adopt a Village' scheme. He and a team of teachers had been making the 7-mile journey on foot each weekend to run a Sunday School in the village. He was also an active Governor of Cheltenham's British Schools and in succession Treasurer and Chairman of the Cheltenham Sunday School Union. He was also a founder member of the Brockhampton Village Institute which brought culture, education and recreation to the local people.

Mr Whitbread sought permission to use the Reading Room as a Sunday School for the Chapel children. He was helped in this enterprise by the Cheltenham Salem Group who came to preach in the Brockhampton Chapel or gave lectures on weekday evenings to the Institute.

The original chapel was a long, single storey, stone building which had been in use for about 70 years when it was decided in 1920 to build a second storey to accommodate the Sunday School. This became known as The Schoolroom and a ceremony was held to celebrate the new building where two foundation stones were laid by R G Hanks and F R Dicks in 1920. It came into use in 1921. Mrs Joyce Cowcher recalled being allowed to lay a brick at the foundation ceremony. She was just a small child and daughter of R G Hanks, Justice of the Peace and a leading member of the Chapel. The family lived at Charlton Abbots Manor House as tenants of Col Rhodes until his daughter Mrs Sadler wanted to live and farm there in 1933. The Hanks family then moved to The Holt in Charlton Abbots. They came to the Summer Gathering each year, this was a big event in the Chapel year. Mostly they walked across the fields to chapel services, occasionally in bad weather they would drive over in the car. Other past chapel goers remembered Band of Hope and Christian Endeavour for older children. Also the annual prize-giving when all the children were rewarded for regular attendance. They also took part in religious knowledge competitions between other Salem chapels and were often first prize winners.

The Chapel was well supported for many years but after the 2nd World War the congregation diminished. It was still thriving however in the 70s and 80s with a number of cars parked outside by the village green during services. The name of the next visiting preacher was posted beside the front doors. Once a year at Anniversary time coaches brought the Boys Brigade Band from Cheltenham to the Chapel. They parked near to Brockhampton Park then formed up to march down the road to the Chapel playing all the way.

The Chapel kept going until 1990 when it finally closed its doors. Even after that the village was allowed to hire it as extra rooms for the annual Produce Show in September. After some debate by Salem Church as to whether it should be turned into flats for old people it was finally sold to a builder who converted it into a private house.

At the end of the Napoleonic Wars in 1815 a new religious wave swept the country and many new churches were built. Wealthy people who subscribed to the building then expected guaranteed best seats in the churches in return. Many pews were inscribed with family names, other worshippers had to pay one shilling for a seat. Later when it was realised that poorer people were excluded from Sunday worship free seats were offered to get them back to the churches. Hence 'Free Churches' came into being, paid for by voluntary subscriptions and some Government money. St Paul's in Cheltenham was one of these churches its founder being the Revd Francis Close, or Dean Close as he is now remembered. It did not happen in this area, although certain people did reserve family pews for themselves, as no new churches were built and the existing ones were very old, Sevenhampton Church c.1150; Whittington Church c.1100; Charlton Abbots c.1250 A.D. They were already sited next to the Manor Houses but not as their chapels; the churches were in place long before the present Manor Houses were built. However, Whittington may well have had a former chapel on the same site as the present church where there was a moated house near to, or on the site of the present Whittington Court.

The Baptist Chapel
Brockhampton Centre Village

St Andrew's Church

John Melland Hall, one time Vicar of Sevenhampton, wrote in 1889 –

> "The Church is dedicated to St Andrew. Said by Sir Robert Atkyns (1712) to have been built by John Camber who died in 1497 and lies buried in the chancel."

The Rev J L Petit, historian possibly of Shipton, says "not so – the architecture of the church ranged from Early English (of a very rude character) to a debased Perpendicular. It is a building of great interest. The front of the south transept has a triplet of lancets, and the chancel some early Perpendicular work introduced. But the principal feature is the curious insertion of the central tower. On approaching the church, it seems of very good dimensions, yet it is considerably narrower than the nave. Its western piers consequently are detached (though there are no aisles to the church) and as they are not very massive, they are strengthened by flying buttresses in the interior from the piers to the corresponding angles between the nave and transepts.

The tower is open to the interior considerably above the roof of the transepts, and has a north and south window; above there is a vaulted roof, and angel corbels with shields. Neither these nor the belfry windows have their lights foliated, though the latter are of a very good composition. The tower presents a fine bold outline, from the stair turret at the south east angle. The south porch is close to the transept, which has a string-course resting on brackets on its west side, stopped by the face of the porch."

The Church was greatly altered in the late15th to early 16th century by the addition of the 3-stage Tower with its cleverly installed buttresses and Nave roof. This was paid for by the 100 shillings from John Camber's Will. It was drastically restored twice. Once in the late 1700s when the Rev. John Lawrence and his brother, the Lord of the Manor, fitted box pews to the Nave and Transepts. Again in the late 1800s by Waller, when the box pews were removed and new bench pews were insalled. This was made possible because some kind of heating was installed to the very cold church. The 19th century screen was added to the West end and a new Priests' doorway fitted to the old chancel 15th century doorway.

St Andrew's in the 19th Century

There is a picture of the interior of the Church in the late 1800s showing box pews in the North Transept and the Nave, North side. On the South side are open pews, two of these could be the choir pews now in the Chancel. A solid fuel heating stove, with a fuel box beside it, was positioned where the Lectern now stands, near the 2nd pillar. Against the 1st pillar was the wooden Pulpit, a more simple structure than the present one, it rested on a cup-shaped stone plinth. A wooden Reading Desk was standing just inside the Chancel opposite to the pulpit. The coat of arms, now on the Nave South wall, was then situated above the inner archway leading to the chancel. Lighting was provided by lamps hanging from the roof, probably oil lamps, which could be lowered to be lighted and then pulled up again.

The floor appears to have been level throughout at this stage, though the altar may have been raised. An ancient stone shelf beneath the East window shows the height of the original altar and floor level. Sir Stephen Glynne, writing in the mid 1800s, suggests that the elevation of the altar by a succession of steps has been made gradually over the years. The Ambulatory was still open at this stage.

Stone Shelf behind Altar showing Altar's height before the floor was raised

The Early English East window of the chancel had been removed by the mid-1800s and replaced by a Perpendicular window. The Early English window was now situated in the South wall of the South Chancel. In 1869 it was dedicated to John Walter Walker of Guiting Power, who died at the age of 12 years. His grieving parents had stained glass fitted to the window which is three lancet. His grave is in the churchyard South side, near to the outer wall of the Manor House garden.

The Revd Melland Hall says: "At the restoration of the south window in the south transept, preparatory to the insertion of a memorial by the Walker family (the subject, St John the Baptist pointing his disciples to Jesus as the Lamb of God), some mural paintings were discovered, together with fragments shewing the general mode of wall treatment – these have been variously described, and may even now test the ingenuity of some of our members: the first, on the left, represents a dog and pomegranate; the second, on the same side, probably the Annunciation, and the lily stem bearing its three white flowers, open and in full bloom; the third, on the right, the head of an angel. It has been suggested, however, that the dog, arrow and tree seem to be part of a hunting scene, whilst beneath it is a portion of an angelic figure with a scroll, or perhaps it may be part of the Agony in the Garden; the lower subject on the right is said to be part of the Descent into Hell."

The East, Perpendicular, window in the Chancel was created as a memorial to Mary Lawrence who died in 1881. Widow of Walter Lawrence and daughter of Christian Splidt. This window is very beautiful depicting the Transfiguration of Christ. In the centre is the shining white figure of Jesus Christ. On his right is Moses carrying the tablet of stone on which was written the Ten Commandments. On his left is Elijah the Prophet. Below are James, Peter and John who were with Jesus at the time, and were very afraid. Above are two angels.

Also in the Chancel, to the right of the Lawrence window, is a single lancet window dedicated to Charlotte Elizabeth, Lady Pollen, died 1877, Aged 73. She was the sister of the Revd John Melland-Hall who was the Rector of St Andrew's at the time.

All three bells were now in situ and are still tolled regularly for divine services:

1. BE YEE FOLLOWARES OF GOD AS DEARE CHILDREN 30½ ins
     W Chandler 1650

2. SANCTE GABBRIEL ORA PRO NOBIS 32 ins
     early 15th century

3. JOHN TIMBRELL, CHURCHWARDEN A.R. 1718 34½ ins

The second bell is medieval, with the legend in Early Gothic characters and must have been installed in the church before the alterations by John Camber. It was also the Gabriel Bell which was rung every morning and evening and was thus called the "day belle" and "kerfowbelle". The midday bell was never rung in England, and the "Angelus", as used abroad, began in France in the 16th century.

Drastic changes were made to the inside appearance of the Church when W.S. Waller restored St Andrew's in the late 1890s. He was the Chief Diocesan Architect for Gloucester Cathedral and the County churches – Verey called him "that Arch Scraper". The walls were scraped and repointed, so any remains of the old wall paintings were removed. However one small portion survived this treatment, that being the Apostles Creed chiselled and painted into the West wall of the South Transept. This has worn away through the years, only a little of it now remaining.

Apostles' Creed in South Transept

The Chancel floor was raised and beautifully tiled with red patterned tiles, these were graded in size with the largest at the Chancel steps, getting smaller and smaller towards the altar. With the raising of the floor the ambulatory was much smaller and so became a Hagioscope or squint. A perfect view of the altar may now be seen from the South transept.

The furnishings of the church were changed totally. The box pews were removed and are said to have been used as panelling in the Sanctuary of Whittington Church. New 19th century pews were installed in the Nave, all facing towards the altar with a central aisle between them. Similar pews were put into both Transepts all facing towards the Chancel steps.

The West end of the church which has a Perpendicular window and two original pilaster buttresses, now had a beautifully carved, wooden screen with a central doorway erected, thus creating a small Vestry. The Pulpit was removed and replaced by a handsome wooden Pulpit carved with the sacred letters I.H.S. (Iesus Hominum Salvator – Jesus the Saviour of Men) on each side. This is supported by a solid, carved stone base. The Reading Desk had as its successor a Lectern which was brought from Whelford Church near Lechlade. This now supports a large copy of the James I. Bible, which is still used for all services.

The Font was the 1660, chalice shaped, Tudor font which had been used in the church for 200 years. In keeping with all these changes the Lawrence family presented the church with a new, very ornate Victorian font in Memory of their parents Walter and Mary Lawrence. This was situated on a solid stone base just inside the main door to welcome the newly baptised into the church family. Sadly the earlier font was removed to the churchyard where it stood for many years in the flower border of the path leading up to the church. In 1933 the P.C.C. decided to bring this Tudor font back into the church where it was mounted on a stone, adjoining a pillar at the chancel steps, by E.W. Barnfield, stonemason and churchwarden. It is now used, to great effect, by the flower arrangers with elegant displays throughout the year, except for the period of Lent when no flowers are brought into the church.

Gifts to the Church in the 19th Century

1872 Christmas	Linen for the Altar	
1873	Shields on Chancel Beams	The Misses Marriott of Brockhampton Court
1873 Whitsunday	Carpet and Hassocks for Altar	Mrs Lawrence
	Kneeling cushions for Communicants	Mrs Craven
1873	Handsomely embroidered Crimson Altar Cloth, With sacred monogram I.H.S.on a vesica piscis of blue velvet: in the corner fleur-de-lys: border ornamented with roses in gold silk: edging of Gold silk fringe.	The Misses Marriott
September	Crimson Hangings for the Reading Desk Antependium (beautifully embroidered after an ancient pattern) for the Pulpit.	The Misses Marriott
1891 July	The Lady Jane Swinburne presented Altar Cross and Alms Dish	
	Vases for Altar and flower holders	F Privett
	4 smaller ditto	C Woods
	Pair of Candlesticks	Mrs Storr
	Altar Desk	Miss Storr

Miss Agatha Lawrence promised a New Font "to replace the present unsightly one".

Canon St John promised the Lectern from Whelford Church.

The Vicarage

In 1850 the Tithe Barn was pulled down in order to build a Vicarage. The Revd Edward Ellerton was the St Andrew's Incumbent at the time and he had the house built entirely at his own cost, except for £200 from Queen Anne's Bounty. This was a fund set up by the Queen in 1704 to help the clergy and church buildings. The Tithe Act of 1725 transferred tithe revenues to this fund. It was a handsome house, a fine example of the best of Victorian building. The earlier Parsonage House, situated to the right hand side of the present gate, was still occupied at this stage and the Priest used it to house his Curates for a short period until this too was demolished.

Our Tithe Barn must have been this size

The Vicarage Sevenhampton

The Vicarage was a very important part of village life in Sevenhampton parish. Apart from meetings on church business, other groups met there regularly. Sunday School was held there each week for the Anglican children and Christmas parties were arranged for them at the Vicarage. The annual Ascension Day garden party at the Vicarage was very much a part of parish life. A warm welcome was afforded to all guests.

Sadly, when the Revd Canon Philip Hobbs retired as Vicar in 1995, the house stood empty for a long while. Then the Church Commissioners sold the property which has now become a private house.

Education

Some early education had been provided by the monks who taught all ages reading, writing and Latin grammar, in the churches or chapels. There was a small charge for this, but some of the clever poor were given a free education.

Robert de Bethune, Bishop of Hereford and former Prior of Llanthony Abbey, was a pioneer in private schooling. He supplemented his income by teaching and in this way was able to set his nieces up in suitable marriages and purchase places in monastic houses for his nephews. His connections with Sevenhampton may have assisted in gaining some education for the local population. He was still Bishop of Hereford when Sennington was destroyed and Sevenhampton church was built.

Charity schools were endowed from time to time by wealthy philanthropists in the larger towns, the earliest being Christ's Hospital or Blue Coat School for orphans in London in 1553 and in 1571 Richard Pate founded the Cheltenham Grammar School. Masters taught Latin and Greek grammar, languages and logic.

DAME SCHOOLS were mostly 18th century where a limited education was provided for the children of the poor (especially younger children before they became economically useful). They were run by elderly women who might teach reading, sewing and other useful aids. These small informal schools had something of a social and economic impact on a village.

In the grounds between Sevenhampton Vicarage and Manor Cottage (now Lea House) were once small cottages. One of these was used as a Dame School – a former Vicar's wife told how the remains were still to be seen in the 20th century until modern building destroyed them. These cottages would have been part of the early Sevenhampton village before the Vicarage was built and the Tythe Barn was still standing.

Private schools were started for the children of wealthier families, mostly for the boys who then went on to attend Public schools and Colleges, such as the Gentlemen's College and Dean Close School in Cheltenham. The girls were given teaching at home by a resident Governess.

The BOTHY at Sevenhampton was a long low 19th century building, below the Church, partly used to house the unmarried male workers of the Manor Estate, but also partly used as a school for local estate children, and accommodation for the headmaster. This was pulled down later when it became redundant.

In 1818 Rebecca Lightbourne opened her Charity School in Whittington and in 1864 Georgina Craven had a purpose-built School to educate the children of her estate workers in Brockhampton, which thrived until she took sick in 1869; the school was then closed, but later became the Reading Room.

Sevenhampton School

In 1870, following the Parliamentary Act which made education for children compulsory, a National School, later known as Sevenhampton Church of England School, was built on Lawrence land in Sevenhampton by the Squire, Christian William Lawrence. This was attended by not only local children but others from neighbouring villages and farms. Many children walked to school in all winds and weather for several miles each day, sometimes arriving very wet in bad weather. They carried food with them as nothing was provided by the school. Solid fuel stoves were installed for heating, the boys were required to collect and chop wood for these. Hot drinks could be produced when the boys carried water in buckets up the steep bank from the spring at the bottom of the field opposite the school, near to the Coln river. The water was heated in kettles on the stoves.

In 1874 school numbers were: Boys 46, Girls 47. At the turn of the 20th century the school had two classrooms, but when the numbers grew to over 100 a new classroom was added to accommodate the pupils.

The first Headmaster was Edwin Hazzard helped by two teachers, and with his wife as the sewing mistress. He died suddenly in 1886 when walking home from the Lodge.

Sevenhampton School, built for Squire C. W. Lawrence

The second Headmaster was Charles Capps with three assistant teachers. He was also Clerk to the Parish Council from 1900.

The numbers continued to rise in the 1920s. Children started school at 5 years old or less and could leave school at 12 years of age. As the numbers continued to rise Pupil Teachers were brought in to gain experience before going on to Training College. Miss Florence Barnfield of Sevenhampton was one of these. She also played the organ at St Andrew's Church for many years.

B T FLETCHER was Headmaster from 1920-30. In the 1930s the numbers began to fall, there was a Headmistress and two teachers. School leaving age was now 14 years.

During the second World War 1939-45 free school milk was provided in 1/3 pint bottles and the children were given real straws with which to drink it. School meals were provided when a Cook and a Meals Supervisor were employed. The 1st cook was Mrs Edna Holloway with Mrs Ethel Locke to assist her. Later Mrs Mildred Jarman was the Cook.

When the war was over the older pupils 11-14 years were transported to Charlton Kings Secondary Modern (now Comprehensive) School. The numbers at Sevenhampton decreased to 20-30 pupils and the school was closed in 1974. The village people tried hard to stop this closure, but their petitions were ignored.

The children of 5-11 years were taken by bus to Andoversford Primary School. The 11 year old pupils who passed the 'Scholarship Examination' went either to Westwoods Grammar School in Northleach or to Pates Grammar School in Cheltenham.

The Sevenhampton School was sold in 1975 and is now a private house.

1800s	Dame School, Sevenhampton – converted cottage near Vicarage
1800s	Bothy in fields below church used as School and accommodation.
1818	Whittington School built for Mrs R Lightbourne
1864	School in Brockhampton built for Mrs G Craven
1870	National School Sevenhampton built for C W Lawrence

Headmasters Sevenhampton School

1886-1886	Edwin Hazzard
1920-1920	Charles Capps
1920-1930	B T Fletcher

Headmistresses

1930s	Miss Sisum	
	Miss Ruth Foyle	
1937-39	Mrs Emmett	
1939-41	Mrs Cathcart	Mrs D Grainger – Assistant Head
1941-1943	Mrs Hollister-Short	
1943-1944	Mrs Harding	
1944-1950	Supply Head Teachers	
1950s	Mrs Collins	
1960-1974	Mrs George	

A young man named George Locke came to live at Sevenhampton in 1896. He was a member of the local Locke family who lived in the area for many years. He kept a diary and tells how they moved here from Naunton in 1896 and recalls his early life in Sevenhampton where they lived in a thatched cottage. He attended the local school at the time when Mr Capps was the headmaster. He was happy at school and must have been a bright child for Mr Capps took a keen interest in

Children of Sevenhampton School with Charles Capps, Headmaster Dennis Locke holding plaque

him, gave him private lessons and assisted in every way to further the boy's education. Mr Capps was very disappointed when, owing to economic conditions, George was obliged to leave school, but he attended night school each winter for a further five years. The first season was free owing to George passing an examination for a free winter session. At the end of each winter session the pupils were given a night school supper by Squire Lawrence. This was always a most enjoyable evening.

He also joined the church choir at the age of seven, but was disappointed to be told he was not old enough to attend the Christmas supper. Thus discouraged he left the choir. He was coaxed back by the organist Miss Williams, who lived at Gassons Farm and was also a teacher at the school. He was a chorister for many years and went on the annual outings to Sharpness, Weymouth, Bournemouth, Portsmouth, Weston-super-Mare, Ilfracombe, Ryde, and London. He tells how he was confirmed at the age of thirteen by the Bishop of Gloucester.

They had a school club where he enjoyed playing in the cricket team against other villages. He remembered, in his diary, boyhood days of playing cricket.

"Probably one boy owned a ball, another possessed a bat or part of one, "I often made one if I could find a suitable piece of board". Stones from a wall or sticks from a hedge would constitute a wicket. Under these conditions we would commence. It really is surprising the disputes we had, one would be bowled out and would declare not out, if that is out I shall take my bat home. Another would declare if he doesn't go out you shan't play with my ball. Sometimes fists have been used to settle the argument, sometimes the game was broken up for the evening, sometimes we affected a compromise, and the game would continue.

There was also a men's club, in which I played later, being secretary of the club in my last season home. Cricket matches were eagerly looked forward to, as in a country place you do not get much change from the daily round the common task. We had enjoyable excursions on Saturday afternoons going to cricket matches, the party usually going together by brakes. As a cricketer I was no good at bowling. I was fair in the field, usually my place was keeping wicket, as a bat I was uncertain, I would never play carefully. Some men can stay in for an hour and not make a run, my motto was do something or come out and let someone else in, my innings would be very short and no runs made, but when I hit the ball sailed far out into the field."

The CRICKET CLUB has lasted for many years into the 21st century. Each Lord of the Manor was generous in allowing a cricket pitch to be maintained on his land by the cricket club. Col Rhodes allowed a pitch in the Deer Park, the handicap here was the young fawns who liked to sleep on the short warm grass of the crease. The players had to lift them off before the game could start. Certain local gentlemen would act as umpires and one was famous for saying "I shan't give him out this time, but if he does it again I shall give him out." Several venues were used in both villages the final one being in The Walks. This club was run by Mr Charles Canon-Smith and a Pavilion was given, by Col. Rhodes, for the Club members' use. The Brockhampton Cricket Club became Mid-Cotswold Cricket Champions in 1926. A photograph was taken of the team and umpires, with Col. Rhodes at the wheel of his Rolls Royce behind them. When the club closed in wartime the pavilion was removed to Mr Canon-Smith's garden at Colnside. Tennis clubs also were available for village players mainly on the Court at Sevenhampton Manor.

● Mid Cotswold cricket champions of 1926 were Brockhampton. In the car is the Rev Norton, Major C. Stacey (president of League) and Col Fairfax Rhodes (president, Brockhampton Club). Standing, Mr Meikle (hon treasurer), C.F. Smith (hon secretary), G.H. Alcock, B. Townsend, T. Denley, W.J. Perry, L. Townsend (captain), A. Avann, A. Holcombe, B. Holcombe, J. Locke, E. Harvey and W. Barnfield (umpire)

The Champion Cricket Team, 1926

VICTORIANA

Almost the whole of the 19th century was Victorian, several generations of Britains knew nothing else. The early years were happy for everyone but after the sudden death of Prince Albert, from typhoid, in 1861, Victoria went into deep mourning and most of her subjects mourned with her. Many of the ladies wore long black clothes for the rest of the century, relieved only by snow white aprons. Working mothers wore black aprons also to keep the white aprons clean. Prince Albert had encouraged building and engineering projects which left their Victorian stamp forever on the country. His Great Exhibition funded many educational museums in London and the Royal Albert Hall, one of London's treasures, was erected to his memory in 1871.

The Napoleonic Wars against France had ended in 1815 but two major wars followed. The Crimean War of 1854-6 – famous for the Charge of the Light Brigade and Florence Nightingale – was a hideous war of great suffering. Two heavy guns from Sebastapol were mounted on stone bases outside the Queen's Hotel, Cheltenham only being removed during the second World War to be recycled for war weapons. The Boer War in South Africa 1899-1902 affected the country in hindsight because communications were slow and the only means of following its progress by the general public were the newspapers. Gains and losses were only known long after the event, unlike the 21st century when, via television, we are on the battlefield with our forces and knowledge is immediate. How much Sevenhampton was affected by world affairs at this time is not evident, but its own famous local casualty, John Fairfax Rhodes, killed in action, had a profound affect upon the village, which gained permanently by the erection of the Rhodes Hall in his memory.

The Industrial Revolution moved on apace with the use of steam power, fuelled by the coal mines and the rise of the Factory System, which in some areas took men from the countryside looking for work. The Agricultural Revolution followed the Enclosure Acts with the loss of common land and the farms themselves started, slowly, to become mechanised. Countrywide the population grew, also the need to provide food for its greater numbers. Sheep farming had declined and dairy farming was widespread. The Corn Laws of 1815 which kept the price of bread unnaturally high, the Repeal of the Corn Laws in 1846 and the Free Trade Act, all had their effect on the food producing countryside. Agricultural improvements followed, diverse crop rotation and better breeding of livestock and because of these advances farming became an important profession. Cirencester Agricultural College started in 1845 to improve the knowledge and skills of farming. The first Young Farmers Club was formed at Berkeley in 1898 and soon spread countrywide. Farming prosperity declined following the bad harvests of 1879 onwards and foreign competition made matters worse, so the farming community also declined.

Taken from a Table of Social and Economic History of Gloucestershire:

Sevenhampton – acreage 3,377

Population – 349 in 1801 A.D., 334 in 1811, 386 in 1821, 465 in 1831, 471 in 1841, 553 in 1851, 543 in 1861, 526 in 1871, 456 in 1881, 399 in 1891, and 400 in 1901.

In the 1841 census there were five farms in the parish:

Whitehall Farm	– John Humphries, farmer
Puckham Farm	– William Humphries, farmer
Brockhampton Farm	– Thomas Denley, farmer
Oxlease Farm	– Richard Bee, farmer
Soundborough Farm	– Charles Cock, farmer

Sevenhampton Manor	– Walter Lawrence Lawrence Esq
Brockhampton Park	– Mrs Laura Craven
St Andrew's Church	– Revd Edward Ellerton

Blacksmith – William Pearce; Whitesmith – William Hartwell;
Grocer – John Mansell; Grocer – Isaac Fardon;
Maltmaker – Thomas Hooper; Builder – John Lovering;
Tailor – Charles Larner; Shoemaker – James Hoar.

By 1851 were added John Mansell, farmer, 30 acres; Edward Handy, farmer, 400 acres; John Smith, farmer, 700 acres.

Interesting additions to the census were:
Paul Daston – Chelsea Pensioner; Relieving Officer – Richard Kendrick;
Tailor and Draper – Thomas Bee; Maltmaker – James Budd;
Baker – George Combe; Grocer – Catherine Bee; Stonemason – David Denley;
Beerhouse Keeper – Esther Denley; Carrier – George Westmancott;
Schoolmistress – Lydia Bee; Shoemaker – Thomas Wood;
Blacksmith – William Pearce and Henry Pearce who was a journeyman blacksmith – so by now the blacksmiths travelled to the farms and country houses to do their work.

By 1871 the mistress of Brockhampton Park was Georgina Colquit Craven with her husband Goodwin Charles Colquit Craven (he had changed his name from Goodwin to Craven)

Sevenhampton Manor had a resident caretaker – Thomas Flush, the Lawrences having moved to live at Sandywell Park.

The Vicar was Revd George Masters M.A.

Parish Clerk – John Davis was also a sawyer

Brockhampton Court House was occupied by the Misses Marriott

George Combe was now Brewer/Maltster/Baker at No 10 house – (later The Brewery) Employing 3 men.

Clement Combe was a tailor at No 3 house.

Two of the Pearce family were blacksmiths at Sevenhampton, but Henry Pearce was a blacksmith at Brockhampton.

Grocer and carrier – Neighbour Williams at No 34 house (now Gassons Farm)

Grocer/Draper/Carrier – Thomas Roffe; Beerhouse Keeper/Stonemason– David Denley; Master Stonemason – James Denley; Schoolmistress – Ann Smith, widow.

The house numbers came originally from the account books of the Lords of the Manor. A few houses retain their number as their postal address, but most have changed to house names. Street names were not used although there are unofficial local names.

Parish Rate Book 1860 – 1862

An Assessment for the Relief of the Poor in the Parish of Sevenhampton and for other purposes chargeable thereon according to the Law, made this Fifth day of November 1860 after the Rate of 5d. in the £1.

There are some forty-five householders listed as ratepayers or occupiers of the properties, mostly rented with nine actual owners. W.L. Lawrence was landlord to c.25 of the houses; Capt. Goodwin of The Park owned 9 properties; Brooks and Walker owned 5; (Brooks was of the Boddington Manor family; they acquired a lot more property in the area in later years. Walker, one time resident but moved to Guiting Power. This was the Walker family who gave a window to St Andrew's Church, fitted into the South Transept in memory of John Walter Walker who died at the age of 12 years). W J Agg of The Hewletts, Aggs Hill owned Puckham Farm; George Combe owned the Brewery House, Malthouse and land; Hester Denley owned her own properties in The Quarry; left to her by her aunt Mrs Pitman, widow of Mr Pitman the Baker. The Revd Charles Chambers was living in the Vicarage.

At the 1891 Census:

A. Humphries, farmer, Manor Farm
Thomas Barnfield, farmer, Lower Farm

William Trevethan, Court Farm
Thomas Jackson, Soundborough Farm
Neighbour Williams, carrier and farmer, Gassons Farm
James Roberts, Oxlease Farm
Caretaker, Wheeler, at Puckham Farm
W. Humphries, farmer, Whitehall Farm
Thomas Combe, farmer/maltmaker/brewer

Innkeepers	The Craven Arms – Fanny Taylor
	The Stag – Job Nash
Shoemakers	Oliver Wood, Cordwainer (Master Shoemaker)
	Thomas Pitts
Blacksmiths	William Pearce Postman A Ruck
	Reuben Andrews

Kellys Directory 1906

Lord of the Manor – Christian William Lawrence living at Sandywell Park
Fairfax Rhodes Esq. At Brockhampton Park.

Vicar: Revd Joseph Storr B.A. living at The Vicarage with 30 acres of Glebe land

Whitehall Farm – Frank Humphries; Manor Farm – Benjamin Thos Hyatt;
Puckham Farm – Andrew Walker; Oxlease Farm – Robert James;
Court Farm – Wm Tippett Trevethan; Gassons Farm – Neighbour Williams.

Sevenhampton School. Headmaster – Charles Capps
Mrs G Tombs – sewing mistress;
Miss Emily Williams – assistant mistress

Post Office and shop – Charles Barnett

Craven Arms – David Denley; The Stag – Mrs Nash.

The Humphris Farmers

This family was well known in farming circles all over the Cotswolds.

John Humphris acquired Whitehall Farm in 1833, but died in 1848. His son John succeeded him until 1861. William Humphris was at this time farming at Puckham.

In 1861 Thomas Humphris of Whitehall farmed 584 acres employing 9 men and 5 boys. By 1867 Manor Farm was farmed by John Humphris; Whittal Farm by Thomas Humphris, and Puckham Farm by William Humphris.

By 1881 Manor Farm was run by Mary widow of John. At Whitehall was William Humphris who farmed 470 acres.

By 1906 Whitehall Farm was held by Frank Humphris; Manor Farm had passed to Benjamin Thomas Hyatt, and Puckham Farm was farmed by Andrew Walker.

The Gloucestershire Graphic, on 30 November 1940, reported the death of Mr Frederick William Humphris, of Owdeswell Farm, at the age of 80 years. He was the son of William Humphris of Whitehall and his family had farmed on the Cotswolds for 300 years.

Until his health failed he had hunted regularly with the Cotswold pack since the age of ten. On his pony, Trixie, he was a familiar sight on the Cotswolds and up to two years before his death he had ridden regularly to church each Sunday.

Before taking over Owdeswell Farm he had farmed at Clapton, Bourton-on-the-Water. He had been a Churchwarden at both Clapton and Dowdeswell Churches.

His daughter, Marjorie, said Mr Humphris was very proud of the long association his family had with farming in the Cotswolds and recalled that his great-grandfather gave a farm to each of his sons.

Frederick also recalled the 'bare fist boxing' – although illegal – which took place at secret locations. He remembered attending one between Nash Cottages and Whitehall, with lookouts posted along the race road against sudden arrival of the law.

One protagonist of high repute from near Oxford was so badly damaged that he was confined to bed for some weeks afterwards. The story ran that the law arrived in the middle of it all and everybody had to make a quick getaway.

Commerce

The whole area was agricultural in the 19th century. In 1891 there were eight farms, mostly dairy, selling their produce locally. Milk, butter, cheese and eggs could be bought directly from the farmhouse; you carried your own jug for the milk, no bottles in those days.

Some farmers loaded churns of milk on to a horse drawn cart and sold milk directly to housewives at their door in the surrounding areas (the original doorstep delivery). There were metal measuring cans hanging on the sides of the churn and the milk was ladled out into the housewife's jug ½ pint, 1 pint or 2 pints at a time.

Large dairies became the norm and the day's milk would be poured into large churns to be collected at the farm gate and loaded on to a lorry. This was a noisy process and some people still living today can remember being awakened in the early hours of the morning by the lorries (after the internal combustion engine came in) thundering through the village.

Eventually it became illegal to sell dairy produce directly from the farm; it all had to be processed in proper dairies. This mainly came about because of the serious rise of tuberculosis among the population countrywide and milk was considered to be the main source of infection. Doorstep delivery has continued into the 21st century, but it is now threatened by the rise of Supermarkets.

Carriers

The Carriers must have been a great blessing to the country people, when so much could be bought in the growing town not available to country dwellers. The carriers' carts were horse drawn and canvas-roofed, carrying a great variety of goods and several passengers who would be dropped at and later

Williams Carrier's Cart

collected from the Crown Yard off Cheltenham High Street, thus allowing them a few hours shopping time. The carriers would call for orders, so the housewife would give him a list of items she required from the town. Next day he would collect the items required and deliver them to the lady. Sometimes he would buy a few extra items such as small fancy cakes and the children, on seeing him return to the village, would beg for a penny or ½ penny from Mother to buy a treat from the carrier's cart.

The Carriers of the 19th century were George Westmancote of the Quarry, Neighbour Williams of Gassons Farm, and the Carpenter brothers also of the Quarry.

One cart owner, driver from the Quarry was known to be a heavy drinker. He stopped at too many public houses on his way home. His horse however made no mistakes and brought his master home safely. When they arrived at the stable (in a barn, now turned into a private house) some kind soul took the horse from the shaft, then fed and watered him, leaving the driver asleep in the cart. When he awakened he is reputed, (by local jokers) to have said in Cotswold dialect:

> "Be oi oi, or be-unt oi oi?
> If oi be oi I've lost an 'orse
> If I be-unt oi, oi've found a cart."

The Old Shop, Quarry Road

The Old Forge, Sevenhampton

The Old Forge, Brockhampton

Shops

Two grocery shops were started by 1841 in Brockhampton, one by John Mansell and the other by Isaac Fardon. Another by Catherine Bee and more shops followed in later years.

Blacksmiths

There were two blacksmiths forges, one in Church Lane, Sevenhampton worked by William Pearce and his family. This is now a private house, 'The Old Forge' below the Vicarage.

The Brockhampton forge, near to the Craven Arms, with Reuben Andrews as the blacksmith, later Alfred Bostock, is now a private house.

Blacksmiths were very much in demand at this time, for not only were there horses for working and pleasure to be shod, but the Smith made a lot of farm implements and household items too.

Shoemaking

Shoemaking and repairing were carried out by Cobbler Oliver Wood, his brothers and family. They lived in 3 adjoining cottages facing Coln Farm House, in Sevenhampton. The centre of these is the only cottage with a thatched roof, although there would have been many more at one time. The Woods family had been in the parish for several generations, owning the Malt House building at one time. Mrs Vera Fletcher is the last of the line, but sadly she too has left the parish. One of the

Woods family, in later years, was the shoemaker and another the shoemender. One older resident told how you took your shoes to be repaired and Mr Wood threw them on to a pile in the corner without marking them in any way. He added "how he knew which shoes were whose when you went back for them, I will never understand".

The Old Shoemakers' Cottages, Sevenhampton

Bakers

The first Baker in the village was Edward Pitman of Quarry Road. He became the baker of the loaves for the Longford Trust, or Donnywell Dole, given out to the needy on Christmas morning. Mr Pitman later became Baker, Grocer and General Dealer at his own home. The other 19th century Baker was George Combe, later to become Maltster, Brewer and Baker in Brockhampton.

Many housewives baked their own bread in those days. Most houses had open fireplaces with bread ovens beside them These are the much sought-after ingle nook fire places in old properties now.

Public Houses

Early in the 19th century a number of households in Brockhampton were listed as Beer Sellers. No doubt many households made ale of some kind for use of their own families, because this was the usual table drink before tea became cheap enough for daily family use. Some must have been sufficiently skilled in home brewing that they were able to sell to their neighbours. Gradually some of these became ale houses where men would gather together to drink the somewhat stronger brew. The Stag in the Quarry Road and the Craven Arms in

The Stag

Brockhampton centre lived on as Public Houses, mainly used by agricultural workers after a hard days work.

A Denley owned and built house became a Public House which changed its name many times over the years. From census forms various:

1856	Esther Denley	Beer seller and dairy	
1856	Job Nash	Beer Retailer	The White Hart
1857	Isaac Fardon	Publican, farmer and grocer	
1879	David Denley	Publican	The White Hart
1879	Job Nash	Publican	The Hare & Hounds
1906	Mrs Nash	Publican	The Stag
1906	David Denley	Publican	The Stag & Hounds

The Stag & Hounds continued to thrive for many years under owners various, but was eventually sold to be converted into a private house in 1965 and was renamed the Hunter's Rest.

The Craven Arms was housed in one of the original Cotswold style houses of the 1640's Paul Pearte era. Two storey, one room width house of the two up and two down variety. The original outside back windows are still to be seen in the bar, opening on to the restaurant area. It would have been, originally, an ale house selling home brew, becoming a Public House during the Craven family's years at Brockhampton Park 1803-1890, and named after them as The Craven Arms. Beer was supplied to this public house by the near-by Combes Brewery for many years. From the census forms beer seller: 1881 Harriet Fardon; 1891 Fanny Taylor; 1903 David Denley (rented), (owned) James Walker of Guiting.

The Craven Arms

The Craven Arms was later owned by Inde Coope & Alsop's Brewery with a succession of landlords. Mr Lewis Wallbank, who took over from a Mr Spencer, was the uncle of Laura McDaid. After the Great War 1918 Mrs McDaid's parents brought their family to live at the Craven Arms and in 1927 her father took over as landlord from Mrs Dolly Wallbank who was by then a widow. They set to work to build up the trade by serving honey teas and taking in paying guests. Mr Wallbank laid out the gardens and made them attractive to visitors. He grew and sold vegetables from his gardens, also kept fantail pigeons which came originally from Suddeley Castle. The family had to work hard and, as there was no water laid on in those days, water had to be carried in buckets from Donnywell Spring. About this time the Pub changed hands again to the Cheltenham Original Brewery – rumour has it that it cost them £84. Deliveries were then easier and a barrel of Cheltenham 3 x's was always on the counter – beer was served from the barrel at that time. During the 2nd World War they took in the overflow of evacuees who came to the village. Son John Wallbank took over from his mother, thus three generations of the Wallbank family had been landlords of the Craven Arms.

The Pub was run from December 1961 by Charles Birkenhead who brought his family to live in the village. Catering in their time was mainly lunches for Dowty staff members working at Brockhampton Park.

In 1977 the Craven Arms was bought by Clive Darvill who then made it into a free house. Ex-builder Mr Darvill enlarged the building with a restaurant and kitchen added to the back on the garden side and so it remained up to the 2nd millennium.

The Old Brewery, Brockhampton

The Tall, Red-Brick Chimney of the Brewery has been a local landmark for several generations.

The Old Brewery was originally a farmstead of several stone buildings probably of the late 1600s. The first buildings were of the long, low, single storey type and could have been separate residences – as are several other examples in the village – and were later used as storehouses. The BREWHOUSE was heightened in the late 18th century and again in the late 19th century.

The MALTHOUSE has a plaque on the wall dated 1769. Deeds show the property owned by John and Jane Wood in the late 18th century. It having been purchased from Sir William Dodwell of Brockhampton Park. In 1853 the premises were conveyed to George Combe, Baker of Bread, by Messrs Wood, Trenfield & Cook.

In 1860 the Parish Rate Book gives George Combe as owner of House, Malthouse and Land. So the malting came first.

The Census for 1871 shows Clement Combe, Tailor of No. 3 Brockhampton and George Combe, Baker at No. 10. The 1876 Kellys Directory lists Thomas Combe, Malster, Baker and Brewer.

The 1884 Ordnance Survey shows an outbuilding South of the Brewhouse. This was taken down and reconstructed as a barn, now the site of 'The Old Cowshed' home of Mrs John Lanfear née Combe.

In the late 19th century a copper with a brick surround was installed in the

Brewhouse and a very tall brick chimney was built. This CHIMNEY is now a local LANDMARK.

Brewing may have started in the dwelling house. The first conversion of the buildings into a Brewhouse would have been by George Combe. Brewing was carried on by four generations – George Combe, Thomas Combe, George T Combe and Reginald G B Combe.

Malt and hops were hoisted into the Brewhouse for storage. The malt was milled in the Malthouse then mashed with hot water in a mash tun. The resulting sweet wort was boiled with hops, brought in from Hereford, in the copper, then cooled and fermented with yeast in a tun. Next racked and put into barrels for storage. The barrels were stored in a cellar behind the house.

Some oldest inhabitants in the village could remember when George T Combe owned the Brewery. He is said to have been a very smart man who wore a gold watch and chain across his waistcoat. His chief brewer was a Mr Thom who lived in New Row. Will Locke was his delivery man taking the beer by wagon and horses to Public Houses in Cheltenham and Winchcombe. He would be allowed a free pint in every pub – fortunately the horses knew their own way home! Local Inns including the Craven Arms sold Combe's beer.

Brewing continued until 1928 when the business was sold, but the malting continued. The family then made up and sold packets of COMBES Home Brewed Beer. The packets contained malt and hops and a sachet of yeast, the buyer just added sugar and water. 144 packets were produced at a time selling for a few pence each. These were delivered by van over a large area by R G B Combe, to village shops, post offices and private customers, travelling as far as Ledbury. This industry too came to an end in 1939 because the outbreak of World War II created a sugar shortage.

The landmark Red Brick Chimney

The Ministry of Defence then took over the buildings to billet troops returning from Dunkirk where they set up their own cookhouse and quarters. The M.O.D. used the buildings for storage for a time. After that the old malt kiln was brought back into use for drying corn, spices etc rescued from boats sunk by the enemy in the Bristol Channel and transported to the brewery in lorries. German prisoners of war were sent to work on this process.

To help produce food which was scarce during the war the farm had a thousand laying hens also 20 sows and piglets fattened to pork and bacon weight.

After the war the Malt House was used again to produce malt for a Tewkesbury Brewer and the kiln was used to dry corn for local farmers. Now modern technology has taken over and all the old skills are gone.

New Row, Brockhampton

A row of six attached, stone cottages was built in 1869 opposite the Craven Arms during the time when the Craven family owned Brockhampton manor. They were called NEW ROW because they were a replacement for Old Row – a row of tumbledown cottages in the lane, beside where the Village Hall now stands, leading to a spring where the cottagers would have drawn their water. These cottages were on land owned by the Craven family and were pulled down, perhaps because the land was needed for other purposes.

New Row, Brockhampton

New Row housed six families and it soon acquired the name of 'Hornet's Nest' because the neighbours were said to be so quarrelsome. They shared outside toilets in the gardens, earth closets only. There was of course no water laid on and the housewives had to go down the lane with their buckets to Donnywell Spring to supply their household needs. Years later when Mr Brookes owned Donnywell Cottage and New Row, he put a ram in the well and pumped water up to a tank in the Craven Arms yard. This tank had a tap on the side and the Row residents were allowed to draw their water from it. The Craven Arms occupants too must have been pleased to use this supply, because Laura remembered that, when living there with her Aunt, she was sent daily down the lane to fetch buckets of water from the Donnywell Spring. This water was always crystal clear and pleasant to drink.

There was no piped water in the villages at this time people relied on the number of springs in various parts of the manor. Villages grew up around these natural water sources, vital to their livelihood, no one could live without water. It was far into the next century before piped water was laid on. On some of the farms wells had been dug, for unless the Coln ran through the land there would have been no water for the animals.

Post Offices

A private postal system existed in the time of Edward III 1327-77 when the mail was carried by a royal messenger service. The first 'Master of the Posts' was in office by 1512. The service was consolidated into one establishment in 1635 when a General Post Office was started in London, mainly for use in London. Letters would be delivered in bundles, often to Coffee Houses, to be individually collected by the addressee.

In 1784 the Mail Coach system was set up with special coaches drawn by teams of horses. The poor condition of the roads made travelling difficult and caused many to overturn. An added danger was the Highwaymen seeking rich pickings. Because of this Mail Coaches each carried a guard armed with a blunderbuss and a horn to warn the toll-gate keepers and the Inn keepers of their approach. Only four inside passengers were allowed on a Mail Coach. It proved very expensive to carry letters in this way and that cost had to be borne by the recipient. The charge was calculated by distance and weight and could sometimes be as much as one shilling – this was a great deal of money at the time, making the service unattractive.

The 1d postage and the adhesive stamp – 'the Penny Black' – were introduced in 1840 by Sir Roland Hill. Your letter travelled for a pre-paid 1d, no matter how far distant. This revolutionised the Post Office, which became a Government Department as the General Post Office, with the mail and a telegraph system, under the Postmaster General until 1969. It then became The Post Office with responsibility for the telephone service until being given to the new British Telecommunications in 1984.

By 1867 mail was delivered for this area to Andoversford to be carried on foot to the villages nearby. Money orders were only available from Northleach.

In 1879 Andoversford had a Post Office and a Telegraph Office. Letters were still delivered on foot.

In 1882 the Ordnance Survey six-inch map marks a post office on the north side of the Brockhampton village, approximately where the Dower House stood. This may have been a collecting point for mail and could have been a small building or a room set aside especially from the Dower House. This must have closed after a short while because the mail was still delivered on foot from Andoversford, a postman would walk daily to Guiting Power and back delivering mail to certain places. He would stop off in Guiting Power to do half a day's gardening, then return to Andoversford by the same route. Denis Locke remembered , as a young boy, being sent by his Mother to meet the postman on the top road, where you could hand over your letters for mailing or buy some stamps from him. This postman, Denis recalls, was very deaf and walked at a great speed, ringing a handbell, singing or whistling all the way and never stopped walking. It was difficult to get his attention and to quote Dennis "you was halfway to Andoversford before you could get him to understand what you wanted".

In 1891 the census gives Alfred Ruck of Sevenhampton Cottages as Rural Postman.

Brockhampton Post Offices

In 1900 Charles Barnett opened a Post Office in his house and is named as Sub-Postmaster. The telegraph was still at Andoversford. He is listed in the census as carpenter and wheel-wright. He was also the village undertaker and a dairy farmer.

By 1920 Louie Barnett, Charles' sister, was named as Sub-Postmistress and now they had a telegraph office also. Louie delivered telegrams herself over a wide area. Village boys were paid, in coppers only, to deliver telegrams as far as Guiting Power. In the towns and urban districts telegraph boys in uniform delivered the telegrams on bicycles to individual houses. These telegrams came to be dreaded by ordinary people, as they

The First Post Office, Brockhampton

The First Postwoman
May Barnett

were known to be the bearers of bad tidings, used only, because of the cost, in dire emergencies.

In his memoirs the late George Locke tells how he started to work for Mr Barnett in 1905 as a postman. He had to be sworn in by a Magistrate and then received his uniform. His duties were to do the Charlton Abbots delivery, also the outlying farms, on foot, from 7.30 a.m. to 11.00 a.m. often in heavy rain or deep snow. Then he worked for the rest of the day in the Barnett workshops, or drove out the ponies.

Local people remember the Post Office as being very dark, having shelves with sweet jars and attended by two very old, gentle ladies in dark clothing.

The Barnett office closed in 1946 and, at first reluctantly, the Lockes took it over, in their home, opposite to the Old Post Office in Brockhampton Centre. Denis Locke was newly demobbed from the services. He was now Sub-Postmaster while May Barnett continued to deliver the mail on foot until 1961. Then his wife Freda ran the office – acting unpaid – while Dennis delivered the mail on foot. He was a familiar sight around the villages with his collie dog for company.

Although the space was limited Freda's Post Office became the local meeting place. W.I. business, information (and some gossip) was exchanged, sometimes taking up a lot of time, to the frustration of some husbands; one of whom was quoted as ringing Freda to ask "could I have my wife back please?".

In 1976 Freda Locke took over as Sub-Postmistress when Dennis retired. Val Smith delivered the mail locally for some time.

By now the familiar red Royal Mail vans started to deliver the mail from door to door, at a much greater cost.

In 1987 the Lockes gave up their Post Office after 40 years service to the local community and were very much missed. Mrs Val Smith volunteered her house as the next Post Office, but the Royal Mail and Planning Authority made so many difficulties that she gave up the idea.

For a year the Post Office business was carried on, for one day a week only, in the Reading Room. With a Post Office official and Heather Hawkes-Reed training beside him.

By 1988 Alan and Heather-Hawkes Reed had converted a room in their home at Brockhampton Quarry to become the next Post Office, also as shop for groceries and

The Second Post Office, Brockhampton – with Denis and Freda Locke

vegetables. They continued in business until the end of December 1996.

The Reading Room entrance hall was converted into a fully equipped Post Office, with Vanessa Holland as its Postmistress as from January 1997. This brought it into the village centre again.

All of the 'Post Offices' gave good service to the area, recently publishing coming events etc., now acting as a Booking Office for the Drama Group, B.A.D.S., performances.

Mrs Holland gives a valuable service to the village, handling the post, pensions, licensing, banking, photocopying, computer work and much helpful information. She is an important part of the village community and as such is much appreciated.

From Freda Locke to Heather Hawkes-Reed to Vanessa Holland the local Post Office has been a happy meeting place for us all.

Railways

Eventually the Mail Coaches gave way to the new Railway System that was spreading rapidly across the country in the early 19th century. Roads were still in a very bad condition despite the Turnpike charges to improve them. It was very costly to send mail and goods by road and soon the railways proved to be cheaper and quicker e.g. the first trains took four hours from Bristol to London, whereas the mail coach took twelve to sixteen hours. Railway Mania gripped the country in the 1840s when many people invested in this exciting new venture.

Rebecca Lightbourne and the Timbrell sisters of Sandywell Park objected to the proposed railway in case they lost part of their land to it. They need not have worried because Rebecca and her sisters were all dead by the time the dreaded railway actually arrived.

Building and track laying had started in this area when in 1864 Walter Lawrence Lawrence was investigating the Roman remains on his land, after he had inherited it from Rebecca Lightbourne. Walter Lawrence was one of the shareholders in the coming railway.

Even then it was not until 1881 that the line from Cheltenham to Andoversford to Oxford was brought into commission. A branch line from Andoversford to Bourton-on-the-Water ran through Sevenhampton parish, as the bridge in Gypsy Lane shows where the line crossed. The line to and from Andoversford ran parallel to the now A.40 road; this part of the road came into being when the hill was cut through to create a high bank to support the railway line above. This became known locally as the 'Deep Cutting' and the locals must have watched in wonderment as this fantastic engineering took place. A new road had long been planned between Whittington and Sandywell to Andoversford, in order to avoid the steepness of Dowdeswell Hill which was difficult for horsedrawn traffic.

A long bridge was necessary to carry the line over the Dowdeswell road. It was a wonderful piece of Victorian architecture with many pillars and arches to support

Andoversford Railway Station

The Viaduct

the rails. Known as the Dowdeswell Viaduct it was an elegant structure, admired by many over the years. This viaduct was destroyed as part of the 'Beeching Plan'. Many people congregated at Dowdeswell on the morning of Monday, 1st May 1967 to see this landmark blown up, leaving a yawning chasm where once proudly it had stood.

In the early years of the 20th century it was possible to travel by train to almost any part of the country. It was very pleasurable to be pulled along behind a steam engine, with its familiar noises, watching the countryside apparently moving in the opposite direction – such nostalgia. The railway was efficiently maintained by a huge staff, who were very proud to be railwaymen who cared greatly for their engines, carriages and stations which were often decked out with flowers in their little station gardens. It was considered the 'done thing', after many hours of travelling, to thank the driver for a safe journey.

Sadly after the second world war the railways were losing out to the roads and the internal combustion engine, so Dr Beeching (a name never to be forgotten) was given the power to destroy a great many lines and stations in the countryside in the cause of economy and hopefully to make the railways pay their way again.

The Police

At the end of the Napoleonic Wars in 1815 thousands of men returned to this country without jobs or homes. The inevitable trouble broke out and the militia was brought in to maintain law and order. There was still much public unrest until Sir Robert Peel became Home Secretary in 1822. He produced a system of policing, which became the model for the future Police Force, with men in uniforms of blue tail coats and top hats, required to prevent crime with only a truncheon and a rattle, but expected to be civil and obliging to all people. Once accepted they became known as 'Peelers' or 'Bobbies' after their founder. The force was so successful in London that the idea spread to many more places. Further legislation such as the County Police Act of 1839 enabled Justices of the Peace to establish police forces in rural areas, but by 1853 half the counties of England and Wales still had no police force. In 1856 the County and Borough Police Act finally required all counties to employ their own police.

Many country districts were opposed to this, especially as the force was to be paid and this meant raising local taxes to meet the bill. Some felt that in their villages law and order was adequately dealt with by the Vestry and its Constables who were unpaid.

A local protest was organised for Sevenhampton parish and sent to Gloucester.

To the Worshipful Magistrates for the County of Gloucester, in General Quarter Sessions assembled, on the 4th day of January, One Thousand Eight Hundred and Forty-two.

The Petition of the undersigned Occupiers of Land and others, in the Parish of Sevenhampton in the said County of Gloucestershire

SHEWETH

That your Petitioners have observed, with much concern, the great increase of the County Rates occasioned by the extensive introduction of the Police Force throughout this County. That your Petitioners are deeply sensible of the expediency of every necessary precaution being taken to ensure the Peace, and, as far as practicable, to prevent the committal of Crime. That in large and populous towns, a Police Establishment may not be considered disadvantageous; but in Rural Districts, your Petitioners verily believe that crime is not of that extent as to warrant the interference of such a force, and that the introduction of Police into those Districts of this County, has created a great feeling of dissatisfaction amongst the Yeomanry and others, whose loyalty and promptitude in assisting the Civil Power, have been found sufficient, in the most turbulent times, for the suppression of outbreaks.

Your Petitioners earnestly pray, that your Worshipful Bench will be pleased to adopt, forthwith, such Resolutions as will relieve your Petitioners from contributing to the maintenance of the Police Establishment of this County.

Signed by the following:

Fulwar Craven		Richard Kendrick, Schoolmaster	
Charles Cook	Churchwarden	John Wood	
John Lovring	Churchwarden	Paul Preston	
John Humphries	Overseer	John Preston	
John Mansell	Overseer	Samuel Hart	
William Humphries		David Denley	
Henry Smith		William Wicksey	
John Smith		Thomas Denley	
Thomas Bee		James Hannis	
Thomas Holtham		Richard Bee	
William Peacey		John Davies	
John Biggs		Richard Marchant	
E Handy		Richard Ruck	
John Lovring		Robert Ruck	
Edmund Lane		William Alsop	
Thomas Wood		Solomon Williaams	
William Yearp		David Cook	
James Bee		Michel Cook	
Isaac Heddon		William Moss	
John Matthews			

Register of Electors Sevenhampton 1832/33

Ashby	Thomas	Lovering	John
Bee	Richard	Lawrence	Walter L
Bee	John	Mansel	John
Bridgeman	John	Matthews	Richard
Cook	Charles	Morris	William
Craven	Fulwar	Smith	Henry
Denley	Thomas	Stanley	Henry
Denley	Isaac	Trotman	Edmund
Denley	William	Wood	John
Humphries	John	Wood	Benjamin

Vestries

By the end of the 17th century Vestries had become established as the rulers of rural England.

For the following 200 years law and order was maintained by the Church through its Vestry, which also looked after the old, the poor and the sick. To fund this they were allowed to levy a Poor Rate under the Poor Law Acts of Parliament of 1572 and 1601.

The Vestry provided relief for the needy, apprenticed orphan children and provided housing for the old and the homeless. If vagrants did not find work quickly, within forty days of their arrival, they were sent back to the parish of their birth, which parish was obliged by law to support them.

Everyone in the parish was expected to pay the poor rate. The Vestry appointed Overseers of the Poor whose duty it was to collect the poor rate from their neighbours. Also appointed were the Churchwardens, Sextons, Keepers of the Pound, Parish Clerks and the Constable. These appointments, made at each annual vestry, were for one year only, unpaid, unpopular, and a man had no right to refuse to serve. Exemption could be bought at a high price, or he might persuade a substitute to serve for him.

The people of the villages regarded the Vestry as the real government and not the Parliament which was too remote to be understood. It mattered more who was the Overseer of the Poor than who was Prime Minister.

The Constable was the immediate law and order officer, formerly appointed by the Court Leet, but later by the vestry as Manorial authority diminished and Parochial authority grew. Over him were the Justices of the Peace who in turn were responsible to the County Sheriff – or Shire Reeve – who later became the Lord Lieutenant of the County. The constable was responsible for the maintenance of the stocks, pillories and lock-ups, the suppression of riots and unlawful assembly and he had the power of arrest. The churchwardens also had the power of arrest and still retain that right although not now used. They could order a man to remove his hat in church. Offenders were brought before the Manor Court; petty crime was dealt with by the Justices of the Peace. More serious crime was heard by the Sheriff either locally or in the County Court.

Sevenhampton had its stocks for punishing local offenders. From Elizabethan times a whipping post was compulsory in addition to the stocks.

The Vestry was not a legal institution but had grown up gradually and was recognised by all without an Act of Parliament. The affairs of the parish were controlled by Open Vestries as well as all church affairs; after Parish Councils came in to being the Vestry continued to look after all church affairs only. Occupation of property qualified a man to vote at these vestries, some had more than one vote if qualified by owning several properties and a woman could vote if qualified by the occupation of property and unmarried.

In its administration of the Poor Law the vestry was not unlike the modern Social Services and, since they were unpaid, handling their own rates and with a direct knowledge of the needy, it was probably more fairly organised.

The Government made many attempts to reform the Poor Laws, including changing the parish boundaries, but the reforms became more muddled and unworkable. They considered local government for many years and finally under the Local Government Act of 1888 they created the County Councils, there followed the

Local Government Act of 1894 which saw the birth of Rural and Parish Councils.

The setting up of Parish Councils was not well received in some parts of the country. All classes of men were allowed to put themselves forward for election to the councils, including the labouring classes. This could have been a problem in the old manorial parishes, but the change was made peacefully and smoothly in this parish as the newly elected council was made up of the same people who served on the Vestry committee including the Lord of the Manor, Christian William Lawrence Esq.

County Councils

The local Government Act of 9 August 1888 created the County Council System of England and Wales – 62 newly elected County Councils were established. This replaced the old system of rule by the Justices of the Peace. These J.P.s handed over their administrative functions to the new authorities, but retained their judicial power in their capacity as Magistrates.

Each County Council would be responsible for administrative and financial affairs and would be controlled by a Chairman, Aldermen and Councillors. To stand for election as councillor a man must be a property owner, either as a Peer of the Realm, or as a Parliamentary voter. (Peers and lunatics were not allowed to vote in Parliamentary elections.)

The County Council were to assess and charge the rates and the salaries of all paid officials including the Coroner and police etc. Also they had to provide Jails, Shire Halls, Court Houses, Judges' Lodgings and County Buildings.

County Councils would be responsible for licensing places of entertainment, providing asylums for pauper lunatics and reformatory schools. They would provide and maintain all roads and bridges in their county and ensure all Government Acts relating to control of contagious diseases and vermin and to the conservation of fish and wild birds. Also the control of weights and measures.

At election time the County Council would divide the county into polling districts and arrange where the election would be held and maintain the lists of all those eligible to vote.

Parish Councils

Local Government Act of 1 March 1894 (or the Parish Councils Act) set up a new tier of local government. Some 6,880 Parish, Rural and District councils were set up and promised great changes in the way Britain is administered.

The new local authorities were given substantial powers, but their spending limited to the equivalent of a threepenny rate.

The establishment of elected Rural Councils would bring an unprecedented degree of local democracy.

Cirencester Division of Gloucester 1894

Whittington Polling District   Parish of Sevenhampton

Name of Voter	Place of Abode	Qualification
Agg William	The Hewletts	Freehold land – Puckham Farm
Brooks John Lovering	Uckington	Freehold House Brockhampton
Combe Clement	Brockhampton	" " "
Hall Alfred Lee	The Cross, Winchcombe	" " "
Hall John	Brock. Quarry	" " "
Lawrence Christian Wm	Sandywell Park	Freehold House Sevenhampton
Pittman Edw John	Brock Quarry	" " The Quarry
Storr Revd Joseph	Sevenhampton	The Vicarage Sevenhampton
Wallker James	Guiting Villa	Freehold House Brock.
Wood Oliver	Sevenhampton	House & land
Andrews Joseph	Hampen	Land & tenement
Andrews Ruben	Sevenhampton	Dwelling House, Sevenhampton
Ashby Thomas	Sevenhampton	" " "
Attwater John Newman	Syreford	Land Millfield, Sevenhampton
Barnett Charles	Brockhampton	Dwelling House
Barnett Albert	Sevenhampton	" "
Barnfield Benjamin	Sevenhampton	Land & tenement
Barnfield Daniel	Sevenhampton	Dwelling House
Barnfield Frederick	Brockhampton	" "
Barnfield Thomas	Sevenhampton	Land & tenement
Bateman John	Sevenhampton	Dwelling House
Bayliss Thomas	Brock Quarry	" "
Biggs Charles	Brockhampton	" "
Biggs George	Whitehall Cottages	" "
Burrows George	Oxlease Cottages	Dwelling House
Buttel William	Hampen Cottages	" "
Combe Clement	Brockhampton	" "
Combe Thomas	Brockhampton	Tenement & Brewery
Cook Thomas	Sevenhampton	Dwelling House
Cross William	Brockhampton	" "
Dean John	Whitehill Cottage	" "

Denley John	Brockhampton	"	"
Denley Thomas	Sevenhampton	"	"
Dyer Frank	Sevenhampton	"	"
Dyer Samuel	Brock Quarry	"	"
Gegg Charles	Brock Quarry	"	"
Elford Alfred	Puckham Wood	"	"
Griffin Henry	Brock Quarry	"	"
Haines Thomas	Brockhampton	"	"
Hale David	Sevenhampton	"	"
Hall John	Brock Quarry	"	"
Hannis James	Brockhampton	"	"
Herbert Andrew	Brockhampton	"	"
Holder Edwin	Oxlease Cottages	"	"
Hughes Richard	Brockhampton	"	"
Humphris Arthur	Manor Farm	Land & tenement	
Humphris Henry	Sevenhampton	Dwelling House	
Humphris William	Whitehall Farm	Land & tenement	
Iles Frederick	Soundborough Cottage	Dwelling House	
Jackson Thomas	Soundborough Farm	Land & tenement	
Jeffries Arthur	Brockhampton	Dwelling House	
Kinch George	Sevenhampton	"	"
Lailey John Edward	Sevenhampton	"	"
Lanchbury Job	Brockhampton	"	"
Lawrence Christian Wm	Sandywell Park	Land, Sevenhampton	
Lockie Harry	Hampen Cottages	Dwelling House	
Merrick Richard	Home Farm	Brockhampton	
Mustoe Edward	Brock Quarry	Dwelling House	
Nash Job	Brock Quarry	The Stag	
Newcomb Hugh M L	Hampen Cottages	Dwelling House	
Newman Thomas	Sevenhampton	"	"
Norris Immanuel Jnr	Sevenhampton	"	"
Norris Thomas	Brockhampton	"	"
Parker Benjamin	Hampen Factory Cottages	"	"
Pates William	Brockhampton	"	"
Pearce William	Sevenhampton	Dwelling House	
Pittman Edward J	Brock Quarry	"	"
Pitts Thomas	Brock Quarry	"	"
Powell George	Hampen Cottages	"	"
Proctor Charles	Brockhampton	"	"
Proctor William	Brockhampton	"	"
Reeves James	Whitehall Cottages	"	"

Roberts James	Oxlease Farm	Land & tenement
Ruck James	Hampen Factory Cottages	Dwelling House
Savoury Henry	Brockhampton	" "
Slatter Solomon	Brockhampton	" "
Smith John	Nash Cottages	" "
Storr Rev Joseph	Sevenhampton	The Vicarage
Tombs Albert	Brockhampton	Dwelling House
Tombs Edward	Sevenhampton	" "
Trevethan Wm Tippit	Brock Court Farm	Land & tenement
Turner William	Brockhampton	Dwelling House
Walcraft George	Brock Quarry	" "
Walton George	Brock Quarry	" "
Walton William	Hampen Cottages	" "
Webb Charles	Sevenhampton	Dwelling House
Williams John	Brock Quarry	" "
Williams Neighbour	Brockhampton	Land & tenement
Wood Oliver	Sevenhampton	Dwelling House
Wood Thomas	Sevenhampton	" "
Capps Charles	Brockhampton	Lodger

Sevenhampton Parish Council

Sevenhampton Parish Council was formed and held its first meeting on 18th December 1894. Five persons signed a declaration of acceptance of office:

> Christian William Lawrence
> William Tippett Trevethan
> Thomas Cook
> George Cook
> James Edmund Roberts

Five councillors were required for this parish; many years later the number was increased to seven. Elected councillors were to hold office for three years.

Mr Lawrence was elected as Chairman, Mr Trevethan as vice-Chairman. Mr T M Trevethan was asked to take the office of Clerk, Treasurer and Overseer.

To form a quorum one third of the members, plus the Clerk, must be present.

The Clerk's salary was agreed at £10 per annum, but in his additional office as Treasurer he was asked to find a security of £100 per annum.

The Parish Council held their meetings in a room at the school in Sevenhampton. Initially they paid a rent of 4 shillings for the first part year. After that the rent charged was ten shillings per year, until after the Education Act of 1902 when education became chargeable on the rates. The P.C. was no longer required to pay rent.

The first record books were supplied by E J Shenton at a cost of £1.2s.3d., and a

Parish Chest in which the books were stored was made by Mr C Barnett at a cost of eight shillings. The Parish Council Records have long since outgrown the Parish Chest.

Northleach was our Rural District Council. They set the rates for the area and it was to them that Sevenhampton's Precept was presented. Parish Councils were restricted in their spending to the product of a threepenny rate. The first precept of £1.10s. was submitted, but by the following year this had risen to £7.

The Council was responsible for repairs to footpaths and bridges, also water supplies such as Donnywell spring. It also took over, from the Vestry, the distribution of the Longford Trust or 'Donnywell Dole', the trust set up in 1770 by Thomas Longford, for the distribution of bread to the value of £1 to be delivered to the poor at Christmas. The supply of this bread was tendered for by local bakers and in 1908 Mr Curtis' tender

Christian William Lawrence
Lord of the Manor, Sevenhampton
1st Chairman of Parish Council

Parish Chest, Sevenhampton Parish Council

provided 54 loaves for £1. The bread was distributed at the Hall by a councillor on Christmas Day morning. Before this date the bread had been supplied by Mr E Pittman, Baker, Grocer and General Dealer of Quarry Road, at fourpence halfpenny per loaf. Mrs Pitman (nee Denley) would stand at her cottage door on Christmas morning giving out the loaves to the needy families.

At the first meeting of 11 February 1895, the Winchcombe P.C. asked for the council's co-operation with them in obtaining a Light Railway from Andoversford to Honeybourne via Winchcombe.

9s.6d. was to be paid to the Returning Officer from the County Council for stationery and services in forming the first Parish Council. Standing Orders that the Parish Council should meet on the first Monday after Quarterdays, i.e. four days per annum.

In 1900 the Clerk, T M Trevethan, resigned as he was moving to Birdlip. C Capps, Headmaster of the local school, was appointed Clerk, Rate Collector and Treasurer to the Council. No mention was made of the turn of the New Century to 1900. Queen Victoria was still on the throne of England and her Diamond Jubilee had been celebrated quietly in 1897.

In 1901 an Annual Meeting was open to all eligible voters when there was a dispute over the method of voting in the new Council which was by a show of hands. A poll was demanded, but since there was not a third of voters present requesting this, the demand was not sustained. Many voters withdrew from the meeting hence the

Northleach Rural District Council

small numbers of votes cast. G T Combe 5, E Godwin 5, B T Hyatt 5, W Trevethan 5, J E Roberts 4, E J Pitman 3, G Tombs 3. The first five were elected as the Council for the next three years. C W Lawrence was not nominated because he was away in Italy, because his position as Ambassador had taken him abroad.

The suggestion of secret poll elections was turned down in many parishes because of the cost entailed and the fact that the local rates would not cover it. A rate rise was unacceptable, but it was difficult for men, who though entitled to vote but were also locally employed, to hold up their hands to vote against the Squire, the Parson, or other employers. In some areas any more than the required five were discouraged from being nominated thus making an election unnecessary. The situation generally was not solved until halfway through the 20th century with further Acts of Parliament. A Local Government Act of 1933 empowered County Councils to order a poll procedure if parish councils requested it.

At the Coronation of Edward VII in 1902 the local Parish Clerk was instructed to write to O E Part Esq, tenant of Sevenhampton Manor expressing thanks and appreciation of the Council for his kind offer with regard to celebrating the Coronation in June next. He opened his grounds – much larger then than now – to the villages for a day's fun and games for the children and picnic teas afterwards. The longest serving councillors were from the Combe and Hyatt families who were represented on the Parish Council from 1899 to 2000 A.D. Benjamin T Hyatt, Councillor, left the parish in 1928. He was followed as Parish Councillor by his son Thomas Hyatt who was Chairman a number of times. In 1979 his daughter Mrs Anne Jackson

Parish Council 100th Anniversary

and later grandson Thomas became the Hyatt Councillors. George Thomas Combe was elected Chairman and when he died late in 1930 the Revd Norton stepped in as Chairman. Then in 1934 his son Reginald G B Combe became a councillor and was many times Chairman. He was also elected as a School Manager, Overseer of the Poor and Sevenhampton representative on the District Council at Northleach. He was followed on the Parish Council by his daughter Mrs Val Smith and his son-in-law John Lanfear who was also Chairman for many years.

Col Fairfax Rhodes purchased Brockhampton Park and manor in 1900. In 1904 he joined the Council and he too became Chairman until his death in 1928. Harry Vernon, father of John and Ethel, was appointed Parish Clerk in 1930, a post he held for very many years and was awarded an inscribed silver cup for his long and faithful service to the community.

End of the Victorian Era

At the end of the 19th century Queen Victoria was still on the throne but was by now a very old lady. Her Golden Jubilee was celebrated in June 1887 and her Diamond Jubilee in 1897 marked by a chain of bonfires across the country. Sevenhampton seemed to have joined in with Whittington, because of the Lawrence family owning both villages. A procession headed by the Denley band started from the Vicarage, where the Revd Anthony Lawrence was in residence, to the centre where a sheep was roasted and games and races were organised. Dancing was accompanied by the Denley String Band and the Jubilee Anthem was sung by the Church choir. The Queen's birthday was celebrated annually, together with Empire Day on the 24th May. The World Atlas showed many countries coloured in red denoting the British Empire. Victoria and Albert had brought the family life into great regard during their years together and strived to improve moral life generally after the decadence of the Georgian years. The Crimean War of the 1850s was long over and the Boer War lasted through the turn of the new century. These would have involved the Regular Army but not general recruiting as in later years.

The Victorians were great builders with a style of their own, Victorian buildings were elegant, sturdy and practical. Strong bridges were needed to accommodate the new railway system. The line from Cheltenham to Andoversford had to be taken across the main road to Dowdeswell with embankments on either side especially made for this. An impressive Victorian Viaduct was built at this spot which supported passenger and goods trains in both directions for some eighty years. The line crossed Sevenhampton parish via the bridge in Gypsy Lane. Coal was used to provide steam for the railway trains, also for steam ships and industry at this time. Domestic coal was brought by the trains in trucks and some was delivered to Andoversford Coal Yard, where it was fetched in small carts by householders. Electricity was in its early stages of supplying power to some buildings. Bicycles became a popular form of transport, fixed wheel at that time. Tricycles too were popular, the Revd Joseph

Storr was said to have used one to get around his parish, one elderly parishioner remembered how he paid them, as young boys to clean it on Saturdays. A penny-farthing – early bicycle with a very large front wheel driven directly by pedals and a small back wheel – was ridden (or fallen off) in local lanes. Horses or horses and carriages were the usual form of transport, though most people were content to travel for many miles on foot. Walking to Cheltenham, Winchcombe or Northleach was in no way unusual. If you needed to see a Doctor, or get him to visit a sick relative, you had to walk to Winchcombe. In later years the Doctor held a once-a-week surgery in a private house in Brockhampton. In time a District Nurse was resident in the village and she would attend to most local medical needs. She would leave a slate outside her house, when she was going out on her local visits, and on this board you could write your request for help and she would then visit you in your home. The Nurse was highly thought of in those needy days and the people of the parish built a special bungalow for her on land donated by the Smiths of Soundborough. This bungalow is at the very top end of the Quarry, known now as 'Wychwood'.

Sevenhampton Manor House was still owned by the Lawrence family, although the Lord of the Manor, Christian William Lawrence, had moved his household to Sandywell Park, which was a much larger country house than the Sevenhampton one. The great houses still dominated the countryside everywhere and were maintained by vast numbers of servants; women and girls indoors, with men and boys mainly outdoors as grooms or gardeners, although there was some indoor male employment e.g. butlers, footmen etc. So the working population of the countryside were mainly either in agriculture or in service. A few would have found employment at the Brewery. There were teachers, blacksmiths, stonemasons, bakers and carriers. The countryside was self-contained when everyone grew their own vegetables and fruit and usually a pig was kept in a sty in the garden which kept the family in meat and bacon for many months after it was slaughtered, cured and hung from a beam in the kitchen. The parts which would not 'keep' provided an immediate feast which would be shared with neighbours, while they in turn shared with you when it was their turn to slaughter the pig. They would also keep a few chickens in each garden which produced eggs for the family and table poultry. The hens would be slaughtered when they became too old to lay eggs.

Brockhampton Estate was owned by the Craven family until 1890, then leased by Major de Freville for the next ten years to 1900. The Reading Room was still the small, single room in regular use as Library and Institute.

Sevenhampton School was the only school in the parish, reached its highest number of pupils and had to be enlarged to accommodate them in 1900. The two non-conformist Chapels held their regular Sunday services and the Sunday Schools both church and chapel were well attended.

The Vicarage was occupied as from 1850 and became the parish centre after the Tithe Barn had been demolished. Incumbents Revd John Craven, died 1807, and Revd William Pearce, Incumbent 1808-1825, had both previously lived at Brockhampton Park. The Revd Joseph Storr and his family were living at the Vicarage from 1890-1923.

St Andrew's Church was very much as we know it today, with altar, choir stalls, pulpit, lectern, organ, pews, font and vestry, although the older font had been removed to the churchyard. The window behind the altar now had its beautiful stained glass depicting the Transfiguration of Christ and dedicated to Mary Lawrence who died in 1889. The Church, much loved and cared for, was still the centre of the parish with a good and regular congregation.

Incumbents of St Andrew's Church

1204	John the Clerk mentioned by Bigland in connection with division of land
1264	Sir John de Soincot) from
1275	Master Ralph de Pirie) Llanthony Priory Registers

There were no Ministers for a number of years because:

"the Prior and Convent succeeded in ousting the Rector, and altogether appropriating the benefice to themselves; no longer content with the portion of forty shillings that previously been paid to them annually by the Rectors. Probably the cure of souls was henceforth in the hands of the Canons themselves, or the Lessee of the manor might be bound to provide a chaplain for the performance of the duties".

1377	Roger de Breynton	
1388	Thomas Frenche	Clerk
1430	Thomas Frenche	
1504	Thomas Morton	Clerk
1522	John Hawkins	

After the Reformation in 1538 came the following Ministers:

1545	Roger Fowler	
1551	John Handley	(said to be unable to recite the 10 Commandments)
1565	Miles Busteed	(Curate at Salperton also)
1584	William Busteed	
1594	John White	(described as sufficient scholar but no preacher)
1597	Elias Woodruffe	
1599	Nicholas Parrye	
1607	Miles Nicholson	
1619	Robert Williams	

1625	Nicholas Tucker
1631	Henry Blackburn
1634	John Williams

1649 1669 THE COMMONWEALTH

1662	Thomas Hook	
1673	-- Dobson	
1676	John Burbyn	
1677	John Farmer	
1681	Charlton Barksdale	(Rector of Hawling also)
1712	Elias Petty	
1713	Gerard Clements	
1723	John Hughes	
1747	Robert Lawrence	
1758	John Lawrence	(held Hawling and Salperton)
1776	William Longford	
1776	John Craven	
1807	Thomas Longford	
1808	William Pearce	(held Salperton also)
1825	Edward Ellerton	
1851	Charles Chambers	
1862	George A Holdsworth	
1868	George Masters	
1872	John Melland-Hall	
1879	Henry Venn Hebert	
1890	Joseph Storr	
1923	Arthur Norton	
1934	John Miller	
1944	B A C Kirk-Duncan	
1947	Hugh McCalman	
1953	Francis Charles Canon	
1974	Philip Hobbs Canon	
1996	Roger Morris	

The Churchyard

To the South side of the Church is the oldest part of the churchyard with the graves of Sevenhampton people identified from 1615 onwards. There would have been many earlier graves but they would not have had the durable headstone or tombs.

Earlier burials would have had stones, without inscription, placed over one end of the grave to protect the head. There are a number of table-top tombs for the families of local landowners, the earliest legible inscription being of Henry Lord who died in 1615. Nearby is a small grave with a flat stone inscribed to a child, Henry Lord, born in 1649 and died in 1650. Of the 17th century were Nind, Ebsworth, Mason and Timbrell all landowners. In the 18th and 19th centuries were Lovering, Trotman, Brookes, Arkell, Denley, Attwood. Another grave of a child, John Walter Walker died 1800 aged 12 years, strikes a sad note His grief stricken parents dedicated a church window to him in the South Chancel.

After burials were no longer possible inside the church, some of the Lawrence family were buried to the left of the churchyard gate. Christian William Lawrence, the Last Lord of the Manor was buried, with His Mother and sisters, in a tomb with a large cross and ornate carved stone railing. Sadly this has since been broken down.

The Craven family, of Brockhampton Park, are buried in graves with coloured marble crosses and edgings near to the South side of the South Transept near to the old Vicarage gateway. The East window in the Chancel of Charlton Abbots Church commemorates Mrs Georgina Craven, also in this chancel are memorial plates to her husband Goodwin Charles Colquit Craven and son Fulwar Colquit Craven.

On the right-hand side of the churchyard gate are the graves of the Coomb family, brewers and farmers of Brockhampton. On this area was once the original Church House before the Vicarage was built.

Several former St Andrew's Vicars lie near the old Vicarage gateway. Revd Joseph Storr died 1923; Revd Arthur Norton died 1934; Revd Hugh McCalman died 1953. Canon Francis H Charles died 1978 is near to the Lawrence tomb. Also Bishop David Porter, died 1997, who retired to Sevenhampton though still assisting the local churches. He was also a fine artist, as many portraits of local persons and landscapes proved.

On the North side of the church, near to the Manor House wall, are many graves of the Humphries family, farmers, who at one time farmed a number of farms in the Sevenhampton and surrounding area.

A new churchyard burial ground was opened in 1927 when burial space became scarce in the old churchyard. Mr C Smith of Soundborough gave the stone and Mr W Smith helped build the surrounding wall. A Right of way gives access to this churchyard from Brockhampton at Donnywell, across Manor Farm fields. This was also used as a walkway to church in fine dry weather. In 2000 this burial ground was becoming full and a new area was much needed.

Sevenhampton
Old English – Seofon–ham–tun = "A village with seven homesteads"

The Parish of Sevenhampton/Brockhampton grew in a strange fashion. Upper Sevenhampton grew larger around the church as started in 1150 AD. The valley of the Coln divided Sevenhampton and because the lowland beside the waterway was not suitable for building, the village extended on higher ground on the other side – oddly it became known as Lower Sevenhampton.

The Coln would have been wider and deeper then. An early water-mill is documented above it, near to the present water-splash and Saxon bridge and was taxed at 13s.4d. in 1291 AD.

BROCKHAMPTON – Brokhamtone, or Brockington = "farmstead of folk dwelling by the brook" (English Placenames of Gloucestershire).

There would have been some sort of early village on the Brockhampton side of the Coln, for it is shown on some early maps at the same time as Sennington. The central village grew up around the water springs, one at the bottom of the lane beside the Reading Room and the other at Donnywell beyond the now local landmark of the Old Brewery chimney.

The top end of the village grew around the Quarry which was being worked in Sennington times, 800-1140 AD. Its stone was used to create the village down the years. These hills were never short of stone, used mainly for Roman Villas, Churches and Manor Houses at first, but by 1650 'The Cotswold Style' came in and after that all new buildings were of local stone. The colour varies from quarry to quarry and this brings greater interest to Cotswold villages.

The church was always the focal point of a village, the oldest ones being simple one room wide erections, but, when wealth was generated by the large sheep population, the churches became larger and grander bit by bit. Sevenhampton church was enlarged and altered many times, the last major changes came in c.1900.

Sevenhampton Church of St Andrew

1150 AD   Norman church built – this part is now the Nave.
           2 Norman doorways and windows
           Pillaster buttresses at West end 12-13thC
           Original Stone Altar brought down from Sennington

Manor and Church owned by Hereford Cathedral and Llanthony Priory

1348   Black Death/Bubonic Plague
           Door and windows on North side blocked up

           Church extended Eastwards
           1st to about present Chancel steps
           2nd extension formed the Chancel with Early English East window and
              Priests' door on South side

1400   Church now at present and final length

BELLS

GABRIEL Bell early 15th C   'daybelle' and 'kerfowbelle'
housed in Turret
Inscribed
"SANCTE GABRIEL ORA PRO NOBIS"

1650   CHANDLER Bell
Inscribed
"BE YEE FOLLOWAIRES OF GOD AS DEARE CHILDREN"

1718   TIMBRELL Bell
Inscribed
"JOHN TIMBRELL, CHURCHWARDEN A.R. 1718

Late 15th C   Transepts added – making church Cruciform
Used as Chantry Chapels with an altar in each

1497   Death of John Camber, Wool Merchant
1498   He willed 100 shillings for improvement to St Andrew's.
Tower erected, supported by flying buttresses

1504   Church building completed
Dedicated to St Andrew by Bishop of Hereford

1533   Reformation. Henry VIII

1534   Dissolution of the Abbeys

1538   All Baptism, Marriage, Burials to be listed

1547   Dissolution of Chantry Chapels Under Edward VI.

Privy Council ordered:
1548   Relics and images removed. Walls whitewashed
Protestants texts in black& white

1549   Book of Common Prayer in all churches

1550   Stone Altars replaced by Wooden Tables – Edward VI
Sennington altar used as roof to Ambulatary

1551	Queen Mary ordered Edward's texts to be removed Apostles Creed remained on S. Transept W. wall
1570	Queen Elizabeth ordered Bibles in English and Books Of Common Prayer be placed in all churches
1598	Incumbents to make transcriptions of previous entries into Registers and send copies to Diocesan Registrars
1611	King James Bible introduced – 'Authorized Version'
1640	Bishop Laud ordered Altars to be railed off
1640	The Commonwealth banned Fonts in all Churches
1660	Restoration of the Monarchy. Charles II re-instated Fonts. Chalice-shaped Font placed in St Andrew's Church
1771	St Andrew's altered and restored. Box Pews introduced
1830	Tithe Commission Act taxes to be paid in money Vestries to be responsible for Law and Order
1850	New Vicarage built. Tythe Barn pulled down
1861	Hymns Ancient and Modern first appeared
1890s	Waller Restoration new pews,. pulpit and lectern
1892	Victorian Font given by Lawrence family
1929	Benefice extended to include Charlton Abbots
1975	Hawling and Whittington added to Benefice 'The Foresome'
1981	Alternative Services Book published
1996	Coln River Group of Parishes formed. One Priest-in-Charge

Late 19th Century Renovations

In 1891 W.S. Waller, the County Ecclesiastical Archivist for the Bishop of Gloucester, turned his attention on St Andrew's, Sevenhampton. He had already made drastic changes to many of the County churches and destroying many old historic features in the process. The Revd John Melland-Hall writes of the mural paintings which would have once adorned the walls. These were pictures of bible stories for the benefit of those who could not read, thus teaching them the historic background to the scriptures which would have been read to them by the Incumbent priest. Some of these paintings were on the walls when the Early English window was moved from the Chancel to the South Transept.

At this stage St Andrew's still had its full complement of Box Pews, in Nave and Transepts, installed at the Lawrence renovations of 1771, which can still be seen in a.sepia photograph of 1892. This picture shows clearly the 1840 Lectern; the simple Pulpit on its stone pedestal with a bench beside it; the Royal Coat of Arms, with Dieu et Mon Droit and Honi Soit Qui Mal Y Pense, above the Chancel Arch.

The floor is of the same level throughout. For heating – an iron stove raised on a small dais with a lidded coal scuttle beside it. For lighting – a lamp, probably paraffin fuelled, is shown suspended from the ceiling on a chain, which could have been lowered for lighting or refuelling. The walls were scraped and plastered.

The floor was raised by one step where Nave and Chancel meet and another elevates the Altar still higher. There is an ancient, narrow shelf behind the altar which shows what would have been the original altar height. A central aisle was created between the new low pews when they replaced the old box pews and the floor was laid with handsome brick red tiles with gold patterned tiles at centre and edges. The tiles become smaller in the chancel and smaller still near the altar, with the same colouring and pattern throughout.*

Behind the altar the Perpendicular window was transformed in stained glass representing the 'Transfiguration of Christ' by the Lawrence family in memory of Mary Lawrence died in 1881, wife of Walter Lawrence Lawrence, Lord of the Manor of Sevenhampton.

Beneath the Chancel floor are a number of graves to members of the Lawrence family and to members of the Carter family of Charlton Abbots. Also of course John Camber, benefactor of St Andrew's. The engraved stone covering of his grave was removed and hung on the South wall of the chancel.

It was during the Waller changes that the simple Stuart font was removed to the churchyard, to be replaced by the ornate Victorian font commissioned by Miss Agatha Lawrence in honour of her late parents Walter and Mary. This font has been in regular use up to and beyond the second Millennium.

The old heating stove was removed to be replaced by two iron 'tortoise' stoves,

Vestry Screen

*New Pews
with Hassocks
embroidered by
Parishioners*

one in the chancel and one in the nave. These were stoked and lighted by Mr Hooper for many years.

A very beautiful carved, wooden screen was fitted to the West end of the Nave a few feet from the West window, thus creating a Vestry for the clergy to robe, also for storing church items safely. Eventually when, sadly, the Vicarage was sold by the Commissioners, the safe containing the old church Records was removed to the vestry. At the end of the 20th century these books and papers were removed to the County Record Office for safe keeping.

Inside St Andrew's Church showing the special tiles leading up to the Altar

Quote from Canon Philip Hobbs:

"The encaustic tiles were very much part of the Victorian church restorations. They were made in the Midlands with great inventiveness and skill. Note that the pattern becomes more elaborate and splendid as one approaches the altar. Our tiles came with the 1890's restoration when the Cotswold tiles and the grave plates were removed. This fashion was all part of the Oxford Movement or 'High Church' influence of the time – emphasising the Sanctuary and altar as the focal point of the church."

The Church Windows

There are nine stained glass windows in St Andrew's Church.

1869   The Early English window in the South Transept facing South is of three decorated lancets dedicated to John Walter Walker. His grave is in the old churchyard near the Manor garden wall.

1877   A single lancet window in the Chancel, facing South is dedicated in memory of Charlotte Elizabeth – Lady Pollen – died August 7th 1877. She was the sister of Revd John Melland Hall, Vicar of St Andrew's 1872-79.

1881   The Perpendicular, 3 lancet, East window behind the altar, dedicated to Mary Lawrence, represents The Transfiguration of Christ. To his right is Moses holding the Tablet and on his left is Elijah the Prophet. Beneath are the three terrified disciples, Peter in the centre with James and John on each side.

1901   A Perpendicular window in the North Transept facing North is dedicated to John Fairfax Rhodes, son of Fairfax Rhodes of Brockhampton Park, who was killed in action during the South African War. He was buried in a tomb in Charlton Abbots churchyard.

1915   Also in the North Transept another double lancet window, facing East, depicting the Virgin Mary holding the infant Christ, facing her cousin Elizabeth with her son John the Baptist as a young boy. It is dedicated In Memory of Mary – wife of Fairfax Rhodes of Brockhampton Park, who died 4th January 1915.

1919   Following World War I, the Great War, a stained glass memorial window was fitted in the North Transept facing East. Depicting St George and St Alban and dedicated:

"To the Memory of those Men connected with this Parish who gave their lives for their Country in the Great War 1914-1919". Underneath is a tablet engraved with the names of all those who died in the Armed Forces.

Three new stained glass windows in the Chancel are:

1993   In loving memory of Leonora 'Goldie' Paddon. Born 1914 At rest 1993.

1996   Treasured Memories of our Dear Daughter Claire Felicity Hedges nee Wilson 1947-1996

1997   In Prayerful Remembrance of a Devout and Faithful Priest and Father. Ordained St Peter's Tide 1946 Called to Higher Service Stanley Wilson June 1997. He was well known in the parishes where he often took Services.

St Andrew's Church showing the old Box Pews

THE 20TH CENTURY – The Age of Technology

The 20th century came in very quietly. The Boer War was still in progress and a nationwide epidemic of Influenza was taking many lives across the country; in London alone there were 50 deaths per day.

Queen Victoria, now aged 80 years, was still the reigning Monarch of Great Britain and the Empire which covered a fifth of the globe. Her Consort Prince Albert had been dead for 40 years. Her many children had married into most of the Royal families of Europe, the eldest child Victoria, the Princess Royal, married Frederick Emperor of Germany; the heir to the throne Edward married Alexandra of Denmark; the Queen's granddaughter Alix married Nicholas Tsar of Russia – Queen Victoria became the most revered International Grandmother.

The two ends of the 20th century couldn't be more different. In 1900 villagers lived a very simple existence. There was no water laid on, so water had to be fetched in buckets from springs and wells or from taps in the walls, the latter put in by the Lords of the Manor, fed from the natural water supplies of each village.

There were no indoor facilities, the 'loo' or privy was a hut in the garden containing a wooden seat over a hole in the ground. One old lady from Sevenhampton told how her father planted a hedge from the kitchen door to the loo to give the family privacy. These primitive facilities had to be moved from time to time over a new hole and the old one was filled in thus keeping the soil in a very fertile condition. Also the pig in the sty in the back garden helped to nourish the soil too.

The Rhodes Tap
near to the Village Hall

One of the Taps in the Walls

Heating came from open fires and cooking was done on kitchen ranges heated with solid fuel. A stone hot water bottle warmed the bed in winter and baths were taken, in a tin bath, before the kitchen range. The water was first heated in the kitchen copper also fired by solid fuel, filled by buckets, then transferred when hot into the tin bath again by bucket. The owners of the Great Houses would have bathed in hip baths, with the water, heated in the kitchens, being carried up the back staircases in jugs by the servants. The range was made of iron and had to be blackleaded regularly by the housewife to keep it clean and rust free. The range heated the ovens where all the household cooking was done. Washing was boiled in the copper and ironing done by flat iron (literally made of iron) which was heated on the range. Shirts, collars and aprons were starched and whitened by 'blue' added to the last rinse. (Blue came in soluble squares, made by Reckitts, which when dipped in water a blue liquid was obtained. A cube could be used many times so was economical.) The washed clothes were pegged to a line in the garden to dry, using wooden dolly pegs, or gypsy pegs held together by a metal strip, later came spring pegs. Housework really was hard work at that time Monday was always washing day. Saturday night was bathnight and Sunday was kept for church or chapel, nothing else was allowed, no fun and games and no entertainment. Sunday walks with the family were usual on fine days.

Lighting was by oil lamps fuelled with paraffin supplied by the visiting Lusty Hardware Wagon which called regularly. It also carried pots and pans of every description. Candles also which were used to lighten the bedrooms which were dark and very cold. Children went to bed Wee Willie Winkie style carrying a candle in a candle stick. These candles threw up frightening shadows on the walls.

Both Manor Houses acquired generators to supply electricity for domestic use. Sevenhampton Manor used the Old Barn, now a private dwelling, to house their generators. Fairfax Rhodes later supplied lighting to the Hall from Brockhampton Park supply.

Many cottages had bread ovens built in to the stone fireplace and housewives baked their own bread. But others got theirs from the Pitman Bakery of Brockhampton Quarry, or from Combe's Bakery in Brockhampton, later Ryman's from Whittington. Mr Harries from Guiting Power brought bread and groceries and lastly Watsons from Guiting Power delivered to the end of the century and beyond.

Enterprising firms from Cheltenham, such as the International Stores, delivered goods and Drakes would supply draperies. Singletons mens' outfitters would come and measure customers for a suit, then duly deliver – a made-to-measure suit.

There were local shops of various kinds to supply local needs. Mrs Roberts' shop was a grocery & general store in the Quarry road, the Barnett ladies at the Old Post Office kept some items including jars of sweets. The Old Shop next to the Chapel was also a sweet shop, regular customers being the children coming from or going to school. Later Mrs Minnie Webb opened a shop, in the house, which was once a mill, next to the River Coln in Webb's Lane. This shop was used during the Second World War to provide the rations for registered customers.

The whole area was agricultural so most people earned their living directly from the land as farmers and farm workers. At the beginning of the 20th century ploughs were still drawn by oxen on some farms. Barns had stalls for oxen as well as stables for horses. The oxen, being cattle, were prone to foot and mouth disease. There was no slaughtering at that time, but the cattle were nursed back to health, which often took many months before they were fit to work again. The last oxen were used on Gassons farm early in the century as witnessed by John Smith.

The 1881 Census gives:

Whitehall Farm – William Humphris; Court Farm – William Trevethan; Manor Farm – Arthur Humphris; Lower Farm – Thomas Barnfield; Gassons Farm – Naibor Williams; Oxleaze Farm – James Roberts; Puckham Farm – Andrew Walker; The Brewery – Thomas Combe. The spelling varied according to the enumerator.

In 1900 the first Post Office was opened by Charles Barnett.

In 1901 The Craven Arms was run by Fanny Taylor; the Stag by publican Job Nash, baker and grocer was Joseph Pitman; the caretaker of the Hall was Mrs Norris who lived near to the Reading Room. Some local employment was available at the Hampen Bone Factory making fertiliser for fields and gardens.

By 1901 there were eleven farms of varying sizes in the area:

Whitehall Farm with William Humphris, farmer;
Court Farm with William Trevethan;
Manor Farm with Benjamin Hyatt;
Lower Farm with Thomas Barnfield;
Gassons Farm with Neighbour Williams;
Soundborough Farm with Hedley Combe;
Oxlease Farm with James Roberts;
Puckham Farm occupied by John Dollins farm bailiff, Andrew Walker owner;
The Brewery Farm with Thomas Combe farmer, malster, brewer, baker;
Grange Farm with Charles Barnett farmer, sub-post master, carpenter, undertaker;
Coln Farm with Walter Locke.

Manor Farm

The Hyatt family came first to Manor Farm, from Snowshill, as tenants in 1899.

Benjamin Thomas Hyatt was the resident farmer. He joined Sevenhampton Parish Council in 1901 and became an Overseer of the Poor Relief and a Manager of the local school. At the Parish Council meeting in December 1928 it was recorded that a replacement member was required for B.T. Hyatt as he had left the parish. At his death in 1935 a wheeled bier was presented, in his memory, by his family to be used at village funerals. A letter of thanks to his widow from the Council also said that the bier would be housed in the Rifle Range. Later the Council purchased a dust sheet to cover it when not in use. His son Thomas Hyatt, born at Manor Farm in 1902, had continued to run Manor Farm with his wife Betty after their marriage in 1928. They had two daughters Anne and Gillian. Tom was also a Parish Councillor and several times its Chairman. He was also a Church Warden at St Andrew's for many years and in his later years he became Church Warden Emeritus.

The Hyatt Wheeled Funeral Bier

Thomas Hyatt purchased Manor Farm from Miss Wynnefrede Lawrence in 1928, also much of the Sevenhampton estate land. The final purchase in 1944 of land leading to the water splash crossing of the Coln in Sevenhampton, completed the 'Original Area of Sevenhampton Estate' which brought with it the entitlement to call themselves 'Lords of the Manor of Sevenhampton'. However the vital papers confirming this were sadly destroyed in the fire of London during World War II. Tom and Betty retired in 1969 moving to Spring Cottage in Brockhampton. Manor Farm was then carried on by John Jackson and his wife Anne, nee Hyatt, for many years. Tom died in 1991. The double gates at the entrance to St Andrew's churchyard were given by the Hyatt family to commemorate the Diamond Wedding of Tom and Betty in 1988. Betty died in 2003 just a few weeks short of her 100th birthday.

When it was the turn of John and Anne Jackson to retire their elder son Robert with his wife Lynne became the farmers until the second millennium of 2000 and beyond.

All the farms included some dairy farming and local people could get milk by taking a jug to the farmhouses. (By the end of the 20th century there were no dairy farms left, then cattle and sheep were kept for meat production, with the fleeces for wool and hides for leather.) The sheep were still taken to Syreford to the sheep dip before the annual shearing. In later years the Government forced the farmers to make their own sheep dips with a compulsory chemical included, which may have done well for the sheep, but did a lot of harm to the farmer's health when doing the dipping.

As an agricultural area labour was intensive and the working population moved about quite a lot. The tied cottages, mostly owned by the manor estates, went with the job and recruitment had been done at the Hiring or Mop Fairs where the workers stood, with a symbol of the type of work they were seeking. No doubt the landowners could retain the staff they had if they so wished. Still there must have been a great upheaval in the population in the Autumn at the end of harvest and after the Hiring fair. It would have been a very unsettling period for families and especially for the young children. There was some evidence of the meadow opposite St Andrew's church being used for a fair. Metal fair tokens were found by someone using a metal detector. The annual fairs were an opportunity for relaxation and fun, with games and stalls selling tempting items such as brandy snaps, toffee apples, trinkets and ribbons. It would be just the farmworkers moving house, while stone masons, blacksmiths, bakers, grocers, inn keepers were self-employed and rented their properties from the manor estate. This would account for the many name changes in the registers down the years.

Families

The **Lawrence** family held the Manor House from 1605, purchased from the Carter Family of Charlton Abbots, and the whole manor of Sevenhampton by purchase in 1608, until the final sale in c.1928. Their total holding at its peak included Sandywell, Whittington, Syreford, Sevenhampton and most of Brockhampton.

Paul **Pearte** drew Brockhampton into one manor with the purchase of much of the land from the Chandlers of Soundborough, to build his great house and village from 1639. After came the **Lord** family at Soundborough and the **Nynd** family at Oxlease. The manor of Brockhampton was increased in size when Sir William

Dodwell bought much land from these two families. Anne, daughter of Ralph Dodwell of Brockhampton House, married Thomas Timbrell in 1651.

The **Timbrell** name is the longest surviving in Sevenhampton parish. Baptismal records give 1596 Thomas and 1597 John Timbrell. A Gyles Timbrell, yeoman, was mentioned in the Men and Armour survey of 1608. There were five Timbrell householders in The Court Rolls of 1676. John Timbrell, church warden, presented the church with the Timbrell Bell in 1718. Descendants of Anne and Thomas Timbrell were the three Timbrell ladies who inherited the Whittington and Brockhampton Estates in 1806. There were Timbrells still living in the Quarry area at the millennium, 2000 A.D.

The **Craven** family came into the picture through the Revd John Craven who rented Brockhampton Park from Rebecca Lightbourne in 1803. The next owner of the estate, Walter Lawrence Lawrence sold Brockhampton to Fulwar John Colquit Craven, thus Brockhampton and Sevenhampton became again separate manors, but still one parish of Sevenhampton. The Cravens also bought Charlton Abbots Manor House and estate.

Humphris was the next longest surviving name amongst the local farming community from c.1500. A John Humphries born at Naunton in 1590. A later John Humphries came to Whittal Farm in 1833 when it was part of the Walter Lawrence estate and to Manor Farm in 1867. Thereafter his sons farmed most of the farms in and around the Sevenhampton area. Frederick William, who farmed at Owdeswell was the last Humphris farmer in the area. Mrs Muriel Candler nee Humphris, much loved St Andrew's Church Organist for many years, is the last member of this family still living in Sevenhampton parish.

The **Denley** family were resident in Sevenhampton parish for 250 years.

John Denley, stonemason, settled in Brockhampton in 1750 and married Mary Dobson at Shipton Oliffe church in 1752. They brought up a family of eleven children, whose descendants were stonemasons in and around the village until the millennium. Historian Robert Atkyns said in 1712 there were eight cottages in Brockhampton Quarry. In 1812 there were ten, two having been built by the Denleys.

The 1818 Enclosures awards showed the Denleys owned a lot of land near the Quarry. In 1834 the Quarry Chapel, 'Bethell', was built by the Denleys and paid for by local subscriptions. In 1847 the Quarry was owned by John Lovering, builder of Brockhampton, by purchase. It passed to his descendant Charlotte Walker who sold it on in 1922. Six cottages were bought by Joseph Pitman, husband of Annie Denley. He was a baker and shop keeper living next to Quarr Cottage. The last owner was Burt Denley who died in 1979, thus severing the Denley connection with the Quarry.

In 1903 David Denley became licensee of the Craven Arms, which included seven acres of land which he leased from James Walker of Guiting. David moved and became licensee of The Stag which he called 'The White Hart'. In 1926 the Denley brothers built 'Rockville' from the Quarry stone, also the house called 'Combe', the last house in the area to be built of local stone. Also in 1920 they worked on the new extension, the Schoolroom, to the Salem Baptist Chapel in Brockhampton centre. The last surviving male Denley, Michael, or Mick was also the last caretaker of the Rhodes Hall, living in the Hall Cottage with his wife Carol. They finally left the village in January 2000 to take up residence at St. Merryn in Cornwall.

The family of James **Hannis** moved into The Dower House, Brockhampton in the 1870s. He was a Preacher, stonemason and builder – also the Grandfather of this author. James had a wife and family of eight children and was known for his love of music. Each of his children was taught to play a musical instrument, so he was never short of accompaniment to the hymn singing during his services. He travelled, with his wife, to a number of Cotswold chapels, in his pony and carriage. He was remembered for his fine preaching by Mrs Canon-Smith of Colnside and was in fact documented in Salem Church records as being in charge of Brockhampton Baptist Chapel at the time of his death in 1896. He was buried in St Andrew's churchyard, Sevenhampton.

The **Barnfield** family were well known in Sevenhampton and Brockhampton for many years. They were a family of farmers and stonemasons. In the 1891 census Thomas Barnfield is listed as the farmer of Lower Farm, Sevenhampton. In 1933 it was E.W. Barnfield who brought the beautiful Stuart Font back into St Andrew's church. They did many miles of crafted stone walling and also carved in stone. Their numbers dwindled, some left the village when the Park Estate was sold in 1934, until there was only one family left. William Barnfield lived at The Homestead, Sevenhampton with his wife and five daughters. Three were married to farmers, Flo and Ada never married, but lived out their years in the bungalow, which was built for them, next door. Flo was a school teacher and church organist for many years. Ada was fun loving and an active founder member of the B.A.D.S. May was married to William Barrett of Upper Hill Farm, their children were Heather and Willy. Heather was the last Barnfield in Sevenhampton parish, married to Alan Hawkes-Reed, Steward to the W.W. Bailey, Charlton Abbots Estate, also Warden of St Andrew's for many years. Together Heather and Alan ran a sub Post Office in Quarry Road until 1996. They moved to live in Prestbury.

The **Locke** family arrived in Sevenhampton from Naunton in 1896, as agricultural workers moving to new employment after the Autumn hiring fair. This was vividly reported by George Locke in his interesting diary still in the family possession. The family grew and in the 20th century there were a number of Locke brothers in farming, building etc.and finally as sub postmasters. George's family would have been living on the Lawrence estate, while others worked for the Rhodes estate. George worked as a postman for the Barnett post office and when this branch office closed Denis and Freda set up a sub post office in their own house opposite. This became the village social centre for many years, also information office; W.I. affairs and Drama bookings being part of everyday business, much missed by everyone when it finally closed in 1987. Denis' brother Chris had a fine singing voice in St Andrew's choir. He sang beside Ethel Vernon who also had a beautiful voice, remembered nostalgically by other church worshippers. After Chris was widowed he later married Ethel who is better remembered as Mrs Ethel Locke. In remembrance of the active part the Lockes played in the village, the family presented the Rhodes Hall with a fine clock dedicated to their Locke parents.

The **Vernons** were later arrivals to the Parish moving in the first half of the 20th century. Harry Vernon became a dedicated Clerk to the Parish Council over very many years and was awarded a Silver Cup for his long service. Ethel always remembered, and probably polished, the orginal box which stored the Council minutes and accounts, being kept in their home. They had moved into the Hall Cottage as caretakers when the 1939 war broke out. John had moved to Birmingham at this time, but when he was called into the services he brought his new wife Margaret to live in Brockhampton for the duration. In fact they never left the village again. They were very involved with the church always and John became a Church Warden for many years and also a very active member of the local community.

The **Smith** Family. Very early in the 20th century land belonging to the Salperton estate was sold off. Two brothers, Charles and Jesse Smith bought much farmland each, Charles settled at Soundborough and Jesse acquired Southdown and the two families have lived in the area ever since. It was Charles who, having a large quarry on his estate, gave the stone to build a wall round the new churchyard extension in 1927, his son William helped with the building of it. Another son John (Victor) was a skilled stonemason and he told of how he helped his Father to lay stone from his quarry to repair a long stretch of the Winchcombe road; he said the road looked white with the new stone. John was well known to the people of Sevenhampton parish and other villages for the stonework he did for so many people. When you had a new fireplace someone would ask – is that one of John's? His fireplaces and other work will be a permanent memorial to John. His youngest brother, Allan, after a period in the Guards, married Val Combe and together they took over Gassons Farm, of which Elsdon is a part. In 1973 – 'Plant a Tree in 73 Year' when the Government wanted everyone to plant more trees for the environment, Allan allowed the Parish Council to plant a group of trees on his land, these were small deciduous trees and the Council planted small conifers beside them as a protection while they were small.

Later the conifers were removed and John built a wall around them. The parishioners were allowed access to this group of trees, via a footpath, at any time. The Parish Council agreed to be responsible for the maintenance of this group which has now become a landmark in the area. People did visit as allowed and one year the W.I. held a Summer Picnic there. When Allan died he left the trees, with access, to the Village so that people could enjoy them and the lovely view in perpetuity.

The **Hollands** lived in the parish from 1953, left it for some years but returned to live in Brockhampton in the early 1970s, bringing their handicrafts which they put to good use for the benefit of the villages. Syd is a perfectionist in cabinet making, joining and carpentry. Clem used her accountancy skills as W.I. treasurer and organiser of many events, helping others and working for charities, then as Churchwarden to St. Martin's, Charlton Abbots for many years. They were joined by daughter Georgina when she moved with her family from North Wales, bringing her wonderful crafts of needlework, cooking and catering which she used to great effect for local good. Then in 1989 she started 'The Brockhampton Quilters' meeting regularly at the Rhodes Hall in Brockhampton. Georgina taught patchwork, quilting and appliqué and together with her group built up a great reputation for perfection, as their many subsequent Exhibitions showed only too well. They have become a local institution of their own.

At the turn of the century the main landowning families were Lawrence, Rhodes, Combe and Hyatt.

In 1900 Christian William Lawrence left Sevenhampton Manor to take up residence at Sandywell Court as this was a much larger house. The whole estate had now become known as Sandywell Estate with C.W. Lawrence as Lord of the entire manor.

Col Fairfax Rhodes owned Brockhampton and Charlton Abbots through purchase from the Craven family in 1900 until his death in 1928. The estate then passed to his widow Mrs Mary Rhodes until the sale in 1934.

The Combe family arrived in the area as bakers, then maltsters and brewers when they purchased the Old Brewery in 1853. They continued in production until 1928. By 2000 the land was still owned and lived in by the Combe/Smith/Lanfear family. The brewery house and malt house were sold, but the Brewery with its landmark red brick chimney was converted into a house and lived in by the William Lanfear family.

The Hyatt family arrived in 1899 to Sevenhampton and the same family has farmed Manor Farm ever since. Each generation has played a part in parish affairs, the Church, Council, W.I. as well as farming. Old Sennington is on Manor land and they have honoured the pledge, made by the Bishop of Hereford, to keep the land on which Sennington village was situated in hand for sheep.

Transport

The Manor Houses employed household staff, also outdoor staff such as gardeners and grooms. Horses or horses and carriages were the only form of transport in 1900, although the horseless carriage (motor car) was still in its infancy. Most horses were the heavy working ones like shires with their beautiful wool covered feet. These were mostly bred on the farms, the mares being sired by visiting stallions from the Heavy Horse Society. Lighter horses were used by the carriers and bakers, or other delivery vehicles. Even lighter horses were bred for hunting and racing which was very much alive in the Cotswold Hills. These horses were commandeered by the Army for use in two world wars later in the century.

Bicycles and tricycles came in early in the 20th century preceded by the Penny-farthing with one large wheel (penny) and one small wheel behind (farthing), with a saddle and foot pedals attached to the large wheel. Very difficult to ride (one late former resident remembered proudly that he could ride one of these contraptions).

The alternative was walking – 'Shank's Pony' was very much in vogue then. People thought nothing of walking to Cheltenham and back for work or pleasure, they must have been very fit. They had to walk to Winchcombe if they needed to see a Doctor, or to fetch the Doctor for the very sick. He would then visit the patient, travelling around in his personal pony and trap. The District Nurse started a daily surgery in a local private house. She moved into Rose Cottage and then Spring Cottage for a while, until a piece of ground was given to build her a bungalow at the Top of Quarry Road next to Campden Lane. People remembered her leaving a blackboard outside her cottage – while she was on her daily round on her bicycle – on which they could write and ask her to call on them when she was free. Later the Doctor held surgery locally, on fixed days, in a private house. The last of this service, before the days of the National Health Service, was held at the home of Freda and Dennis Locke, opposite the Rhodes Hall.

The local carriers, Williams of Gassons Farm and Carpenter opposite the Stag and Hounds, Quarry Road, took a few paying passengers with them when they went to Cheltenham to shop, to fulfil orders. A lady in Sevenhampton, Mrs Humphris, owned a horse and trap which you could hire for a personal shopping trip to town. Dennis remembered a promised shopping trip at Christmas time when he was a small child. His mother would take her small brood on such a trip "but only if 'tisn't raining". He would waken up in the morning hopefully, saying "is it raining Mam?" Coming home afterwards up tunnel hill, which was too steep for the horse to pull them all, the boys would have to get out and push.

The Railway was running regularly to Andoversford bringing goods which had to be collected from the station. Also bringing coal which had to be transported to the villages by horse and wagon. Railway passengers from this village were taken to or fetched from Andoversford station in the pony and trap belonging to Mr Barnett.

The railway had built up a wonderful network of rails and stations over the whole country. At one time it was possible to travel anywhere in the country by main line to towns and cities and by the many small branch lines to outlying villages.

These were privately owned railways, very efficient, always on time, run by a large staff who were fiercely proud of their railway system.

After the second world war the railways were Nationalised by the Labour Government. Dr Richard Beeching was appointed Chairman of the British Railways Board to increase railway efficiency. The Beeching Plan in 1963 slashed the network by a quarter, closed 2,128 stations, scrapped 8,000 railway coaches and axed 67,700 jobs.

This was followed locally by the closure of Andoversford station, and the destruction of the elegant Victorian Viaduct at Dowdeswell which carried the railway over the road high above Dowdeswell.

The Motor Car came in with the 20th century bringing the beginning of great change to the country way of living.

Early in the 1900s Col Fairfax Rhodes, the new owner of Brockhampton Park and Estate, introduced the new motor car to the village. Most people had never seen one before and it must have caused quite a stir. Subsequently he was the owner of three cars, two Rolls Royce and one Arrell Johnson. The other 'first' in the parish was Miss Marie Cannon-Smith with her Austin. She used her car to take the local cricket team to their fixtures. Her father organised the team and was often the Umpire. Col Rhodes also used his charabanc to ferry the team for the more distant fixtures.

The introduction of the motor bus in the 1930s made the greatest impact on the local countryside. Miles Coaches of Guiting Power are very much a part of our recent history. In 1896 the Miles' family was in transport with horse and cart. They changed to petrol driven vehicles with a fleet of 3 x 29 seat Bedfords and later a Dormobile. Mr W.G. Miles driving the Stage Service two to five times daily from Guiting Power to Cheltenham. The Dormobile carrying children to and from schools was driven by Mrs Miles. All the family drove for the firm, but in 1968 the Company sold out to Pulhams. Two of the family stayed with the new firm, Hilda, so well known to many local people, as a conductress and David Forbes as a driver. Later under De-regulation a mini-bus was tried on this route by Cotswold District Council, but this proved so unpopular with the passengers that they demanded and got David and Pulhams back again. David is well known for his kindness and courtesy to older passengers and still giving good service at the turn of the Millennium and beyond.

Death of the Queen

In 1901 Queen Victoria died at her house Osborne on the Isle of Wight, on 22 January after a short illness, at the age of 81. She had reigned for 64 years. This caused a problem for the Establishment because no one remembered the procedures for the death of a Sovereign, or the accession and Coronation of a new King. No one under the age of 70 could remember living under another monarch. She was succeeded by her eldest son Albert Edward, Prince of Wales, who now became King Edward VII. He was by then 60 years old. In 1863 he had married Princess Alexandra of Denmark and she became his Queen. He had been a fun loving and sometimes rebellious heir apparent, so much change was anticipated.

The House of Hanover now became the HOUSE of SAXE-COBURG-GOTHA.

The Coronation in 1902 was held on 9th August after a three month delay because of the new King's appendicitis operation. It must have been wonderful for all the countrywide subjects to let their hair down and celebrate the Coronation. Owen Part Esq of Sevenhampton Manor opened his house and grounds to the villages for the day when they held a grand coronation picnic, said to have been much enjoyed by everyone. Special services would have been held in all the local churches. Sevenhampton service being taken by the Revd Joseph Storr, in the newly altered and beautified St Andrew's where they had much to celebrate. The Revd Anthony Lawrence held service at St Bartholemew's in Whittington. He was living with his family in the Whittington Vicarage. He was brother to Lord of the Manors Christian William Lawrence. The Dobell family, wine merchants of Cheltenham, supported and took part in the celebrations. They were living in Whittington Court at the time. When in 1904 Revd Anthony collapsed and died whilst walking along Station Road in Andoversford, his family, who were required to leave the Vicarage because it was needed for the new Incumbent, then moved into Whittington Court.

Lieutenant John Fairfax Rhodes

The Rhodes family of Brockhampton Park had their own tragedy when in 1901 their only son Lieutenant John Fairfax Rhodes was killed in action in South Africa during the Boer War at the age of 25 years. Born in 1877 and educated at Eton College, where his name is on the Roll of Honour, in Lupton's Chantry, for old Etonians lost in battle, he entered the 2nd Dragoons in 1899. He was promoted to Lieutenant in September 1899 and his Regiment was sent to South Africa in October 1899. They served throughout the war in operations of Cape Colony, the Relief of Kimberley and the Advance on Bloemfontein. Sent into action against the Boers at Klippen near Springs, outnumbered and outmanoeuvred. Lt Rhodes was shot in the stomach and fell from his horse badly wounded. He was taken many miles to hospital by ambulance accompanied by the chaplain of the regiment, Father Eustace Hill who records that journey as an agonising bumpy ride. Father Hill stopped the ambulance twice and begged to be left behind with his patient, but the Doctor in charge refused. The ground was rough, the jolting was awful and the patient was in agony, crying out "You're killing me". He died in the ambulance shortly before they reached base camp. He was buried in South Africa and the funeral was conducted by Father Hill.

The famous Cecil Rhodes, founder of Rhodesia, was a relative of Lieutenant Rhodes and he had the body exhumed and brought back to England accompanied by a Sergeant and five men of the Royal Scots Greys. The coffin was carried by train to Notgrove Station, thence by road for burial at St Martin's, Charlton Abbots. The road outside Brockhampton Park was strewn with ferns and straw – to deaden the sound of the wheels and horses hooves in deference to John Rhodes Mother, Mrs Mary Rhodes who was an invalid.

The grieving Father had a fine memorial stone erected over the grave, also a memorial window set in the North Transept of St Andrew's Church, Sevenhampton. J F Rhodes was named under the South African War Memorial Window in the Chapter House of Gloucester Cathedral, also on the Memorial erected in Princes Street Gardens in Edinburgh which

Colonel Fairfax Rhodes
Lord of Manor, Brockhampton

The Rhodes Grave, Charlton Abbots

represents a Trooper of the Regiment in full uniform as worn by the Scots Greys in 1899.

Later Col Fairfax Rhodes extended the Reading Room in 1908 to become the Rhodes Hall as it now is with a Pargetted Plaque on an inside wall to J.F.R. 1877 to 1902.

In 1908 the Rifle Range, provided by Col Rhodes, trained young men in the use of rifles. Many of these young men joined the forces at the outbreak of war in 1914.

The Rook Shoot

Rooks had become a plague early in the century because of their large numbers and menace to crops. They bred mainly in the tall trees of the Deer Park.

Each year the Squire would invite the men of the village, with their guns, to take part in an organised day of shooting. Small boys were allowed to join in by collecting up the dead birds. These they could take home to their mothers to dress and cook. Not all would do this, perhaps because preparing the birds for cooking was hardly worth the effort involved, though I am told Rook Pie was a delicacy.

In earlier years small boys had been employed to walk around the crop fields throwing stones at the rooks to frighten them away.

The Colonel kept a herd of white deer in the Park which became famous because of their unusual colour. They were sometimes a bit of a nuisance and if any escaped they could be counted as vermin and shot. They were a handicap to the cricket

The Rook Shoot

The Deer Park

players too. Colonel Rhodes encouraged the local cricket team and allowed them to maintain a cricket pitch in the Deer Park. Before the men started to play they would sometimes have to lift the sleeping baby deer off the pitch, where they were lying on the short grass because of its warmth on sunny days. Local games were umpired by a local man and John Smith used to tell how when one side called 'howzat' he would say 'I shan't give him out this time, but if he does it again I shall call him out'. The team became very good players however and in 1926 they became top of the Cotswold Cricket League.

Technology moved forward in 1901 when on 11 December Gugliemo Marconi, the pioneer of wireless telegraphy, sent his first signals across the sea from The Lizard in Cornwall. At 6 o'clock in the evening three dots, for the letter 's' in morsecode, were tapped repeatedly on a machine and were received 2000 miles away in St John, Newfoundland. Thus opening a new era in communications – the Radio was born.

Simple crystal sets were the first radio opportunity for the general public. Then wireless sets with earphones attached were the mode. Firstly a high pole was erected in the garden with a long wire, the 'ariel', which fed into the wireless set. This took the form of a box containing valves, condenser and other parts, powered by an accumulator partly filled with acid. The original Radio Times magazine had a picture of such an ariel on the front cover After that came the loudspeaker when all the family could hear the broadcast programmes. The old advertisement entitled 'His Master's Voice' with a terrier dog sitting beside the 'loudspeaker' horn 'listening in' personified the enthusiasm for the new radio broadcasting.

In the towns and cities Theatres and Concert Halls had provided drama and music. Then the Music Halls started bringing a more light-hearted entertainment When the phonograph and the gramophone came in all this became possible as home entertainment. The gramophone machine was hand cranked (wound up) before electricity came in.

Entertainment came to the village first in the Reading Room with its library, coffee room, with talks etc. and later in the full hall. Home produced Concert Parties were put on. The Denley Minstrel Troop played here and in many other villages. Whist Drives and Dances started up – so popular that the Drive took up both rooms set with small tables, four players to a table and the Master of Ceremonies stood in the then only doorway between the rooms to see that the play was fair. This usually involved good prizes and the money raised was used for local charities, including the Hall itself and the local church. When the whist drive was over the main hall was cleared for dancing. Candles were scraped on to the floor to make it slippery enough for dancing. The music was supplied by local people, Mrs Roberts, shopkeeper from the Quarry, played the piano, her nephew played a banjo, Tom Denley was the violinist and Denis Locke was on the drums.

Death of King Edward VII

After a short illness King Edward VII died in 1910. He had been called Edward the Peacemaker because there had been no wars during his nine year reign. Edward visited Paris on a goodwill mission in 1903 and on 8 April 1904 he was the Monarch who signed the 'Entente Cordiale' with France. He was succeeded by his second son George whose elder brother Albert had died in 1892. George V was known as the Sailor King because he was given a maritime education and had served with the Navy, thus he was not trained for kingship. Prince Albert had been betrothed to Princess Mary of Teck and Queen Victoria, who was still alive at the time of her grandson Albert's demise, decided that the new heir should become the husband of Princess Mary. They were married in June 1911.

Old Age Pensions were introduced as from 1 January 1909 for persons over 70 years. Five shillings for single people and seven shillings & sixpence for married couples. This was to be collected at the nearest Post Office and must have made quite a difference to the welfare of poorer families.

In 1913 Brockhampton was closed as a working quarry, but, in 1940, it was opened again temporarily during the 2nd World War when the stone was needed to build a Runway at Staverton Airforce Base.

Also in 1913 Mrs Pitman's grocers shop in the Quarry Road closed finally.

The Flower Show and Fete

The first 'Flower Show' was held at Sandywell Park in 1902, by courtesy of Mr C W Lawrence, where it became an annual event. This was organised by the Sandywell and Brockhampton Horticultural Society. In 1904 the Show was moved to Brockhampton Park by permission of Vice President Col Fairfax Rhodes. It could not be held at Sandywell Park, home of President C.W. Lawrence because of the very recent death of his brother the Rev. Anthony C. Lawrence. By 1908 this had become a real village fair with athletic sports, swings and galloping horses. A demonstration of dairy work, held in a specially erected tent, was an added attraction in 1908. The officials were Mr C W Lawrence President; Col Fairfax Rhodes vice-President; Mr E Whitbread hon. Treasurer; Mr A McLean hon-Secretary; Committee members – Rev J Alcock, Mr C Barnett, Mr W Barnfield, Mr G T Brown, Mr C Capps, Mr G T Combe, Mr J Clifford, Mr W Finch, Mr G Fletcher, Mr Abbot, Rev J Storr, Mr F Humphris, Mr R G Hanks, Mr T Hyatt, Mr W Lane, Mr J Larner, Mr Roberts, Mr H Jones, Mr A Mills.

The Exhibits in 1908:

"Flowers or plants in pots; Cut Flowers, Fruit – blackcurrants also red or white, gooseberries, desert apples, cooking apples, pears, plums, rhubarb. Vegetables – potatoes round or kidney, broad beans, dwarf beans, runner beans, peas, cabbage, carrots, parsnips, cauliflowers, onions, eschalots, lettuce, beetroot, turnips, cucumbers, vegetable marrows, tomatoes, celery, leeks, and herbs, all in separate classes." (as published in the *Gloucestershire Echo*).

Everyone grew their own flowers, fruit and vegetables at that time and allotments were rented from the estates for extra growing space. So prizes for the best kept gardens and cultivated allotments were awarded. There were also classes for poultry – orpingtons, wyandottes or leghorns – eggs, honey, butter and table poultry.

Handicraft classes included – home-made bread, currant cake, dish of boiled or steamed potatoes, pair of knitted socks, patchwork quilt, home-made undergarment, marking, button holeing and herringboning. Children's classes were darning, an apron, and a dressed doll.

There were agricultural prizes for – hedge laying not less than 100 yards; drilling not less than 30 acres of corn; to carters for farm horses and harness turned out in cleanest and tidiest manner, to be seen in the field at work; building and thatching a rick or ricks not less than 15 squares; single and hoe not less than 2 acres of roots. So this part of the judging would have to be done well before the show day.

By 1913 it had become the Flower Show and Fete with a comprehensive Sports

Programme with 150 yards race for married men under 40 years – 1st prize a 9 gallon barrel of beer, 100 yards for men over 40. A sack race, egg and spoon race, thread and needle race, a boot race, high jump and bowling for a live pig. A scout display by the Brockhampton Troop including the building of a floating pontoon to cross the lake. There was Horse Jumping and Yeomanry Sports. Mr Tom Hyatt won a riding whip in the Horse Show.

War broke out the following year in 1914 and the show was not held again for several years. When the war was over the show was started up again and continued annually until war broke out yet again in 1939. The show was then suspended until after the second war and was resurrected again in 1945.

The Show's name became The Sevenhampton, Charlton Abbots and Hawling Parishes Produce Show and Fete. The venue changed a little from time to time. The outdoor Fete was held in the field behind the houses opposite the Rhodes Hall or else in The Walks. Some villagers remembered when the show items were staged on trestle tables in the lane outside the Hall. Before the Hall was extended, the Reading Room was used for the teas In the 1970s the Produce Show became too large to be contained in the main hall, so it utilised the School Room above the Baptist Chapel. Later when the Chapel closed and was standing empty, first the School room then the main hall was used to display some of the produce. When Mrs McKenzie lived at the Court she kindly loaned her field, annually, to be used for the sports and sideshows. After she died and her property sold, the new owner continued offering the field to the Produce Show. A marquee was hired each year, to be put into the field for Show items to be displayed. Another was hired later to house the tea room, thus freeing the Reading Room for show items, such as the childrens' exhibits. The hall extension too was brought in to service.

The Entry Sections of vegetables, fruit, flowers and cookery (in recent years men have entered, and won, the cake competition) continued. More sections were added to include handicrafts in different mediums, photographs, drawings and paintings. All of which showed the very high standards achieved by local people. For each section a cup was presented to the entrant gaining the highest total points.

The fields sports recently are less ambitious than the 1913 variety, it has changed with the times gradually. Bowling for the pig has become field skittles – back-breaking work for the 'sticker-up'. Childrens' sports continued for many years, also a Fancy Dress Parade for the children, with usual Bo-peeps and Batmen. Once we had 'The Lion, the Witch and the wardrobe' as a group and 'Lady Godiva (a boy) rode in on Horseback led by a friend (another boy). Some older ideas like dwyle-flunking (a somewhat messy game involving buckets of water and dusters tied to sticks) were tried out. Background music was at one time the province of Mick Denley, with a running commentary on the field show, but after he left the village music was provided by James Candler from modern recordings. But we have had hurdy-gurdies and street organs, silver bands, Morris men and Scottish dancing from time to time.

Side shows are a regular feature with book stall, plant stall and gift stall. The inevitable raffle, plus icecream tent and a barbecue.

So the Produce Show prospered from post-War to Millennium. It has the largest committee of any local activity, indeed it used to be said that if you dared to show up at the Annual Meeting you were automatically on the committee! A great deal of hard work is put in by the committee and helpers over a long period of time, but it always proves worth the effort by the end of each highly successful Show Day.

THE HOUSE OF WINDSOR

The Great War 1914-18

Trouble was brewing in Europe when the Hungarians living under the Austria/ Hungarian rule for many years showed their resentment of Austrian rule and wished to break away to join their natural kinsmen of Serbia. This came to a head when the heir to the throne of Austria, Archduke Ferdinand, was murdered on 28th June 1914 at Sarajevo. The Austrians blamed Serbia for this and declared war on Serbia in July. Serbia appealed to Russia who came to her assistance. Germany, whose government had blocked an attempt by British statesmen to find a peaceful settlement, entered into the war on the side of Austria. France and Russia then entered into the fray on the side of Serbia.

Germany then decided to attack France, but since her borders were heavily defended, they marched through neutral Belgium. Since Britain had plighted her word to defend Belgium, she was then obliged to go to war on Belgium's behalf. War was declared by Great Britain on Germany and Austria on 2nd August 1914. Thus began four years of slaughter and destruction involving armies from most of the world, many of them from countries which were still at that time part of the British Empire.

This was greeted with great excitement by the young men of the time, many of them rushing to join the army to take part in the great conflict which 'would be over by Christmas' so it was said.

In Sevenhampton parish the Rifle Range at the Rhodes Hall had proved a very popular feature for several years. The men of the area had become highly skilled at target shooting, their teams taking on rival visiting teams, some with military training, and usually winning. Their skills were soon to be put to the test for real when some of them joined the wartime forces as volunteers. Little did they know of the horrors that were to come; as countrymen they were used to digging the soil, buy not living in it, eating, sleeping and waiting always underground in open trenches in all winds and weathers. The thrill must have warn off very quickly in the daily mortal danger from gunfire and explosions all around. The horses commandeered too must have lived like pit ponies when they were not galloping into danger. Many of these came from the Sevenhampton area.

The front line gradually extended from the Belgian coast to neutral Switzerland. The fighting was fierce and the death rate so high that the British army was becoming decimated. More men were needed to replace the fallen and the Kitchener recruitment drive with posters pointing a finger and slogan 'Your Country Needs You' brought many recruits. In January 1916 conscription was brought in of all adult males between 18 and 41 years. All men had to be registered and when your papers came through the post you had to go no matter how you might have felt about the fighting. Conscientious objectors, those who refused to go, were given a hard time, even imprisonment in some cases. The losses among the fighting men left many widows and fatherless children and girls of marriageable age now faced a life of spinsterhood which up till then was regarded as very unacceptable.

So many men left civilian life that women had to be encouraged to fill the men's jobs left vacant. Many women worked on the land, as The Land Army, some became VAD nurses or drove ambulances near the battlefields, or else they joined factories making armaments to supply the forces. Alice Barnfield, daughter of Fred, and some of her friends from Brockhampton found work at the Woolwich Arsenal in London. Food became scarce and some rationing was introduced. The first pig club was formed, most households were already pig keepers, and special pig rations were available from the Rhodes Hall to produce pork which helped with meat rations for the population. In 1916 the British Summer Time Bill was passed, usually called Daylight Saving. Clocks were to be put forward by an hour in the Spring to give the factory workers an extra hour's daylight when they finished their days work. The clocks were to be put back one hour in Autumn to normal Greenwich Mean Time.

There was a tremendous shortage of men when the war was over. Almost all families in the country and empire lost at least one member, as the many war memorials up and down the country stand witness to. One million men killed and a further one and a half million men wounded. The wounded men were a sad sight in the town, legless men were begging for a living on the streets. They did not come back to 'a land fit for heroes to live in' as had been promised to them.

Sevenhampton had its losses too; ten names are listed on a Memorial in the South Transept of St Andrew's Church.

Sgt Albert John Mills D.S.M.	Grenadier Guards
Sgt Albert Attwood	Gloucestershire Regiment
Pte Daniel Mustoe	Gloucestershire Regiment
Pte Edward C Holtham	Gloucestershire Regiment
Pte Charles Briggs	Gloucestershire Regiment
Pte Thomas Taylor	Gloucestershire Regiment
Pte Harry Barnfield	Royal Marines
Pte George Albert Webb	R. Warwickshire Regiment
Pte Harry Emanuel Dyer	R. Warwickshire Regiment
Pte Alfred Thomas Harvey	R. Warwickshire Regiment

The stained glass window above the plaque is of St George and St Alban, dedicated to those who died connected with this Parish 'who gave their lives for their Country' in the Great War 1914 – 1918.

A Spanish Influenza epidemic broke out throughout the country. It was said that it claimed more lives than had the war.

The War Memorial in St Andrew's Church

King George V was Monarch throughout the Great War years. In 1917, because of widespread anti-German feelings, the King was advised to change his German family name of Saxe-Coburg Gotha and the Royal Family became – The HOUSE OF WINDSOR.

Peace At Last

Armistice was declared at the 11th hour of the 11th day of the 11th month in 1918. Religious services were thereafter held on each anniversary for many years; mostly at war memorials which had been erected countrywide,when two minutes silence were reverently observed, by all people remembering those who had died. A severe Peace Treaty – The Versailles Treaty – was drawn up and signed by the winning Nations on 28th June 1919. The harsh conditions of the treaty robbed the Germans of all that they had won by fighting, leaving them impoverished and resentful, thus sowing the seed for further conflict one day. The League of Nations was formed in 1920, at the Paris Peace Conference, in the hope that World Peace could be preserved in future.

Europe opened up again and became the playground of the wealthy. The Women's Suffrage Movement, formed before the war and fighting for equality for women, succeeded in one of their aims – Votes for Women over 30 – was brought in by The Representation of the People Act passed by Parliament in February 1918. They had achieved some of their aims by the work they undertook for the war effort, filling in men's jobs while the men were overseas fighting. So naturally they continued to do so after the war, this time because of the shortage of manpower caused by the slaughter. Women reflected their new-found freedom in the new fashions. Now called the Flappers with their above-the-knee skirts, they abandoned the long tresses worn in plaits, earphones (wound in circles over the ears) or buns at the back of the head and cut it all off for the new 'Eton Crop', very like a man's short haircut. They took to new dancing including the Charleston, leg twisting and energetic, but not ladylike. Whist Drives and Dances became very much the local entertainment in the villages as a relief from the strain and hardship of the war years. Also Concert Parties with local people performing with gusto to entertain audiences at the Rhodes Hall. The Cinema became the next general entertainment.which meant travelling into town. Previously villages gave shows with lantern slides, but they were 'still' pictures soon to be overtaken by the 'movies'.

In 1920 a new room was built on to the Baptist Chapel in the centre of Brockhampton with a flight of steps leading straight from the road. However later it was decided that this access was too dangerous and this was changed to sideways steps along the wall for greater safety.

Christian William Lawrence, Lord of the Manor of Sevenhampton, died in 1920. This part of his estate, which was inherited by his niece Wynnefrede Lawrence of Whittington, included the Manor House, farms and village of Sevenhampton. She later sold the Manor estate in 1928 and the Manor gardens became part of the Manor Farm.

For a few years the Manor House was empty so the Agents gave permission for the tennis courts to be used. Some of the villagers worked very hard to get them in good order and a tennis club was formed for the benefit of Sevenhampton parish. This lasted for two seasons until the Manor House was sold and the tennis club had to find another home. The only near-level ground was in a field behind Webb's house /shop, so a new court was made there by permission of Mr Hyatt owner of the field. A summer house, owned and given by Col Rhodes, was used as a pavilion for both tennis and cricket clubs. After several years the club moved again to a field in Baker's Wood Lane belonging to Major Mitchell of Brockhampton Park. When in 1939 war broke out again the Tennis Club closed and the Summer House/Pavilion was removed to Mr Canon Smith's garden at Colnside.

A swimming pool was installed, next to the tennis courts. On the land where Church Cottage and The Chestnuts now stand. Water for the pool was pumped up from the springs at the bottom of Church Lane. Mr Clarke, father of Wally and Leila, was caretaker of Sevenhampton Manor House while it stood empty. It was he who planted the once-famous chestnut trees. Mr Tom Hyatt recalled his twenty-first birthday was celebrated in the Manor House at this time.

Sale of Sevenhampton Manor Estate

The Estate was sold by Auction on Thursday 2nd June 1927 at the Plough Hotel, Cheltenham.. This was done in 5 Lots and included Home Farm, Manor Farm, the Stag and Hounds Public House and about 10 cottages. The sale also referred to Water Rights. As there was no mains water at this stage, pumped water was provided by the owner of the Manor Estate and the residents were required to pay an annual charge for this service. This resulted in a general change of ownership – the Hyatt family buying the larger part of this estate.

Early in the 20th century the parish still had two working forges, one in Sevenhampton and one in Brockhampton. There was a need for two blacksmiths in the parish because so many horses were working on farms, or as hunters and for transport, in pairs pulling carriages or ridden singly. In 1925 the Old Forge, near to the church, which had been worked by the Pearce family for several generations, finished its working life and was closed. This too has been converted into a private house again, latterly lived in by Mrs Wendy Lee.

The other blacksmiths forge was situated near the corner of Craven Arms lane. This was firstly used by Reuben Andrews and later Alfred Bostock. The families lived in the house next to the forge. Some villagers still living could remember watching the blacksmith at work, during their childhood. It must have made fascinating viewing when there was little entertainment in country places.

Sale of Brockhampton Park and Estate

Brockhampton Park and Estate was owned and managed by Col. Fairfax Rhodes until his death in 1928. His widow Mary continued to live in the house until 1934 when she moved to Cheltenham. The House and Estate were put up for sale. An Auction Sale was held at the Plough Hotel in Cheltenham on July 26th 1934. The estate houses and farms were sold singly and many resident tenants purchased the properties in which they were living. Some villagers chose to leave the village to purchase houses elsewhere. The Manor House and gardens, including the lake and woodlands were sold as one unit, the first purchaser being Major Stephen Mitchell of the Three Nuns Tobacco Company.

During World War II 1939-45 the Park was used by the Government to house wounded service officers. They became known in the village by their hospital-blue suits and as they recovered they took part in village events, even putting on a Variety Show in the Rhodes Hall. Later in the war the Park was used to house pupils of Cheltenham Ladies College. During their stay extra hassocks and hymn books were acquired by St Andrew's Church to accommodate them.

After the war Mr & Mrs Dodwell bought the Park and changed it into an Hotel, followed by Mr & Mrs Gardner who ran it as a Country Club – later they moved to Sevenhampton Manor. It was again sold to Mr Cannon as a residence.

In 1955 Brockhampton Park was bought by Sir George Dowty, of Aircraft Engineering fame, originally as a residence. He never in fact lived in it, but took up residence at Arle Court. He used the Brockhampton house as offices for his Research and Development Unit. Sir George had a great fondness for the Park and with his Head Gardner, Hedley Jarman from Kew Gardens, and his staff, took great care to preserve the ornamental gardens, parklands and woodlands, to the joy of the villagers, visitors and passers by.

When Dowty's left Brockhampton the house was bought by Mr Kerry Hamer and his associate Mr Pearson. They tried to convert the house into flats, each buyer required to finish the changes and decorate his own flat. This proved very unworkable and the scheme fell through.

Lastly the house was sold to a large building firm Barratt Commercial Ltd, who sympathetically changed the Listed Building into a number of luxury flats. The assembly rooms downstairs and the beautiful staircase were left untouched for communal use of the apartment owners. Also the exterior of the building remains in its original attractive form. The gardens and lake were also retained as originally intended.

Brockhampton Park ceased to be the centre of village life and as agriculture declined and the original farmworkers died or moved away much change occurred as cottages were sold, enlarged and sold again. Prices rocketed so that young villagers, on marrying, could not afford to buy them, so had to move elsewhere as first time buyers. Gradually the old familiar village disappeared and people came to live in it from far and near. Some joined in the various village activities which had kept the community together, but as the 20th century moved on the social activities grew less.

In May 1935 King George V with Queen Mary reached their Silver Jubilee, 25 years upon the throne. There were celebrations all over the country with parties and a chain of bonfires across the hills. In this parish villagers were entertained with a garden party at Brockhampton Park. Bunting decorated the streets in various places. In the evening the King spoke to the Nation over the wireless, as he had been doing with his Christmas broadcast each year since 1932.

Year of Three Kings

The year 1936 proved to be a momentous one. King George V had been in poor health for some time. Bulletins on his condition were posted regularly on the Palace gates and one evening over the radio came the never-to-be-forgotten message "The King's Life is Passing Peacefully to a Close". He died at Sandringham on 20th January 1936.

The Prince of Wales was proclaimed King Edward VIII in 1936, but he was never crowned. He wanted to marry his lady friend, twice divorced American Mrs Wallis Simpson, but this was not acceptable to Parliament or the people. So on 10th December 1936 King Edward Abdicated. He made a farewell speech to the people over the radio. This left the throne to his brother Albert, Duke of York, who was married to Elizabeth Bowes-Lyon. He became King George VI. Thus 1936 saw three Kings on the throne of England.

King George and Queen Elizabeth saw the country through the 1939-45 War, visiting the people at bomb sites in London. The Queen declared herself glad when Buckingham Palace, was bombed while they were in residence, because that made her equal to so many of her subjects whose homes had been bombed.

In 1939, before war broke out, Sevenhampton parish came first in the 'Best Kept Village' competition. The prize was a garden seat which was placed at the junction of Webb's Lane and the Winchcombe Road, which at the time was a bus stop.

Women's Institute

In Sevenhampton parish a branch of the Women's Institute was born in 1936. Mrs Miller, wife of Rev John Miller, saw the need for a ladies group to give the housebound ladies an interest outside the home. It had to be non-political, and non-sectarian, because not all families belonged to the church, it could not be the Mother's Union, so the Women's Institute was chosen. This Movement was started in 1897 in Canada, at Stoney Creek, Ontario, by housewife Adelaide Hoodless, because children were dying from ignorance of hygiene. She started a women's group to help each other with their domestic problems, classes on domestic science were started for local women. The idea caught on and spread rapidly. Other W.I.s sprang up and in 1915 the first British Institute was formed at Llanfairpwll in Anglesey. Later Institutes were springing up throughout Britain.

In Sevenhampton parish in December 1936 a Formation Meeting was held in Rhodes Hall, Brockhampton by Miss Allen V.C.O. (Voluntary County Organiser) from Gloucester County Office, invited by Mrs Miller. Founder members were Mrs Miller, Mrs Walter Barnfield, Mrs David Simpson, Mrs Crocombe, Mrs John Barnett, Mrs Louis Barnett, Miss Ethel Vernon (later Mrs E. Locke) Miss F.M. Canon-Smith, Mrs Tom Hyatt, Mrs R. Green, Mrs Hanks, Mrs Bloodworth, Mrs Hooper and Mrs D Grainger.

They gave themselves the title of "Sevenhampton, Brockhampton and Charlton Abbots Women's Institute". Later changed to "Sevenhampton & District W.I.." The W.I. is a Registered Charitable Organisation raising money for good causes by holding events such as Craft Exhibitions, Jumble Sales, Sponsored Country Walks, Coffee Mornings etc.

Sevenhampton & District Women's Institute
Mrs Miller and the Founder Members

The first meeting was held in February 1937. The first President was Mrs Miller; first Secretary was Mrs D. Grainger, and first Treasurer was Mrs Bloodworth. The committee meetings were held at the Vicarage. Membership Cards were printed, handed to, and signed by each member promising to pay the Institute the sum of Two Shillings (ten new pence) yearly. The W.I. met in the evening on the first Monday of every month. Meetings started with the singing of Jerusalem and a Roll Call, and ended with singing of the National Anthem. (They had a piano and a pianist in those days). There was a Speaker or Demonstration arranged for each meeting, followed by a social half hour with tea and buns or biscuits.

Each Institute was affiliated to the National W.I. in London through the County W.I. in Gloucester, founded in 1919. Local Institutes formed themselves into Groups which work together and hold general meetings twice a year. The Cotswold Group was made up of Andoversford, Chedworth, Compton Abdale, Guiting Power, Naunton, Sevenhampton, Shipton and Withington. Each Institute in the Group takes its turn to be Hostess for the year, when they would organize a General Meeting in their own village and provide an interesting Speaker, followed by a special supper prepared by the local members. Often a Group Competition was arranged around a theme agreed jointly and for many years this proved most successful. This showed the high skills of the ladies competing in cooking, needlework, art, flower arranging and other crafts. This joint meeting was held in the Spring and a second Autumn meeting was usually a coffee evening each arranged by the hostess Institute at their individual meeting place.

The National Institute holds an Annual General Meeting each year at the Albert Memorial Hall in London (it was moved for a few years to Birmingham, but London proved to be the most popular venue) to which each individual Institute was entitled to send a delegate – as numbers grew one member was required to represent two Institutes. She would be briefed by each on how they wished her to vote on the year's chosen Resolutions, already voted on by local meetings from a short list , these were intended for Government Departments to enable them to understand country-wide opinions on many topical subjects. The delegate duly reported back to her two Institutes.

Originally delegates travelled by train and stayed for a night in London. Later they arrived in coaches which returned home the same day. It was a great pleasure to be a delegate duly labelled with your home Institute's name. You were given coloured cards to hang around your neck – two saying Yes and two saying No. After eash Resolution was presented and discussed it was subjected to the voting. You held up a card for each Institute and perhaps you would have Yes in one hand and No in the other.. The singing of Parry's Jerusalem – the W.I. anthem – sounded wonderful in the Albert Hall especially when the delegates from Wales sang a verse in Welsh. At lunch time the ladies took their sandwiches outside and sat on the steps of the Albert Memorial for a picnic, if it was a fine day. In the early days the ladies all bought new hats for their special day. Entering the Hall very slowly, then guided down the steps to your seat feeling rather like the Chelsea Pensioners at the Remembrance Festival. Distinguished speakers are invited, sometimes from the Government. It was a Minister of the Environment who asked the W.I. to undertake a countrywide survey of all the old churchyards because the headstones have so much historical detail which was fast becoming lost through pollution. The oldest legible inscription in St Andrew's, Sevenhampton churchyard was that of Henry Lord 1615 A.D. The finished book of the local churchyard survey is held at St Andrew's Church, Sevenhampton While the total account from all Glos. W.I.s , with printed cards filled in for each stone, giving as many details as possible with drawings or photographs, were presented to the County Archivist, David Smith, to be held in safe-keeping at the County Record Office.

Each Institute holds its own Annual Meeting when it reviews the year's work, presents the agenda for the following year and elects a new Committee and President.

Also organises its Christmas or Birthday Party, outings to interesting places and Open Meetings to which husbands and friends are invited.

The W.I. owns its own training college "Denman College" to which members may apply for their chosen course, lasting a few days, or a week, from a range of many practical and intellectual subjects. A single or shared room awaits you, each being furnished and supported by a British County. Gloucestershire has a single room in a newly built annex. Meals are taken in a pleasant dining hall and the standard of food, being W.I., is of course excellent.

It is still a well-supported, charitable and meaningful organisation to which local ladies are made very welcome.

The W.I. has been the backbone of most local occasions usually supplying the catering as required. Particularly so was the occasion of the 50th anniversary of V.E. Day in 1995 when a nostalgic Exhibition was staged by Mrs Stewart, W.I. Member and Parish Councillor, at the Rhodes Hall showing the story of the 2nd World War with examples of the parts played by many local residents in the Services or on the Home Front, proved interesting and informative. This was accompanied by an all day restaurant set up by the W.I. as a Wartime British Restaurant, well remembered by many. The food was as near as possible to wartime food, including Woolton pies (Lord Woolton was

V.E. Day 50th Anniversary
W.I. Ladies running a British Restaurant

Captain 'Mainwaring' Denley on duty all day

Minister of Food during the War) and as near as possible to wartime prices.

The W.I. ladies in charge wore white overalls and white turbans and took it in turns to do a shift of cooking and serving. They were very strict with the customers and made them form an orderly queue and await their turn to be served. Captain Mainwaring (alias Mick Denley) was on duty all day long and from time to time he left the Hall to go outside to sound the 'All Clear' on the borrowed siren.

Electricty & Water

There was still no piped water laid on to the village in 1936 and no kitchen at the Rhodes Hall. At their pre-war meetings the W.I. fetched water from the wall tap nearby, heated it in kettles on the tortoise stove for hot drinks and washed up in an enamel bowl and drained the cups on a tin tray. However electricity was brought to the area in 1938. St Andrew's Church had mains electric lighting installed in 1939. Previously the two Manor Houses had their own supply provided by their own generators. Sevenhampton Manor's generator was housed in the Old Barn – now a private house. Brockhampton Park allowed limited use of electricity from its own supply to the Village Hall by permission of Col Fairfax Rhodes.

Mains water was finally installed in 1953 (only 1,500 years after the Romans piped Syreford water to Wyckham pre 400 A.D.) The local countryside was carved up with ditches dug to take the mains water pipes. This happened again in the second half of the century when local fields were carved up to carry gas pipes (North Sea Gas) to towns and cities. However, this came very near though never actually to Sevenhampton Parish.

The Second World War 1939-1945

London 3rd September 1939

> At 11.15 this morning, 15 minutes after the deadline for Germany to stop all aggressive action against Poland and begin to withdraw from Polish territory, the Prime Minister, NEVILLE CHAMBERLAIN declared that –
>
> "no such undertaking has been received and consequently this country is at WAR with GERMANY".

We were all preparing Sunday lunch and were terrified as this announcement came over the radio.

Britain was never to be the same again; the SECOND WORLD WAR changed our way of living.

We were aware of the rise of Adolf Hitler, who became Chancellor of Germany, and his great appetite for ever widening his German Empire. The newspapers, radio and cinema newsreels told how country after country fell to his powerful forces. The many atrocities became public knowledge only after the war was over.

The British Government had tried their hardest to keep Peace, through our Prime Minister and the Munich Treaty of March 1939, signed by Hitler promising not to make any more territorial demands. Chamberlain waved a copy on his return from Munich saying "Peace in Our Time". Britain, through the League of Nations supported a Disarmament Programme and was ill prepared for war. However, Hitler broke all his fine promises and immediately his troops marched into and overcame Czechoslovakia. He then turned his eyes towards Poland, making a pact with Russia to divide Poland between them. Fear of Russian Communism gripped Parliament when Hitler invaded Poland on 1st September and war was inevitable.

The BRITISH EXPEDITIONARY FORCE crossed immediately to France to help reinforce France's Maginot Line, 200 miles of fortifications built along its border with Germany.

Before war was declared the British population was being prepared. Sandbags were filled and placed as protection around public buildings. Trenches were dug in park land so that town workers could take cover against the expected air raids. A siren on a public building would sound a warning, when you were instructed to move quickly to a place of safety. Anderson shelters, small, steel built and tunnel shaped, were available for householders to erect, partly sunken, in their gardens for use in air raids. They were fitted with bunk beds, because bombing came nightly after sunset.

Each member of the public was issued with a 'Gas Mask'. An ugly contraption to be placed over the face to filter air into the lungs in case poison gas should be used against us. These fitted into small, square cardboard boxes with a string attached to wear over the shoulders, like a shoulder bag, which had to be carried on your person at all times. Babies were given a larger box inside which the baby could be placed, covers and all. All a bit frightening to babies and children. Later in the war gas masks were produced with Mickey Mouse faces hopefully to keep children happy.

We were all issued with Identity Cards with our name, address and personal number, to be carried at all times. Also we were given a personal Ration Book which entitled us to a given amount of rationed food per week. The standard ration was:

Butter 2 oz (57g); Margarine 4 oz (113 g); Lard 2-4 oz varied.
Milk 3 pints (often 2); Cheese 1-2 oz (28-57 g).
Sugar 8 oz (226 g); Tea 2 oz (57 g); Eggs 1 sometimes 2.
Sweets 12 oz (140 g) Per MONTH.

You registered with your local shop, Mrs Webb grocer in Sevenhampton, and your food came from this source throughout the war years.

To some poorer people in the cities this gave a better balanced diet than they had known pre-war. People living in the countryside were better off than those living in the towns as most people had a garden and could grow vegetables, also keep chickens for eggs. In the towns peopled queued for everything, including bread and potatoes. If something different appeared off-ration a queue quickly formed hoping to buy a small share. This is where the famous British QUEUE was started as a fair way of distribution. We became very orderly people and woe betide those who tried to step out of line – Queue-jumping it was called. As the war dragged on shop shelves emptied completely but the shopkeeper might have a few items for his 'regulars' under the counter. This is where the wartime expression 'UNDER THE COUNTER' arose.

In 1939 butter and bacon were the first to be rationed, sugar soon followed. Meat was rationed in January 1940.

Cottagers were allowed to keep one pig in a sty. Any scraps left over were to be saved for the pigs, so nothing was wasted. Pig Clubs were formed in the country villages. The Sevenhampton one was organised by Councillor Reginald Combe of Brewery Farm, and he gave out the special pig food supplied by the Government to all local pig owners.

The Blackout

Immediately on the outbreak of War all lights were extinguished. All houses, workplaces and public buildings had to put up blackout curtains to ensure that not a chink of light could be seen from outside. You could be fined heavily for allowing a light to show. Local affairs at the Hall were arranged for moonlight nights as far as possible. Cars, buses and all road vehicles were ordered to mask their headlights with special covers, like small venetian blinds, which gave very little light for a driver to steer by. Travelling after dark was very difficult.

Signposts

All signpost destinations were removed so that if German parachutists landed they would not know where they were. Unfortunately we did not know either!

CHURCH BELLS could not be rung while the war was on because they were to be used as a warning should the Germans ever invade our country.

The Call Up

Everyone had to register at Employment Exchanges by age group. This was given out over the radio and in daily newspapers, so you registered, when your age group was called upon, at your local Labour Exchange in the nearest town. Then the call-up papers were received by post telling you where to report for war duty. When your family saw you again you would be wearing your service uniform.

A number of local young people were called into the Forces; the Royal Navy, the Army or the Air Force. The ladies joined the W.R.E.NS. (Navy) the A.T.S. (Army) or the W.A.A.F. (Air Force). In the beginning volunteers were allowed to choose which force they wished to serve in. Later when conscription came in and there was no choice any longer and many local young people, of all ranks, found themselves serving in many parts of the world, the deserts of North Africa, the jungles of the Far East, Burma, India, etc.

Civil Defence

This war, unlike previous campaigns, was not fought solely on the battlefields. The whole country was involved and the Home Defence Forces had a very big part to play, especially after Dunkirk when the Expeditionary Force was driven out of Europe and many men were rescued from the beaches by our army of little ships who bravely sailed to bring

Civil Defence Team, Brockhampton

them home. They were attacked by the German Luftwaffe while they were taking the suffering troops on board. We were now open to attack and invasion by the triumphant Germans.

The war was now being fought on our own territory by air raids with high explosive bombs and fire bombs and the civilian casualties were about to outnumber the service ones, in the largely populated areas. The Civil Defence was to become heavily employed in all its various groups.

Those not already in the forces, and the older able people, had joined the Home Defence groups. These were the A.R.P. Air Raid Precautions, the L.D.V. Local Defence Volunteers – later to become the Home Guard (Dad's Army), the Special Police, the A.F.S. Auxiliary Fire Service and the W.V.S., Women's Voluntary Service. Also the Red Cross. Many had received pre-war training for their service.

Sevenhampton had a full compliment of volunteers Home Guard, Fire Watchers, Special Police and Air Raid Wardens. Mr Tom Hyatt was appointed Head Warden for the area. In 1940 the A.R.P. were supplied with the following equipment:

1 stirrup pump
2 steel helmets
2 curtains
1 waterproof coat
1 pair trousers
1 pair rubber boots

This was the standard set for each village.

Most places had loud sirens to give warning of an air raid. When they sounded people had to take shelter in Anderson shelters in the gardens, or else in cellars.

Handbell rung by Warden as Air Raid Warning

London people took to the underground stations for safety. Sirens were not regarded as practical for widespread country areas, so instead the Air Raid Warden would ring a loud clanging bell to give warning to all on his patch

The Luftwaffe began a full scale assault on Britain firstly attacking the aerodromes hoping to put the British Air Force out of action. Starting on 18th August 1940 London was bombed and burned by incendiary bombs for 57 consecutive nights. In September hundreds of German bombers raided the London Docks to destroy our shipping. There followed attacks on all the big cities which mostly lost their entire city centres. After they attacked Birmingham and were flying home some of their stray bombs were dropped in the Sevenhampton area. When this happened Ethel Locke, who was the Rhodes Hall caretaker at the time, said that all the young people using the Hall dived under the table for shelter. Three bombs were dropped on Brockhampton in November 1940. At Isingwell (where the River Coln rises) beyond The Walks; in a field behind the Old Quarry and at Whitehill where a cow was killed.

This dangerous period became known as The Battle of Britain, when ferocious air battles were fought daily by our brave young air force pilots taking on an increasing number of enemy bombers with their accompanying fighters. Our losses were many but the enemy losses were greater.

The B.B.C. broadcast daily the numbers of enemy aircraft destroyed – this gave us a tremendous boost. Our own casualties were not mentioned for fear of giving information to the enemy.

Speaking of our brave pilots Prime Minister Winston Churchill said "Never in the field of human conflict was so much owed by so many to so few". Winston Churchill was a wonderful wartime leader. He kept us going with his, now famous, wartime speeches which were broadcast regularly over the radio.

As this was a farming community the land and land workers were commandeered by the Government to produce more and more food for the population as a whole. This became very important as so much of our merchant shipping was sunk daily by German U-boats (submarines) and our food situation became desperate. Some of our local ladies joined the Women's Land Army which played an important role in food production and released many able-bodied men for the fighting forces. Their smart uniform was fawn, brown and green and they undertook all kinds of farm work from dairying to tractor driving. Some went in to forestry producing timber for the factories and others in market gardening, bringing much needed food. They worked extremely long hours especially at harvest time when they would be helped by the local population mainly housewives but including school children also. Boys from Cheltenham College were brought to camp here and help with the harvest. They also picked fruit for the Toddington jam factory.

In Brockhampton the W.I. ladies were given instruction in jam making at the Rhodes Hall to use up surplus fruit. They made many pounds of jam under professional supervision. This was then sent to the shops to help out the rations, some of it locally and was eagerly sought after by the hardpressed housewives. Some found its way to Mrs Webb's grocers shop.

Farmers were instructed by the Ministry of Agriculture what to grow and where to grow it. This changed the total appearance of the countryside as fields were now used for crops, whereas before the war most of the land was for pasture or unused as scrubland. The whole area became laid out in the beautiful patterns as we now see it.

Everyone in the area was involved with the War Effort one way or another, normal duties during the day and Local Defence throughout the hours of darkness.

Evacuation

The cities sent their children away to many safer inland destinations until the war was over. Mostly whole schools with their teachers would travel together. They became known as 'Evacuees'.. This parish had very few as they were sent to areas with a large school when the local children would attend school for half a day and the evacuees would attend for the other half. A few people would come to the country for short periods as paying guests, mostly as a respite to escape the heavy bombing they had to endure.

As the war progressed there were many Prisoners of War to be housed in camps in many parts of the country. Some of these were brought daily to the Sevenhampton parish to work on the land. They were other people's sons, mostly nice young lads with whom the population became friendly.

All through the war collections were made regularly to help the fighting fund. Also people were encouraged to give up any domestic metal items they could spare to be melted down to make weapons. Sevenhampton churchyard lost its metal railings which had surrounded some of the graves. Last of all a collection was made anticipating the return of the service people of the parish. On 1st January 1946 a public meeting was held with three items on the agenda: 1. The Sevenhampton and Charlton Abbots Welcome Home Fund; 2. Fixing a date for re-starting The Produce Show and 3. A Report on the School.

The Fund had realised the grand sum of £240. 18s. 5d. The date for the Produce Show was fixed for 14th September 1946. The Revd Duncan gave a report on the School, which was proposed to be closed under new development plans. The School Managers suggested that Salperton children should attend the school. This raised the numbers and the Education Committee approved, so the school was saved.

All but one of the service men and women came home safely at the end of the war. Lieutenant John Hood of the Royal Fusiliers was killed in action in 1940. His family lived at The Court House during the war. A memorial to him was placed next to the 1914-18 War Memorial in the South Transept of St Andrew's Church in Sevenhampton. In thankfulness that all other Service people had come safely through the difficult and dangerous experiences while serving their country and no further War Memorial would be required, money was put into renewing the church transept roof as a permanent remembrance.

Peace after 6 Years of War

German forces finally surrendered and the War in Europe officially ended on 8th May 1945. The fighting against Japan continued in the Far East; this too ended when the Allies dropped the deadly Atomic Bombs on Hiroshima and Nagosaki on 6th August 1945.

The lights came on again in Britain, which was bliss after the years of blackout, but it took a very long time to get back to anything like normality. Food was scarce and still rationed. Our servicemen were spread across the globe and many foreign, allied servicemen were still in Britain, also many were prisoners of war. Our towns and ports were shattered by the bombing and many city centres were reduced to rubble. The enormous cost of the war had left Britain empoverished, relieved` only by American lease/lend policy (receive now/pay later) which had helped considerably through the later war years, but this was at a cost.

The troops were demobilised as they returned to these shores; each was given a gratuity and a 'demob' suit chosen from a range of styles, very basic and practical rather than smart. Men returned to young families they did not know and the children had to learn to live with a father they had seen only occasionally, if at all. Men and women, mostly of wartime marriages, had to adjust to each other and this was not easy. Men needed to return to the jobs they had left when called-up, because now they had families to support. Most of these jobs had been filled by women during the war years and they were reluctant to go back to being housewives.

A great housing shortage soon became evident. Women mostly lived with their parents for the war duration, so with children the houses became very overcrowded. Evacuated families had to return to cities where many houses had been destroyed. A clever idea of pre-fabricated bungalows (manufactured in sections to be put together on site) solved many of these problems. This was never done is Sevenhampton parish however, because being an agricultural area most people returned to the cottages they had left. In July 1945 the Parish Council proposed that a row of cottages should be built, but this was turned down by the County Authorities because of a lack of proper drainage.

Post War Britain

After the celebrations of the ending of the war people expected life to get back to what it was before the war, but it did not. The first years were difficult because the country was impoverished and deeply in debt – mostly to America – to cover the cost of the war. Food was still rationed until 1953, even more strictly. 'Austerity' was the word on everyone's lips.

The biggest change came from the General Election of 1945 when the Labour Party gained a landslide victory. Mainly through the votes of the returning servicepeople, who regarded Winston Churchill as their wartime leader, but who now looked for a change in the country's affairs. Clement Attlee was the new Prime Minister.

The parliament soon implemented the 'Welfair State' – the brainchild of Liberal William Beverage. The National Health Service was born on 5th July 1948 offering free medical service to all, including dentistry.

In Education the school leaving age was raised to 15 years and the 11-plus examination was brought in to test all children for Secondary Education. Before the war leaving age was 14 years from Primary Schools and very few children took the scholarship examination to the Higher Schools.

Next the Railways were nationalised, which meant they would be run directly by the Government, becoming British Rail. The Coal Mining Industry too was nationalised and the National Coal Board came into being in January 1947.

The New Look by Christion Dior became the fashion in 1947, with long skirts after the drab Utility Clothing of the war years. Although the Clothing Ration continued until March 1949.

The highlight of the Post War Years came with the Royal Wedding of Princess Elizabeth and Lieutenant Philip Mountbatten at Westminster Abbey on 20th November 1947. He then became the Duke of Edinburgh. The public, apart from those in London lining the streets between Buckingham Palace and The Abbey, would have followed the occasion on the radio. Then later we would have been able to follow the celebrations on screen at the local cinemas.

Death of King George VI

The King survived the strains of war-time Monarchy, celebrated his Silver Wedding in 1948 and the Wedding of his elder daughter in 1947 and opened the Festival of Britain in 1951, which was a turning point to better times for his subjects, but his health was failing. Princess Elizabeth had to undertake many of his public duties and she, with Prince Philip, was representing her father in Africa when the news came that King George had died in his sleep at Sandringham in the early hours of 6th February 1951. Elizabeth returned to Britain as Queen Elizabeth II.

The Royal Wedding of Princess Elizabeth and Lieutenant Philip Mountbatten took place at Westminster Abbey on 10th November 1947. Philip was formerly Prince Philip son of Prince of Greece, having been brought up in England by his Uncle Lord Louis Mountbatten and on joining the Royal Navy he became a British citizen as Lieutenant Philip Mountbatten.

Coronation of Queen Elizabeth II

After her accession in 1952 Elizabeth was crowned Queen in a colourful ceremony in Westminster Abbey on 2nd June 1953. Attending the service were British Royal family including her Mother, who now became known as the Queen Mother, and her two children Prince Charles and Princess Anne, Foreign Princes, Heads of State, Peers and other dignitaries gathered from all over the world. She was anointed with holy oil by the Archbishop of Canterbury and crowned with the Crown of St Edward.

Crowds lined the London streets all day to watch the procession to and from the Abbey. All the precious Royal coaches were brought into service for the day, which was a wonderful spectacle, in spite of the rain which lasted all day. For the first time the whole proceedings were broadcast to the world by the new Television. At that time television sets were not generally owned, so if you had a set in your home you would have entertained many people all day long. The country certainly celebrated by Street parties and other entertainments. Bunting was put up on almost every house in the country, parks and gardens were planted out with red, while and blue flowers. Afterwards everyone remembered where they had been on Coronation Day. Those who had been children at the time were given Coronation Mugs to mark the occasion.

Some were lucky enough to have been in London at the time and one local lady, Mrs Joan Ames, remembered being on duty with the Red Cross in London all day.

Winters

The most memorable being 1947 – referred to in the press as "The Big Freeze" and the coldest winter since 1880/81 when Sevenhampton Parish was completely cut off by extremely deep snow. No supplies could be brought into the area, so many young people got together to walk to Andoversford to collect food which they brought back on sledges, the snow being so deep you couldn't tell where the road was. There were power cuts Nation-wide, mainly because coal was piling up at the pit-heads but couldn't be moved because of the heavy snow. When it happened again in in 1961/62 Dowtys were at the Park and they cleared the Winchcombe road at Sevenhampton to keep their business going. If you tried to drive through it you found high walls of snow above head height on either side, like a white tunnel. Deep snows continued into the 70s and 80s, but more recently weather changes, possibly due to global warming, have brought warmer, drier winters.

Villagers walking through deep snow to fetch provisions from Andoversford in 1947

The Century Club

At the middle of the century Clubs were being formed for Pensioners all over the Country, to give older people an interest outside the household. There they could meet to be entertained by a variety of speakers on many subjects, have afternoon tea and conversation with friends new and old. These were far more cultured than the pre-war clubs for old people where they sat around and sang songs together.

It was decided that such a club was needed in Sevenhampton Parish, so through the auspices of the County Council one was formed to meet in the Rhodes Hall, Brockhampton. It just so happened that this was the one hundredth club to be organised in Gloucestershire, therefore its natural title had to be "The Century Club". This proved to be somewhat misleading for would-be members who believed they had to be very old to join. In fact it was open to all pensioners, 65 for men and 60 for women, to include people from Sevenhampton, Brockhampton, Whittington, Hawling and Charlton Abbots.

The Century Club had its formation meeting at the Rhodes Hall on 13th May 1958. It was formally opened by Lady Dowty, wife of Sir George Dowty, the then owner of Brockhampton Park, in the presence of Miss Stephanie Evans-Lawrence of Whittington Court. A bouquet was presented to Lady Dowty by Mrs Lillian James, 78, the oldest of the new members.

Miss Evans-Lawrence became the first Chairman, Mrs Vera Charley the Secretary, with Mr L C Goodson as Treasurer. The Steering Committee were; Mrs Goodson, Mr C G Purser, Mrs F Charles the Vicar's wife, Mr H Vernon, Nurse Hannah, Mrs S Mace, Mrs B Carey, Mrs R Combe, Mrs J Boyd, and Mrs D W Grainger meetings

LADY DOWTY OPENS OLD FOLKS' CLUB.—Lady Dowty receiving a bouquet from 78-year-old Mrs. Lillian James after she had officially opened the new Century Club in the Rhodes Memorial Hall, Brockhampton, yesterday. Looking on are Mrs. V. Charley (left), hon. secretary, and Miss S. Evans Lawrence (chairman).

100th Old Folks' Club opened at Brockhampton

The Opening of the Century Club by Lady Dowty

were to be held once a month on the second Tuesday and always in the afternoon. A monthly Agenda of Speakers or Events was drawn up and the meetings would end with afternoon tea. Miss Ethel Vernon (afterwards Mrs Ethel Locke) was appointed Caterer. Some interesting outings were arranged and parties at Christmas or special occasions.

At the turn of the century the Club was thriving healthily, although most of its first members were no longer with us. There was some discussion on changing its off-putting title. Early members resisted, so a compromise was decided upon and its new title became 'The NEW CENTURY CLUB' in honour of the New Millennium.

The Club had survived for nearly half a century and seen several changes of Chairman, one being Mrs V Hobbs who took a lively interest in guiding the Club for many years – her delicious ginger cake was famous. In 1995 when Mrs Hobbs left the village Mrs Jenny Stringer of Whittington Court became Chairman. She kindly invites the members twice a year for tea at Whittington Court at mid-Summer and again at Christmas to a party for which the Court is a handsome, old world setting.

The cost of membership is kept deliberately low, so to aid with the funds a monthly raffle is held. This raffle is unique in that each member brings a small gift and buys a raffle ticket, in that way everyone gets a prize!

The Leisure Club

The Rhodes Hall had become shabby and neglected mainly because it was under-used and therefore under-funded.

The idea of a Club with many activities began to take shape, so at the 1975 Produce Show a large board was displayed at the Hall doorway asking Residents to suggest possible activities which they would actively support.

The first General Meeting was called for the 17th November 1975 which was well attended and a decision was made to call the new club The Leisure Club. A committee of ten members was voted in, these were Chairman Leslie Agius, Vice Chairman Sheila Bartlett, Honarary Secretary Doris Austin, Hon. Treasurer Vic Taylor, with Molly Foster, Mildred Jarman, Ethel Locke, Nigel Pearson, Ian Stewart, and Alan Timbrell. This meeting discussed what activities should be arranged and they set out the three main aims of the new club.

1. to foster community spirit
2. to encourage the varied interests and talents within the villages
3. to support the Hall and to contribute to its upkeep.

Their first activity was to refurbish The Hall so the members set to work with a will painting and redecorating it in their spare time to give it a new look. Margot Partington made new curtains to complete the facelift.

The activities decided upon were: Drama, Bridge, Whist, Table Tennis, Tennis, Keep Fit, Yoga, Flower Aranging, Handicrafts, Winemaking, Musical Appreciation, Chess, Country Dancing and a Youth Club. So many choices that sometimes your chosen ones overlapped and decisions of choice had to change. Numerous people offered their services to run each individual activity so the whole idea sprang into effect very smoothly.

Added to this repertoire were many social functions such as the annual Christmas parties, dancing and social evenings, quiz evenings, treasure hunts, talks and debates. Each event was well supported and were happy occasions when all the members from the five villages involved got to know each much better. The community spirit was high at this time.

The Leisure Club thrived for many years, but faded slowly through population changes. Bridge classes and bridge games run by Jeff Jenkin continued for longer than most. The only activity which lasted to the end of the Millennium was the Drama Group, still producing plays and entertainments every year and has never lost its vital enthusiasm and vitality.

The Brockhampton Amateur Dramatic Society

Those in the Leisure Club wanting to form a Drama Group got together in 1975 to assess the possibilities. Early in 1976 the first performance – A Village Vaudeville – was attempted which, while it was tremendous fun for the 'actors' and audience, showed most of the group up as complete novices, definitely not good enough to be called amateurs at that stage. It also proved that the group was a non-musical, non-singing team.

Following the inevitable inquest they decided to stick to acting and after much deliberation voted themselves a name 'Brockhampton Amateur Dramatic Association' or the B.A.D.S. Full of enthusiasm and varying degrees of untapped talent, finding a suitable play was a daunting task.

However, by great good luck they found they had a playwright and poet in their midst. He was Morton Foster, a recent resident in Brockhampton, who used his great talents to work writing a play-cum-pantomime called 'In Baker's Wood' which was put on in the Hall and proved a success, followed by 'The Magic Quarry'. These plays had a local background and were well received in the area, so much so that the cast went on location, performing their plays in near-by villages.

Mr Foster, knowing the area and the actors much better by now, went from strength to strength writing up a little local history in 'The Inn on the Salt Way' and 'The Story of Belas Knapp Long Barrow'. Much of each script was written in verse and the author wrote his characters around the actors themselves. These plays were very satisfying to the performers and gave the audience a good story to follow. By using

The Cast of 'The Inn on the Salt Way'

local writers the Club had no royalties to pay and were therefore able to contribute funds, raised by the performances, to help furnish the hall with new chairs and other items.

A very good team of background workers surfaced. Artists painting imaginative scenery, undaunted by requests to build and paint unusual props for each new show proposed, such as the large boot (for The Old Woman who lived in a Shoe) designed and painted by the Candler family. Lighting and sound experts who excelled themselves as time went on. Costumes were made and stored by lady members. After many doubtful attempts at stage making, a new professional stage was acquired with the help of a grant from the Sports Council.

This was to be stored in sections, after use, in the new extension to the Hall installed by Allan Hawkes-Reed and John

B.A.D.S. 'The Inn on the Salt Way' programme

183

Austen. This had a trap door into a small storage cellar, so the stage could be taken down and stored after each performance run. Other helpers came in the form of make-up ladies, usherettes and box-office lady, and tea-ladies provided refreshments during the interval.

The B.A.D.S. continue to thrive in the village, with a totally new cast from the early beginnings. The interest and enthusiasm is still there and the performances have become more sophisticated and far less amateur.

The Day Centre

The idea of Day Centres, to help Disabled, Elderly, Lonely and Housebound people to get together once a week for a social meal together, came through the Gloucestershire County Council. This was taken up for this area by Mrs Violet Hobbs, wife of the Vicar of St Andrew's, Sevenhampton.

A successful coffee morning was arranged by Mrs Redston at Brockhampton Court to raise funds needed and Mrs Hobbs was then able to open the Day Centre on 19th April 1978. Volunteer drivers offering cars to collect people from their homes, over a wide area, to bring them to the Rhodes Memorial Hall every Wednesday, arriving at 11 am. for coffee, then a hot lunch at 12.30 p.m. The meals were collected by another voluntary driver from the Community Meals Service at Moreton-in-Marsh. The first driver was Denis Locke, later John Vernon and at the end of the century Bob Holland.

The Centre did a good job of caring for these otherwise isolated people and the highlight was in 1981 when pensioner Mrs Alice Waters, of Hawling, blind, disabled (both legs amputated) and diabetic, came second in the finals of Gloucestershire Woman of the Year Award Competition. Entered by Sevenhampton & District W.I. , Alice, described by Mrs Hobbs as an inspiration, attended the Centre every week and visited and encouraged people less disabled than herself. The Awards were presented by Princess Anne at a ceremony at The Gloucestershire College of Art and Technology.

Initially the Centre was visited by a Physiotherapist and Chiropodist regularly. Handicrafts were introduced by Mrs Trevett who encouraged members to make various items, such as covered coathangers, aprons, peg bags etc which were put into a Sale of Work with Coffee Morning at the Hall each November, to raise more funds for the Group. On meeting days the members chatted together, some played whist or did crossword puzzles until early afternoon, when they would be given tea and biscuits before their drive home again. Annual outings were organised to the Arboretum or open gardens, with lunch at or near the chosen venue. A Christmas Party was also held every year.

Chairman Mrs Hobbs left the village when her husband retired in 1975. Mrs Mildred Jarman became the new Chairman, with Secretary Mrs Rita Rhone and

Treasurer Mr John Swain with Mrs Joan Ames and Mr John Vernon as committee members. They renamed the Centre as the Luncheon Club. Now they had social lunch once a week as before and raised funds by holding Garden Parties at members' gardens annually.

In 1966 the Reading Room Library, having closed because it was no longer viable and the supply of books was not available, remaining books and bookshelves were sold to the villagers, after many years of serving the local people with books and newspapers. Many years later the need was covered by a mobile County Library with a vehicle which called once a fortnight with a large, ever-changing supply of books and later still included cassettes and video tapes on hire.

The Parish Council in the 20th Century

The Parish Council has been the backbone of the community throughout the 20th Century. In 1994 we celebrated 100 Years of Local Councils, with a small exhibition plus wine and a special cake, also a church service at St Andrew's

From the Vestry, when the Church was responsible for local law and order, to 1994 when through many changes, the Council was, through its District Council, much more controlled by Parliament itself.

In its early days the Council work was relatively simple, caring for the lanes, verges, hedges and drains. Local employees did the job well (drains did not overflow then) far better than later in the century. There were very few cars, so the roads were not dedicated to the convenience of motorised transport, the horse was still King of the Road. When the road through the stream or the pathway outside the school were in need of repair the council would approach the Lords of the Manors, C.W. Lawrence for Sevenhampton or Col Fairfax Rhodes for Brockhampton, who owned most of the land, to supply materials for the repair work, which they duly did. Local labour was always available to do the necessary work. John Smith remembered repairing part of the Winchcombe road through the parish with his Father, using broken stone from their own quarry at Soundborough. The council held jurisdiction over rights of way and bridal paths, so if they were ploughed up at any time the council would ensure that paths were reinstated as the law insisted.

From its beginnings in 1894 the council took over the handling of the Donnywell Charity and appointed, by tender, the baker to supply the bread annually. In 1920 Workman of Shipton offered to supply 26 x 4lb or 52 x 2lb loaves. Mr Lawrence paid the £1. required by the Charity.

Two councillors were appointed as School Managers to serve for 3 years at a time. Two Overseers were found from among the councillors and part of their duty was to collect the rates locally. They were also required to make the Poor Law Collection to support the local poor. This was formerly the responsibility of the Vestry. The rate books and accounts were audited annually and the appointment of the overseers was reported to the Guardians at Northleach. In 1922 the Sevenhampton Parish Council protested most strongly against the heavy and and increasing rates and trusted they would be materially rediuced, or the ratepayers would be quite unable to pay them. For the New Rating Authority in 1927, B.T. Hyatt and G.T. Combe were elected as our first representatives on Northleach Rural District Council. Later to be held by their respective sons T. Hyatt and R.G.B. Combe.

In 1905 the council sought and received from the County Council permission to establish a Rifle Club at the Rhodes Hall. Precept for that year was £11. The Telegraph was brought to the parish in 1911. In 1915 the Parish Elections were postponed by the Local Government Board because of the Great War. The first election after the war was in 1919, when the Returning Officer charged 6s.6d. The Clerk's salary increased from £10 to £12 per year. Precept £13.

Mr C. Capps, School Headmaster and Parish Clerk died in 1928. His position was filled by B.T. Fletcher who was also the new Headmaster. In 1930 Harry Vernon, father of John and Ethel, was appointed Clerk to the Council, a position he was to hold for 35 years. The council presented him with a Silver Cup for his services. Subsequent clerks from 1965 to 2000 have been Mrs M. Candler, Mrs K. Taylor, Mrs R. Stewart, Mrs L. Ball and Mrs A. Van-Rossem.

Council meetings were held in a room at Sevenhampton School for many years. After death of Col Fairfax Rhodes they asked his widow Mrs Rhodes for permission to hold their meetings at the Reading Room. The council received a letter from the Trustees of the late Fairfax Rhodes asking them if they were prepared to take over the Hall as from 2nd June 1934 as directed in accordance with his Will. This was agreed to.

Mr Nairne was appointed to take over as Hon Secretary and Treasurer.

On the proposition of Mr Nairne it was unanimously agreed to that the Reading Room be named "THE RHODES MEMORIAL HALL".

Repairs and upkeep of the Hall coming under the Council's care, a form from Lloyds Bank re Reading Room Account was signed by Horsfall, Combe and Vernon.

A special meeting was held, attended by 56 persons, when a Management Committee was formed viz:

For Charlton Abbots	R. Hanks, L. Gladwell and Mrs Overton
For Brockhampton	D. Locke, L. Newman and Mrs Barnett
For Sevenhampton	E.E. Bloodworth, E. Harvey and Miss Hathaway

Mr Nairne was unable to undertake the duties so Mr R.G.B. Combe was appointed as Hon. Secretary and Treasurer.

Over its lifetime the Parish Council organised Four Coronation Festivities, Royal Anniversaries etc. It watched over the countryside during two World Wars when food was in short supply. It encouraged cultivation of more land for vegetables. In

1933 Allotments were provided on disused, formerly Shenton's, land near the school, for residents to grow yet more vegetables. Rents were paid to the Clerk. The council organised a pig club, during each war, handing out the special Government suppied pig rations to pig owners thus producing meat and bacon to supplement the weekly rations for all. After the second war the council turned its attention to the provision of Council Housing. The first application was turned down by Northleach Rural Council on the grounds of unsuitable drainage. In 1946 the problem was overcome and four houses were built, at the lower end of the Quarry road near the centre of Brockhampton, on condition that these were allocated to agricultural workers only. Most of the working population at the time were employed in various capacities on the farm lands. Houses five and six could not be started until fencing was put up to stop cattle straying on to the road from the fields behind. This too was settled and the last two houses were built and allocated in 1953.

The Cotswolds, in 1966, became an Area of Outstanding Natural Beauty, A.O.N.B. This restricted building in the area to natural stone – so no red brick here!

In 1971 Britain went Metric on 15th February. Gone was the venerable old system of £.s.d. – pounds, shillings and pennies. For a new system of pounds and pence We all had to carry small conversion tables until we got used to the new system and while we were still getting over this shock Britain was taken into membership of the E.E.C. – the European Economic Community, the document being signed by Prime Minister Edward Heath, without a mandate from the British people. It came into force on 1st January 1972.

A number of local boundary changes were suggested including in this parish a redrawing of the line separating it from the Tewkesbury area. In 1969 the residents living on the Winchcombe road, beyond Brockhampton Park, were asked if they would like to become part of Sevenhampton. They declined however, so the houses beyond the stream, which is the dividing line, come under the jurisdiction of Tewkesbury Borough Council.

Local Government Act 1/4/74 (Heath Govt)

"The biggest shake up in local government in almost a century comes into force today with the redrawing of almost all county boundaries along the lines set by Lord Radcliffe-Maud and his commission. Town Charters dating from the Middles Ages and counties recorded in the Domesday Book have had their ancient identities erased. Only 10 of 45 English counties and one of 13 in Wales remain unchanged.

Yorkshire and Lincolnshire, England's two largest counties, lose their distinctive ridings (thirdings from Old Norse). Part of Yorkshire's East Riding is joined to Lincolnshire over the river Humber to become Humberside.

Hereford is joined to Worcestershire as one county. Four English counties disappear completely: Cumberland, Huntingdonshire, Westmorland, and Rutland, the smallest county, is joined to Leicestershire."

Cynics pointed out that today is April Fools Day!

Gloucestershire was divided up into five district authorities viz: Gloucester City, Cheltenham & Tewkesbury, North Cotswolds, Stroud and the Forest of Dean. Sevenhampton Parish was in the North Cotswold area. North Cotswold District Council came into being with its new centre at Cirencester, with a branch office at Moreton-in-Marsh. Cirencester came to be known as 'The Capital of the Cotswolds'.

The new council was financially prudent and operated, temporarily, from a number of scattered premises in Cirencester, until they acquired the Old Workhouse in Trinity Road, which they converted into offices, bringing all their business under one large roof.

When we became a Conservation Area permission had to be obtained from the District Council Planning Department for all new building, alterations or extensions to existing buildings. Also permission for the cutting down of trees above a certain girth.

On 6th June 1975 the Wilson Labour Government offered the electorate its first referendum in British History on whether or not to stay in the E.E.C. Britain returned an overwhelming Yes vote.

In 1973 the Government began to worry about the Environment, just a little. They asked the country to plant trees wherever possible. The slogan 'Plant a Tree in 73' rang around the countryside. Then came the next request, 'Plant some more in 74'. Sevenhampton Council planted a ring of trees on Elsdon Bank on a piece of ground donated to the village by farmer Alan Smith, husband of Val and father of Brian the current farmer.

On the 8th May 1995, while the whole country was celebrating the 50th Anniversary of Victory in Europe and Japan, Sevenhampton P.C. held its individual celebrations with free drinks on the Village Green and the presentation to the Village of a Garden Seat for the use of people waiting for a bus, or just resting during a walk, also a new Notice Board hung on the Arrow Shed wall – made by local craftsman Syd Holland. Later a detailed map of the village, made by Liz Francis, Artist and Designer and Val Smith, was added. At the Hall an Exhibition by R. Stewart of the whole War story, with artefacts, many provided by those people locally who had served all over the world and on the sea and in the air. Also the parts played in local defence of all kinds here in the parish. Capt Mainwaring (alias Mick Denley) was on duty all day, only leaving the hall to sound the siren – so realistic the ladies in the kitchen dived under the table taking cover. The ladies of the W.I. manned a British Restaurant, as near as possible to the wartime ones, all day long. A Service of Commemoration was held at St Andrew's Church in Sevenhampton.

Another special Service was held to welcome the end of the 2nd Millennium. The whole world celebrated this time, with fantastic scenes on television throughout the day, ending the day, in this village with a bonfire at midnight in The Walks.

St Andrew's Church in the 20th Century

As the 20th Century began St Andrew's Church was very much the centre of village life. Although the two chapels catered for the Non-Conformist people, the others attended St Andrew's regularly and the church was much involved in village activities.

Sevenhampton School was a Church of England school, so many of the children also attended the church Sunday School. They would take part in the beginning of the Matins Service on Sunday, but during the hymn before the sermon they were led out to the Vicarage for Sunday school by the Vicar's wife and her helpers.

Almost everyone walked to church and several footpaths were used regularly for this purpose. From Lower Sevenhampton the path beside the watersplash, across style and meadow to Church Lane served many. For certain weekday occasions the children would come from the school in Sevenhampton, two by two, across the fields and stream to the church.

The church had a choir at one time to sing at all services. This was something of a youth club too, in the early years, they had an annual outing and special suppers just for the boys. Later the choir became adults only, until that too disbanded.

Harvest Festival was a well supported occasion with much local produce, vegetables, fruit, and homemade bread, also corn sheaves in the chancel. This was later distributed to the housebound sick and to Winchcombe Hospital. Followed by Harvest Supper in the Village Hall, when wholesome food was cooked and served by the church ladies.

Christmas and Easter, the great church Festivals, saw the church beautifully decorated by the ladies, with much happy singing of carols and hymns. A choir group was formed, made up of all ages of church-goers, to sing carols around the villages as Christmas drew near.

During the 2nd World War, when some of the Cheltenham Ladies College pupils moved into Brockhampton Park, extra books and hassocks had to be obtained to accommodate their needs for Sunday Services.

Incumbents in the 20th Century

1890-1923	Joseph Storr	1947	Hugh McCalman
1923	Arthur Norton	1953	Canon Francis Charles
1934	John Miller	1974	Canon Philip Hobbs
1944	B.A.C. Kirk Duncan	1996	Roger Morris

At the turn of the century the Revd Joseph Storr was the Incumbent. He would have overseen the drastic changes to the church walls, furniture and fittings made by W. S Waller. The Church Restoration, started in the late 1800s, overlapped into the 20th Century. The present pews, said to be 20th century, would have been the final addition. Joseph Storr lived, with his family, in the still fairly new Vicarage. He travelled around his parishes on a tricycle. Dennis Locke remembered that as a boy he was paid one penny on Saturdays for cleaning the famous tricycle.

The Revd Storr was Vicar during the 1914-18 Great War when the church was still very involved in Local and National affairs. There would have been very many special services during this time and the bereaved would have turned to him for solace as the news of the many casualties became known. The War Memorial, a Plaque and Special Window, were erected in the South Transept and dedicated to the 10 local servicemen who died, was blessed and dedicated by Joseph Storr. The flower arrangers usually place a vase of flowers beside this memorial when decorating the church. Joseph Storr died in 1923 and was buried on the South side of the church near the Chancel.

The next Priest-in-charge was the Revd Arthur Norton from 1923. He died in 1934 and was buried near to the Vicarage gateway. During his years the Benefice was extended to include Charlton Abbots. Burial space had become scarce, so in 1927 a piece of land, behind the Vicarage and adjoining the old churchyard, was adopted and surrounded by a new stone wall. Mr C. Smith of Soundborough gave the stone from his own quarry and Mr W. Smith helped build the wall. The land was ceremoniously consecrated by the Bishop of Gloucester and was soon brought into use. By the end of the second millennium this ground too was almost full and a further extention would be made on ground given, from their farmland by the Hyatt/Jackson family. A right of way gave access to the churchyard from Brockhampton at Donnywell across Manor Farm fields.

During this period, in 1933, the bells of St Andrew's church were found to be unsafe and the firm of Thos. Bond of Burford were commissioned to repair, rehang and quarter turn them. The bill for this work was £45. Pearce Boulton, of Brockhampton Quarry, sexton of the church for many years, who died in March 1990, in his 100th year, was known to be able to ring all three bells himself, simultaneously, by using two hands and one foot. The 1660 Stuart Font was brought back into the church in 1933 after a sojourn of many years in the churchyard garden.

Next in 1934 came the Revd John Miller. He took an interest in local history and assisted Mrs Helen O'Neil, archaeologist, to dig and discover the lost village of Sennington. With his wife, he started to change the layout of the front and oldest part of the churchyard. They altered the pathways: first the one from the main gate to the back of the Manor House was filled in and a new one cut from the lane gate to the Vicarage gate at the East end of the church. The pathway from the Vicarage gate which led to the Priest's door in the Chancel now led to the Porch entry and the

Priest's door, no longer used, was sealed off. J. Melland Hall says in 1889 "In this pathway, near the chancel door may be seen an ancient coffin lid and the fragment of an effigy, probably a lady. The former measures 6ft 6ins in length, 30 ins at the head and 20 ins at the foot. It is slightly coped and shows traces of a raised Calvary Cross. The head of the effigy is represented resting on a cushion. Both supposed to be of 13th century date". This has been walked over by so many feet over the years that it is now hardly recognisable. This churchyard project was taken up by Mr & Mrs Lefaux in the 1960s when some of the footstones were moved and gardens of roses and gentians were planted on each side of the main path from the lane gate to the porch. These gardens have been lovingly tended by a succession of parishioners ever since and are now a great attraction known by many. The County Plate for the best kept churchyard was won by St Andrew's church in 1986.

It was during John Miller's time that the Country was drawn into another War, that of 1939-45 against Germany, and the Church was again to play its part in keeping up the morale of the population. He died in 1944 after a very active 10 years service and was buried in the new churchyard, but chose to lie the opposite way round to the other bodies because it was his wish to face his congregation and his church.

The church was lighted by candles and oil lamps until the coming of electricity to the area. Electric lights were fitted in the church in 1939. The old iron 'tortoise' stoves were the only source of heat for many years. Mr Fred Hooper was the stoker and he would light the stoves the day before services were to be held in winter, in order to make the temperature reasonable for the clergy and congregation. Electric heating was installed in March 1961, new central heating pipes put in during the 1990s make the church pleasantly comfortable at all services. One tortoise stove remains, though unused, in the Chancel, the other was removed from the Nave in 1976.

The next Priest in 1944 was a young man Revd B.A.C. Kirk-Duncan, here for three years only, he was in charge as the War in Europe ended in June 1945, also as the War with Japan finished in August of the same year. His wife had served for several years in the WAFFE and they left the village after the bad winter of 1947. He held the first Thanksgiving Service for the return of Peace to Britain. There were no new names to add to the War Memorial because all our Service men and women arrived home safely, eventually, from all over the world.

In 1947 the Revd Hugh McCalman, an ex Army Padre, became Vicar of St Andrew's living at the Vicarage with his wife and four children and it was during his stay that the church decided on a practical memorial to the war. In 1949/50 the Transepts were re-roofed. Copper was used instead of the traditional lead, following the precedent set by Chichester Cathedral, thus making a considerable saving on an already costly undertaking. The villagers came to the aid of their beloved church again and undertook a memorial fundraising. A grant was received from the Incorporated Church Building Society on condition that "all sittings should remain free". Mr McCalman died in 1953 and he too was buried in St Andrew's churchyard.

Canon Francis Charles became the next Vicar, coming to Sevenhampton from his Matson parish in Gloucester. His wife was a Teacher of Domestic Science at Gloucester College. They had two daughters Alison and Penelope. It was during Canon Charles' first year in office that the Coronation of the young Queen Elizabeth II took place. This great occasion involved everyone in the country and while the villages held parties the church held celebration services to mark the occasion involving Canon Charles as the Minister. Four years after Canon Charles became Priest of Sevenhampton and Charlton Abbots, Hawling was joined to the Group, so now he became Priest of three parishes. The Canon had artistic leanings for he designed and created an Altar Cloth specifically for the Lenten period. It shows the Crown of Thorns, the Nails and the Scourges used in the Crucifixion of Christ. In 1962 he designed a sanctuary carpet which was made up by parishioners, these people are listed in a frame hanging on the South Wall of the Chancel. The following year they made kneelers to his designs, these being Saints of the New Testament on the South side of the Nave and of the Early Church on the North, with Psalm 150 'Praise Ye The Lord' in the Choir Stalls. After 21 years Canon Charles retired because of ill health in 1974. He had to leave the Sevenhampton Vicarage with his wife and they went to live in near-by Whittington. He died in 1978 and is buried in St Andrew's old churchyard near to the Lawrence graves.

Another very beautiful altar cloth and pulpit hanging to match was designed and embroidered by Margot Partington, of Combe, Brockhampton. This was given to the church and dedicated to the memory of Mr & Mrs R.G.B. Combe, parents of sisters Val and Gill. The embroidery is carried out mainly in gold.

Music was provided by a harmonium until 1974 when it was removed to Charlton Abbots church. A pipe organ was installed in the North Transept of St Andrew's. This had been purchased from Tarlton Methodist Chapel and rebuilt by Peter Hutchings of Wooton-under-Edge, at a total cost of £625. Flo Barnfield, teacher and a member of an old Sevenhampton family, was the organist at St Andrew's until her death. The present organist is Muriel Candler, who started first on the harmonium, which was placed in the North side of the chancel, then on the pipe organ, in the North Transept, when it was installed in 1976.

In 1974 the next Incumbent, formerly a farmer, was the Revd Phillip Hobbs; later he too became a Canon. In 1975 when Whittington became part of the Group, he took charge of the four parishes, to be known as 'The Foursome', which were St Andrew's, Sevenhampton, St Martin's, Charlton Abbots, St Edward's, Hawling and St Bartholomew's, Whittington. Previously he had been Vicar of St James' church in Tredworth and whilst serving there in 1961 was appointed Chaplain of Gloucester Prison, which in itself was a busy undertaking. As well as conducting services at the prison he became the prison's entertainment officer. He later became an M.B.E. for his dedicated service, receiving his medal from Her Majesty Queen Elizabeth. Married with three daughters and a son he lived in Sevenhampton Vicarage and

Altar Cloth – designed and embroidered by Margot Partington

*Dedicated to
Mr & Mrs R G B Combe*

*Pulpit hanging
by Margot Partington*

193

played a great part in the work of the four villages.

In 1977 Queen Elizabeth celebrated her Silver Jubilee having been on the throne of Britain for 25 years. At St Andrew's the Royal Coat of Arms was restored and rehung on the South side of the Nave to commemorate the occasion.

The Nave and Chancel were re-roofed in 1979/80, financed by Government grant, Historic Churches Preservation Society, the Warneford Trust, individual donations and money raising events.

In 1981 the Alternative Services book was first published – alternative to the Book of Common Prayer. This was tried and rejected by most of the congregation of the four churches in the group. It was used occasionally, however, for the sake of worshippers, leaving the area for college etc., who might meet up with these services elsewhere.

In 1985 the W.I. Movement undertook a churchyard survey countrywide to document the positions and information on the very old tombstones in the churchyard. The information on St Andrew's was catalogued and presented to the Gloucester Record Office. Sevenhampton W.I. researched and made a book of local information, sketches and photographs and presented it to Canon Hobbs on Ascension Day, the 8th May 1986. This book is now held at St Andrew's church, Sevenhampton and is a useful reference book for people tracing family histories.

Handing over the Book of the Churchyard Survey to Revd. Canon Philip Hobbs

The Hobbs family opened the Vicarage for a Garden Party and sale in aid of church funds after the Ascension Day communion service in the church each year. The Revd Phillip was an excellent and interesting speaker and his sermons were given from the heart without notes.

In 1990 central heating pipes were put into the church under the pews. This meant the congregation was warm and comfortable no matter how long the services and sermons lasted.

A thriving Sunday School was maintained throughout Canon Hobbs time, but declined in recent years as there were very few children in the parishes. Help came to the Vicar when two of his congregation, Bob Andrews and Carol Norden became Readers capable of taking some services in his stead. In the 1970s a Bishop came to live in the village on his retirement. The Rt Revd David Porter took an active part in the running of The Foursome. He was also a talented painter as many of his local portraits prove As a member of the Fosseway Artists he exhibited his work annually. Sadly he died suddenly whilst working in his garden in 1978 and he too is buried in St Andrew's churchyard.

Canon Hobbs, a much loved Vicar, continued to run his parishes for 21 years. In June 1995 he retired, with his wife Violet, to live in Woodmancote, near Cirencester. We then had an interregnum for well over a year, during which time sterling work was done by Reader Bob Andrews keeping the local churches going and taking many of the services himself. He was helped by Reader Carol Norden who was licensed at Cirencester in 1996. It was at this time that the Sevenhampton Vicarage was sold, by the Church Commissioners, to become a private residence; this meant the loss of house and garden for extra church activities, also the loss of parking space as the lane in which the Church stands is very narrow.

In October 1996 the Revd Roger Morris was appointed Priest in Charge of nine parishes. These being Sevenhampton, Brockhampton, Charlton Abbots, Whittington, Hawling, the Shiptons, Salperton, Dowdeswell and later, when their Vicar retired, Withington joined the Group. This was now to be known as The Coln River Group. Formerley a Scientist, Roger served his curacy with the Northleach Group. The service for his licensing as Priest for the Coln Group was held at St Andrew's, Sevenhampton by the Bishop of Gloucester. Roger lived initially at the Vicarage in Shipton until a new Vicarage in building at Andoversford was finished. A fine purpose built Church Centre was erected at the same time next to the Andoversford Vicarage. Ten parishes were a great undertaking for one man to cope with, but Roger brought new life and enthusiasm and many changes were made.

A changed way of life generally needed a change of approach to keep the churches viable. He started a new magazine, which he called CHI RHO, pronounced CAIRO as in the capital of Egypt. Basically it is two Greek letters: CHI which is the X shaped letter and RHO which is the P shaped letter. Together, they are the first two letters of the Greek word CHRISTOS which means Christ. Early Christians used the two letters

Parish Magazine – Chi Rho

to show that they were from the church. Coincidentally, if we wanted to spell Coln River using Greek letters then we would end up using the letters CHI RHO.

Roger organised many occasions at the new Church Centre including children's events. In 1999 he had the help of two clergymen Revd John Ellis of Andoversford, who was also Chaplain to the local Branch of the British Legion and Revd Guy Bridgewater of Withington. Of Readers there were four – Bob Andrews and Carol Norden of Brockhampton, John Millard and Joan Goodworth of Withington.. He was joined by Revd Andrew Axon as his Curate, licensed at St Andrew's on 1st July 2001. Andrew later held the parishes together diligently with no other priest when Roger left for Coventry.

Revd Roger Morris brought his ten parishes safely through to the end of the century and the Second Millennium.

Parish Magazine – The Foursome

The Foursome

The Foursome was the Group of Parishes made up by St Andrew's, Sevenhampton; St Martin's, Charlton Abbotts; St Edward's, Hawling, and St Bartholowew's, Whittington. St Andrew's was the central church of the group, with the Vicar living in the Vicarage near to this church. Firstly it was a long, low Norman building – now the Nave – built in c.1150, with a stout, studded doorway beneath a Norman lintel with chevron markings. The early Nave – with a bell turret housing a medieval bell of 15th century, had a Porch with stoup and benches for weddings and funerals and later a fine Tudor Arch – was extended to its present length, then Transepts added making the Church cruciform, and lastly the Tower, all before 1500 A.D. The

Church was dedicated to St Andrew in 1504 A.D. by Bishop Costello of Hereford. The church Registers date from 1555 and St Andrew's has served (and is serving still) the Sevenhampton Parish for eight hundred & fifty years.

St Martin's, Charlton Abbotts

A small country church, in a perfect country setting, consisting of nave, chancel, vestry and porch, with a bell turret on the western gable containing one bell of 1346 by John of Gloucester and bearing the name of St Martin in Lombardic characters. St Martin's was added to the St Andrew's Benefice in 1929.

At the time of the Domesday Book of 1085, Cerletone (countryman's town) belonged to Winchcombe Abbey – hence Charlton Abbots. "St Mary of Wincelcumbe holds Carleton in Gretestan Hundred … worth 20s." The Abbot purchased a 'Free Warren of Charleton' in 1251 and continued in possession until the Dissolution of the Abbey in 1526. The monks founded a walled in leper colony, close to the church – now part of the Manor gardens – to isolate the sufferers. Leprosy was a serious and contagious disease, said to be caused by a 'Surfeit of Severn Salmon'.

After the Reformation of 1533, Charlton became the property of King Henry VIII who granted it to Thomas Seymour of Suddeley. In 1573 Queen Elizabeth I granted it to Thomas Tracy of Toddington who sold it to John Carter Esq. He it was who built the Manor House in the 16th century and the Carter family lived there for several generations. In 1722 a John Carter of Charlton Abbots and in 1726 his wife Alice were buried in the chancel of St Andrew's, Sevenhampton. The Carters held the impropriation of St Martin's, which was still in the Deanery of Winchcombe. In 1712 Thomas Atkins, historian, reported that "the chancel is quite down and the church has been disused near 12 years. The inhabitants bury at Winchcombe and Sevenhampton". Still in the 18th century the church was restored keeping the original West wall and South doorway, also the 13th century tub-shaped font which now stands on a 19th century base.

St Martin's was restored again in 1880 when the two round-headed windows were put in on the South side. The stained glass in the Early English window in the chancel is a memorial to Georgina Maria Craven, of Brockhampton Park, who died in 1878. Two plaques in the chancel commemorate her husband and son, Charles Goodwin Colquit Craven 1889 and Fulwar John Colquit Craven 1890.

St Martin's Church is still greatly loved and cared for and the churchyard regularly groomed. Members of the congregation embroidered kneelers for it in the 1980s. If you attempt the steep, sometimes treacherous path, you will be rewarded by the sight of a peaceful, welcoming, tiny church in an idyllic setting of fields, farms and hills.

St Edward's, Hawling

St Edward's joined the St Andrew's benefice in 1957.

In Domesday Book the village was referred to as Halling, which was given by Edward the Confessor to Countess Goda. Taken over by the Normans it paid an annual rent of £8 and was taxed at 10 hides. Hawling was given by the Normans to the Abbey of Winchcombe who held it until the Dissolution of he Monasteries. Ownership then passed through hands of successive Lords of the Manor until, in 1913, the manor was split up, many of the farmers buying their own holdings.

Hawling church, which has Norman foundations, was rebuilt in c1764, except for the pretty Perpendicular tower embattled, with pinnacles and gargoyles. The fabric of an early church can be seen in the nave wall East of the South porch and the doorway has remains of late Norman jambs with transitional capitals and hollowed abaci (the crown of a column). The interior is very simple. Though restored after 1873, it was not Gothicised, presumably through lack of funds. There is a 19th century tiled floor. and a Venetian window of clear glass, as are all the windows in the church. The Georgian window behind the altar is of c.1764. Two north nave windows are Georgian and have two lights. On the south are a four-light window with concave mullions and a one-light Perpendicular window near the tower west window Georgian with a round head, set under an older pointed drip-mould on the outside. The Font is chalice-shaped, presumably c.1764. The Pulpit mid-18th century, with Gothic oak panels. Plate Chalice and Paten cover 1716 by Richard Green. Monuments a collection of brasses to the family of Henry Stratford 1649.

St Edward's church stands in a large churchyard, with many interesting memorials, in which there is a magnificent 700 year-old yew tree.

St Bartholomew's, Whittington

St Bartholomew's joined the Foursome in 1975.

There has certainly been a church at Whittington since Saxon times because there is a Saxon arch just opposite the main North door.and it is thought that the door of the Vestry may have been part of the original church.. The West wall of the church stands only a few feet from the Tudor Manor house and the main West door has long been blocked up.

The West end of the Nave has a South aisle which is very narrow and a two-bay arcade, one arch of which is restored Norman, the other Perpendicular with good head stops. There are three life-sized effigies in local stone, one a lady wearing the horned headdress of the 15th century, the others of two knights in armour. Each wears the hauberk chain mail and long surcoat, with right hand on sword and legs crossed in the conventional manner. They are both called Richard de Crupes, father and son, both Lords of the Manor of Witetune. Built into the West wall of the Vestry is a Norman chevroned arch. There is no chancel arch but until the time of restoration of c.1872 by Waller there was a rood screen.

The old brasses below the altar rail are of Richard Coton and his wife Margaret, dated 1556, in the "reygne of King Phillypp and Queene Marye".

The Font of 1200 is a plain octagonal bowl and pedestal. The Pulpit is 18th century panelled oak. The Plate – chalice, two patens and Flagon 1783 by Wakelin & Taylor. Outside is a Medieval Cross with a tall shaft, which may have been a preaching cross.

How the church acquired the name of St Bartholomew is not known for certain, but it is thought that after the Restoration of the Monarchy, Charles II in 1660, the use of the Book of Common Prayer was demanded in every church by August 14th St Bartholemew's Day. The then Rector of Whittington, Dr Ingram complied with the Act, though nearly 2000 clergymen refused to do so and forfeited their livings. The Book of Common Prayer has been used at this church ever since.

Since 1996 when these four churches were united with the other five churches to form the Coln River Group, all of these nine churches had full Sunday services, with good congregations up to 2000, the New Millennium.

END OF THE SECOND MILLENNIUM 2000 A.D.

So we reach the end of the Saga. We have come a long way together from B.C. as new primitive arrivals. Still in the 1st Millennium we were a united set of village country folk living a simple country life on the hill at Sennington, when this was our whole world. We lived in a close community, as families in our simple houses, near to our animals, caring for them and each other.

We have lived through the reigns of, and been affected by many, monarchs and their ambitions. The many changes involved have been difficult to adopt. Wars and civil wars have torn the population apart, each generation losing many of its sons. Many generations later would see the coming of the New Millennium. Surprisingly the two villages have also survived as a fairly close community and this in itself is no small achievement.

Sevenhampton Parish is still a pleasant, happy area in which to live. The farmers created the attractive landscape. Now as 1999 becomes 2000 A.D. there are landowners, but only two farmers actively farming the land, Robert Jackson of Manor Farm and Brian Smith of Gassons Farm. Early in the century much of this area was scrubland, but two world wars and Government directives for producing more food have seen many changes in land use. Careful management by the farmers have produced the AREA OF OUTSTANDING NATURAL BEAUTY which we see and love today. If the farmers are not helped and encouraged we could quickly revert to scrubland again.

As a Conservation Area we may build, repair or extend our properties only in Cotswold Stone. Almost bringing us into another New Stone Age.

The writer of this Saga staged, in late 1999, an Exhibition in the Rhodes Hall taking us through 2000 years of local history. This displayed, in script and artefacts, how we have reached this important date in our history. 2000 years of advancement from over-simple to over-complicated. The idea behind staging the Exhibition was, with the fast approaching millennium, to show what this united parish had to celebrate.

How We Celebrated The New Millennium

As millennium fever built up around the world in 1999, the local Millennium Committee organised fund raising events to cover the planned activities.

Georgina Oldham organised two Candelit Suppers at the Hall, cooking and serving unbelievably good food to a crowded company each time.

A Quiz Night at the Hall arranged by Anne and Bill Jenkin, with Quiz Master Ian Finbow was another huge success.

The Brockhampton Quilters held a "Past, Present and Future" Exhibition in

St Andrew's Church, in aid of the Church and Millennium funds. The Quilters designed a Millennium Wall Hanging for the Rhodes Hall.

A new stylish, Cotswold stone pillar box, designed by Martin Podd, our local Architect, was in place on our 'Village Green' (a tiny, grass triangle), in time for its grand opening, in December 1999, by a Post Office Official who cut the red ribbon. His wife was dressed as a red pillarbox, old style. Post Mistress Vanessa was in attendance with First-Day covering special stamps and the oldest resident, of 96 years Mrs Betty Hyatt who posted the first letter. The youngest resident, newborn baby Daniel Lanfear was present too. We all drank a celebration glass of red wine – in the rain.

Val Smith and Liz Francis produced a Field Map of the area. This was eventually hung in the new bus shelter at Gassons

The Women's Institute ceremoniously planted a young Yew Tree in the churchyard as their celebratory offer. This tree was grown from a cutting from a very ancient. historic Yew Tree.

The Jacksons planted young trees on Manor Farm in the shape of M.M. – 2000 A.D. They also held a Barn Dance in July 2000 for all ages, as a Millennium Event, which was a greatly enjoyed evening by everyone present.

A service was held by Revd. Roger Morris at St Andrew's to mark the Millennium. A table was set up at the Chancel steps with three candles representing Past, Present and Future. They were lighted by Past – Ros Stewart, Present – Wendy Lee, and Future – by young Sarah Cooke; each read a relevant Bible passage before putting taper to candle.

St Andrew's also was to have a new burial ground on farm land donated by the Hyatt family adjoining the earlier churchyard extension, which by 2000 had very little grave space left. A new List of Incumbents was drawn up from John the Clerk in 1204 to Roger Morris at the end of the 20th century. This was to be etched on to a specially made board to be hung in the church. Resarched by R. Stewart and Organised by Warden Gill Hyatt. The ground was to be consecrated and the board dedicated later, by the Bishop of Tewkesbury the Rt. Revd John Went, at a special service in St Andrew's Church. These were both part of St Andrew's Millennium celebrations.

On NEW YEAR'S EVE the B.B.C. television presented an all-day broadcast bringing in the New Century as it arrived all around the world, starting at 10 am G.M.T. from the Pacific Islands as their Millennium was first to arrive. The programme moving westwards as 1999 became 2000 A.D. All nations had their organised celebrations with fantastic firework displays everywhere.

We as a Parish had our own firework display in the Walks, set up and lighted by Robert Jackson. Many of us stood around the fire with torches at midnight on this cold, dark, damp evening, chatting with friends and visitors and the usual Oohs and Aahs as the fireworks lit up the sky and exploded. The display became twice as effective as it was backed up by a firework display at Brockhampton Park. When the fireworks were finished and the bonfire burned down, many of us repaired to the Village Hall where a Champagne Breakfast awaited us. Cooked and served by Kit Gregory and her team of helpers and much appreciated by the diners, in a wonderfully cheerful and hopeful atmosphere, we wished each other A Happy New Year and the whole world

"A HAPPY NEW YEAR"

and a

"WELCOME TO THE THIRD MILLENNIUM"